Love, Ellen

Love, Ellen

A Mother/Daughter Journey

Betty DeGeneres

HARPER

NEW YORK • LONDON • TORONTO • SYDNEY

HARPER

Published by Rob Weisbach Books
An Imprint of HarperCollins Publishers, Inc.
10 East 53rd Street, New York, NY 10022.

Library of Congress Cataloging-in-Publication Data
DeGeneres, Betty, 1930–
Love, Ellen : a mother/daughter journey / Betty DeGeneres.—1st ed.
p. cm.
ISBN 0-688-17688-7 (alk. paper)
1. DeGeneres, Betty. 1930– . 2. Parents of gays—United States—Biography. 3. Mothers and daughters—United States—Case studies. 4. DeGeneres, Ellen. 5. Lesbians—United States—biography. 6. Lesbians—United States—Family relationships—Case studies. 7. Women comedians—United States—Biography. 8. Television actors and actresses—United States—Biography. 9. Homosexuality—United States. I. Title.
HQ75.4.D44D44 1999
306.874'3—dc21 98-50367
CIP

Printed in the United States of America

30 29 28 27 26 25 24 23 22 21

BOOK DESIGN BY PAULINE NEUWIRTH, NEUWIRTH & ASSOCIATES, INC.

To my kids: Vance, Ellen, and Anne.
And to all those whose parents have rejected them.
I love you all.

Acknowledgments

MIM EICHLER-RIVAS. I love Mim Eichler-Rivas. I thank her for her powers of organization and structure—for inspiring, prodding, and pushing me. Thanks to Rob Weisbach for his guidance and encouragement and thanks to the whole terrific team at Rob Weisbach Books. Thanks to Elizabeth Birch and the Human Rights Campaign for filling my life with love and giving me the job I think I was meant to do. Being the first non-gay spokesperson for the National Coming Out Project has been the most fulfilling work I could ever imagine. Thanks to David Smith for keeping me on schedule, telling me where I'm going and when, and being my number-one cheerleader. David, and everyone at HRC, gave me confidence that I could do this work long before I should have been confident. Thanks to Bob Witeck and Wes Combs for their inspired speech writing. Thanks to Jan Sonnenmair, photographer extraordinaire. Thanks to Bob Barnett and Jacqueline Davies for their expertise. Thanks to all of you, my dear new friends, for telling me your stories. And thanks to all of you, whose names I will never know, who shared your feelings of hope and despair with me.

Thanks to my sister Helen, my son, Vance, and my daughters, Ellen and Anne. Thanks for your excellent advice and your love. I couldn't live without them.

Thanks to all in our family, who have always been supportive and proud. And last, but certainly not least, thanks to all my friends across the country—both old and new. You know who you are. I love you all.

Finally, I must acknowledge Matthew Shepard. His tragic death affects every human being. His suffering leaves us all diminished—and we must never forget him.

Contents

Go without hate, but not without rage. Heal the world.

—PAUL MONETTE

PROLOGUE

Coming Out, the First Time

PASS CHRISTIAN, MISSISSIPPI
1978

THREE WORDS, SPOKEN two decades ago by my daughter Ellen at the age of twenty, changed my life forever. In an instant, her bombshell shattered many of my long-held beliefs about who she was, who I was, and about life itself.

Nothing in the months, days, hours, or minutes leading up to that moment could have prepared me for what she would tell me that day. Twenty minutes earlier, just before Ellen suggested we go for a walk on the beach, we had been enjoying a large, relatively uneventful family gathering in Pass Christian on the Mississippi Gulf Coast.

This small beach community is an hour's drive from New Orleans, Louisiana, where I grew up and raised my two kids, Vance and Ellen. It is where my oldest sister, Helen, lived for many years with her family in their lovely, comfortable home on West Beach Boulevard, facing the water. The house, set far back from the boulevard, has a wide screened porch and a large front yard full of shade trees. Inside, the spacious living room has a well-used fireplace and the large dining room opens onto a cozy sunroom.

From the time our kids were small, Helen's was an ideal place to gather for holidays and other happy occasions. At Thanksgiving, Christmas, summer picnic reunions, and other celebrations our number would swell, with grandparents, cousins, uncles, aunts, nieces, nephews, and a few neighbors and friends. Lots of us! Yet we never felt that we were intruding or had overstayed our welcome.

For those winter holiday feasts, the dining room always managed to accommodate us all; afterward we'd share long, leisurely hours by the fire. In warm weather, we always ate outdoors, at picnic tables in the front yard. We have home movies of all the children swinging on a rope tied to a tall tree branch. They'd stand on a picnic table to catch it as it swung by.

To escape the heat we could sit on the screened porch or relax in a hammock. Of course, when it was really hot, everyone headed for the beach—to sit on the sand or swim or go sailing in the Sunfish.

The house on West Beach Boulevard has a wealth of cherished memories for me. Like old photographs, many of those happy moments have faded in my mind with the passage of time, the different years blurring one into the next. And yet, I can vividly recall this particular life-changing visit, which came at the end of the summer of 1978.

At the time, I was living eight hours away in Atlanta, Texas, with my then husband, whom I had married after divorcing Vance and Ellen's father several years earlier. Vance, the older of my two kids, couldn't be with us; he was in Yuma, Arizona, finishing up his two years of service in the Marines, after already having started to make a name for himself in comedy writing and rock music. Ellen, however, was able to make it. She was living just an hour away in New Orleans at her dad's house, so she rode over to Helen's with us.

That meant a chance to do some catching up. Living so far away from each other was hard on both of us. We were always extremely close and missed the luxury of being together on a daily basis. In those days, Ellen was still struggling to find a direction for herself. After graduating from high school, she had tried college for all of a month, only to conclude that wasn't for her. She then embarked on what would ultimately become one of the longest lists of jobs known to humankind—everything from vacuum cleaner salesperson to oyster shucker—before finding her true calling. But even then, Ellen had a knack for describing even the most mundane details of her struggles and making them sound hilarious or dramatic. That weekend was no exception. So I had no reason to suspect that anything was different or out of the ordinary about Ellen.

Nor did it seem unusual when, after we all finished dinner late that afternoon, El said to me, "Let's go out for one more walk on the beach."

When we crossed West Beach Boulevard and walked down the steps of the seawall, I began to sense that she had something on her mind. Probably, I imagined, it was her latest job, or maybe a new boyfriend. But we weren't really talking much as we walked across the broad, sandy beach down to the hard-packed sand by the water's edge. The cool salty breeze felt wonderful as we walked along and my daughter, at my side, was a pretty sight. With her straight blond hair and her sparkling blue eyes, she really was the essence of the girl next door. What a treat to be together, walking along quietly.

But suddenly Ellen stopped, and I turned back to see why. She had tears in her eyes, which alarmed me. As I walked toward her in concern, she began to cry, and it was then that she sobbed with a depth of emotion I will never forget and spoke those three words: "Mom, I'm gay."

In my mind, everything stopped. This was the biggest shock of my life and the last thing I had ever expected to hear. Still reeling, I reached out to comfort her. She was upset and crying, so I did the most natural thing a mother would do—I took her into my arms and hugged her. No mother wants to see her child in pain.

Reassuring her that I loved her was my first priority. But it would take time for the words she had just spoken to sink in. There was no way I could comprehend or process or accept this news immediately. My shock was coupled with disbelief. As close as we were, this was not the Ellen I knew. On the other hand, if we had been living in the same city and had been in more constant touch, I probably would have had some clues.

It was my turn to talk, but I didn't know what to say. A hundred different thoughts and emotions were racing through me. In my mind I was frantically reaching, searching for any question, any argument, that would bring her back to her senses—back to being the lovely, young heterosexual daughter she always had been.

Heterosexual daughter. That thought gripped me. It is such a natural assumption that we don't even have to consider the word. It isn't even in our usual vocabulary. We just are. But now, I had to consider another word that wasn't in my usual vocabulary—homosexual. *My homosexual daughter*—just thinking those strange words brought on a new wave of emotion that I recognized as fear. I feared for Ellen's well-being, given society's prejudiced and negative attitudes. Though I had almost no exposure to gay people at all, I knew the derogatory names used for them, and I didn't want my daughter called those names.

And, then, of all things, as I was hugging Ellen and waiting for her tears to subside, the most frivolous but upsetting thought came out of nowhere. Now, I sadly realized, El's engagement picture would never appear in the New Orleans newspaper.

In those days, whenever I was home for a visit, I'd always look at the engagement announcements of young women in the *Times Picayune*, and I would often recognize the maiden name of the mother—a friend from high school or college. I had always fantasized about seeing Ellen's picture there and about her marrying some fine young man and about myself as the proud mother of the bride.

In retrospect, it's ironic that although Ellen never had an engagement picture in my hometown paper, in years to come she would be a featured celebrity not only in the *Picayune* but on the covers of magazines and papers all over the world. At that time, however, such fame was far beyond my fantasies. I felt as if a dream had been shattered.

Only later would I understand that my disappointment

was not for Ellen. It was for me. I was the one whose marriages hadn't worked out according to expectations. Why on earth should she have to fulfill my dreams? Why not love her and support her as she fulfilled her own?

When I finally found my voice, I asked, "Are you sure?" The question hung in the air. It sounded judgmental. I softened it, saying, "I mean, couldn't this just be a phase?"

Ellen almost smiled. "No, Mother," she said. "It's not a phase. I'm sure."

More questions followed: "How do you know?" "How long have you known?"

Ellen tried to answer truthfully. "I think I've always known, but I didn't know what to call it. Now I do. I'm gay, Mom."

It was getting dark, and when we started back to the house, she reminded me of a movie we had seen together a couple of years earlier. As I recall, it was *Valley of the Dolls*, or something like that. Ellen said, "You know that scene when the two girls were touching and hugging, I thought that was gross. I'd never seen anything like that before. But then it happened to me, and it wasn't gross, Mom."

She told me more about her first experience. She also told me that a friendship formed after her return to New Orleans was more than that. Ellen felt that she was in love.

Even as I tried to understand, I was in a state of denial. "But, Ellen, boys have always liked you, and you're so popular. You just need to meet the right one."

She shook her head. "I've dated a lot of nice boys. That's not who I am." Ellen's expression was wistful and solemn, yet also relieved—as if a burden had been lifted off her. I was feeling many things at that point, but relief wasn't one of them.

We walked back into the house. We were not the same mother and daughter who had left thirty minutes before. We looked the same, but we were not. Nobody else knew—not for a while. Now we had a secret.

Every family of a gay person has its own story. This was ours, a story that would develop and unfold in many surprising ways.

I've heard that some parents are able to accept this news about their sons or daughters readily, with equanimity, even with happiness. I'm sorry to say that I wasn't one of them. Like most parents, I went through a process. It took me time to think about this, to sort out what was important, to get past my terrible ignorance and learn about homosexuality. Though somewhat familiar with the myths and fallacies that are all too common, I needed to learn facts. Two of the most important facts I would learn were, first of all, that as a rule people don't choose to be homosexual; and second, that being gay is normal and healthy. But embracing these truths would take time.

As I grappled with this new information about Ellen, some of what I went through was not unlike the grieving process that follows the death of a loved one—which is also a process of growth. Of course, what was dying wasn't a loved one, but my own expectations about the way Ellen should be. And in their place, room was being made for the truth, about her and about me.

Though this process was hard and sometimes painful, what matters is that I did recognize it as a process, and I allowed it to take its course. Another important thing is that during this whole time I loved my daughter as much as I ever had, and she loved me. We kept the lines of communication open. This is vital, although not necessarily easy.

A short while after that day on the beach, early in my struggle, I spoke to Ellen on the phone, and more questions came out. Was it something in her upbringing? Maybe, I suggested, it was the kind of people she was hanging around with.

"What do you mean?" Ellen said angrily.

"Well, how well do you know them?" The disapproval in my voice was obvious.

Her tone was hurt as she asked, "What are you so unhappy about?"

"It's just that I always dreamed of seeing your engagement picture in the paper," I confessed, the words spilling out. "It worries me that you won't have a man to provide for you and look after you. And what about having your own children?"

The conversation was going downhill fast, and we got off the phone hurriedly.

A few days later, I received this letter from Ellen:

Dear Mother,

I've had a horrible day since I talked to you on the phone! What you said upset me very much. . . . I'm really sorry if I'm not the daughter you hoped I'd be—that I don't have my engagement picture in the paper and am 3 months' pregnant! And I'm not being sarcastic either! And I know this must hurt you a lot—and it's hard for you to accept.

But think about me too! I love you so much—you know how much you mean to me. When you're upset about something, I feel just as much pain. Don't you understand I care so much for you—but I can't change my feelings.

I am in love—I didn't force it—it just happened and I'm not about to break away from the only thing in my life that keeps me going just for you or society or anything. I'm very happy and I'm sorry you can't approve—I know you can't understand—you probably never will. No one can ever understand anything until they've experienced it themselves. You were brought up totally different—lifestyle, generation, surroundings, people, environment, etc. . . .

I just want you to know you're not the only one who gets upset when we don't see things eye to eye. All I ask is that you try to believe me—I'm not sick. I'm not crazy. It just happened, and my friends are not sick—they're normal, healthy, good-looking, well-dressed, polite, young adults who also strayed from society's rule. I just wish you could meet them and see how your image of "them" is so wrong. . . .

I hope we have a lot of time alone together—we really need to talk.

Love you much,
Ellen

She was absolutely right: we did need to spend time talking. And so we did. As we did, I was able to remind her that I accepted and loved her unconditionally. Maybe I would never totally understand, I admitted, but I was going to do everything in my power to try.

Over the next years, we corresponded, we wrote poems to each other, we talked on the phone, we laughed, and we cried. We never lost close contact. "Love, Ellen," or some form thereof, was how she signed off every time she ended a letter or said good-bye after a talk. That love was never taken for granted, on either side.

Ever so slowly, as I met her friends and her partners, I relaxed, seeing how very happy she was—and is. Along the way, I learned many lessons not only about what it means to be gay but about what it means to be human, lessons about love and courage and honesty.

This has been an amazing journey, the journey which began so shockingly for me that day in 1978 on the beach in Pass Christian. The twists and turns in our road have led to many surprises, including Ellen's professional success in movies and as the star of her own television series.

When El became famous, interviewers would often ask her, "Were you funny as a child?"

"Well, no," she would answer, "I was an accountant."

In fact, Ellen was always funny, talented, and creative. And she was sensitive, serious, and even shy at times, too.

So, to the question I've been asked countless times—"Did you have any idea your daughter was going to grow up to be a famous comedienne and actress?"—I've had to answer no. If I had known she was going to grow up to be Ellen DeGeneres, I would have taken more pictures.

As our second-born, Ellen has always felt we were so tired after all the photographs we took of Vance that she got shortchanged. Ooops. She's right. Now, with cameras always following her wherever she goes, maybe she's making up for it.

One of the things I did know about Ellen, long before she was famous, was that whatever path she chose to pursue, she certainly had the talent, energy, intelligence, honesty, courage, and love to be great at it—and to be a great human being.

The big surprise was the fact that, after her own personal coming out, Ellen would later risk her fame and fortune to go through a second coming out process on a much different, much more public scale. If anyone had told me back in those long-ago days that El would one day be one of the most famous lesbians in the world and an activist fighting in the battle for equal gay rights, I don't think I would have believed it. And if anyone had predicted that I would be playing my own part in that battle, I *know* I wouldn't have believed it.

For that matter, if anyone had told me as recently as a year ago that within a few months I would be starting the most exciting, rewarding work of my life, I wouldn't have believed that either. I was almost sixty-seven years old, single, and recently retired after a decade of working as a speech pathologist. I'd always thought this was supposed to be a time for slowing down, spending leisure-filled hours on the golf course, perhaps even catching up on my reading. Fat chance.

In the fall of 1997, not long after Ellen made history by coming out to the world and portraying the first openly gay leading character in a TV sitcom, I jumped into the fray. I was offered the opportunity to become the first non-gay spokesperson for the Human Rights Campaign's Coming Out Project, and I simply could not say no.

What a year it has been! I have had the pleasure of meeting so many gay men and women who have generously shared their stories with me and who really feel very special. They do feel "different," and they're proud of their differentness. They celebrate who they are, as well they should. They're leading happy, successful, fulfilled lives under far less than optimum conditions. Sadly, sometimes those conditions include having been rejected by their family and kicked out of their home—the one place in the world where we should all feel safe.

One of the funniest and most poignant moments in Ellen's television coming out was an exchange between her character, Ellen Morgan, and a therapist played by Oprah Winfrey. Ellen bemoans the fact that when people come out of the closet, no one gives them a party or a cake that says, "Good for you, you're gay!"

Wouldn't it be wonderful if we did? If I had it to do over again, knowing what I now know, I would. I wish I could have done that for my daughter in 1978.

Coming out has been described as an earthquake that shakes the world not only of the person coming out but of everyone around him or her. It has also been described as less a declaration of sexuality to the rest of the world than a personal act of self-love. It is, without a doubt, a discovery of self and a rite of passage that should be celebrated—not only because your daughter or son has taken this courageous step toward being her or his own person, but because you are being given an opportunity to do the same.

Coming out is a gift.

• • •

IN THE EARTHQUAKE of Ellen's public coming out in 1997, one more unexpected opportunity came my way—an offer for me to write a book about my work for HRC, and about my experiences as a woman, a mother, and now an activist. Again, I couldn't say no. I had only to think of how many times in my travels across the country young people have approached me to say how wonderful it would be if only I would write a book they could give to their parents. I have also received many letters to that effect from people of all ages. Here's one:

> Please write a book for families struggling with their kids/siblings coming out. This past Thanksgiving holiday made me realize that some of my family members could use a good book on this subject, and I am sure Betty DeGeneres is the right person to write it! Betty, please write your own story about struggling with your own daughter's coming out and how it made you feel, and how you came to terms with it. I wish I had such a book right now to send to my Mom and siblings. . . .
>
> It's tough when you hear things like "I'm ok with you being gay, but I don't think it's natural," which my sister told me. . . . She also said it was a choice I had made and only shared her negativity and disparaging thoughts. Acceptance, love, and support are all I want, as do many others like me. . . .

So, at one of my speaking engagements, when a reporter asked, "Is it true you are writing a book about homosexuality?" I answered, "No. I'm writing a book about love and acceptance." I smiled and added, "And about me and my kids." I was referring to all my kids—not only to my own children, but to all the people, young and old, who have become part of my extended family.

Under that umbrella, I intend to cover a lot of ground here, providing many stories: bits and pieces of this and that; a poem here and there; other people's stories; letters; even a recipe. Because I have an important message, I think it's only fair that you know something about the messenger—me. So, as we get to know each other, I'll be pulling a few things out of the old memory trunk, just for fun, or to make (to quote my famous daughter) "my point . . . and I do have one."

As you will come to see, I believe that we all have the power to make a difference in each other's lives and in our own lives. That was a lesson that took me a long time to learn, and it too is a part of my story.

Still, at its heart this book is all about love—specifically, about loving our children, *all* of our children. You might think that such a book should not be needed. What could be more natural, more innate, than loving your children?

You take care of them from the time they are born, or, if adopted, from the time they are yours; you help them to grow into the very best persons they can be. And then, one day, one or more of your children may come to you, as a loving parent, with their own self-discovery—the news that they are gay or lesbian. You can rest assured that they haven't come to this decision lightly. Because of society's negative messages, they may have been struggling with this realization for years. When they finally work up the courage to be honest with you about who they are, it's because they need your love and support more than ever. They need to know that your love is pure and unconditional. Such love is something they are not likely to get from anyone else in the world—only from a mother or father.

I'm not saying it's easy. That's why I want to tell you more about the struggle and the subsequent growth process I went through after Ellen came out to me as a lesbian. I want to share with you all the wonderful stories of acceptance I hear as I travel back and forth across the country. But lest we imagine there is no battle left to fight, I must also tell you some very tragic stories of rejection.

I hope our collective stories will be helpful to parents, grandparents, siblings, spouses, and offspring—in fact, all family members and friends—to better understand and accept their gay family members. I also hope this book will be helpful to gay men and women to better understand how their non-gay relatives feel, the not-so-easy process they may go through. I hope it will serve as a reminder that we all need to give each other time—time to adjust, to assimilate new information, to grow more comfortable with each other.

On a broader level, another aim of this book is to educate the general public about the immeasurable value and worth of our gay family members. For those parents and other relatives who are just beginning the process of understanding, or who are still struggling with new information about a gay loved one, I know that the concerns about "what will people think" are very real. I remember having to agonize over who to tell—or whether or not to tell at all. I want you, like me, to be able to be proud of your gay sons and daughters in a society where they can be judged on their own merits.

After all, when people meet me, and like or dislike me, it's because of what they get from my personality or demeanor, not because I'm heterosexual. The same should be true if they meet someone who's gay. That's just extra information about the person. And we shouldn't have to say that's information others don't need to know. They need to know precisely so that it won't matter anymore, so that we can allow our gay sons and daughters, gay relatives, and gay friends to be their full, complete selves and not to have to pretend they're like "us" so we won't feel uncomfortable.

It is my great wish that through education we can achieve equal rights for all our gay citizens. As I write this, only ten states have antidiscrimination laws based on sexual orientation. Fifty states should have these laws. A person who's doing good work should not be fired simply because he or she is gay, or evicted from his or her home for the same reason. And we should make sure that Congress passes and enforces the federal Employment Non-Discrimination Act.

The conservative William Bennett has referred to equal rights for gay citizens as the next frontier for liberal Democrats. I think that's ludicrous. It may surprise him to learn that I was a Republican most of my life, and I came from a conservative, traditional background. Equal rights for gay citizens is the next frontier for all fair-minded people. Some argue that these are special rights, but that's a smokescreen for bigotry and prejudice. Until our gay sons and daughters have basic equal rights under the law, they are treated as second-class citizens. And we don't have any of those in the United States of America.

Whether you agree with me, disagree, or aren't really sure, I hope you'll let this book open your heart and your mind, maybe even allow it to change you. Above all, I hope that you will come away with a feeling of complete acceptance—for your gay children, family members, and friends. Please don't allow yourself to miss out on so much joy and love.

PART I

1930–1978

It's about civility—something very common when I was growing up, but not anymore.

—JACK VALENTI, ON ACCEPTING DIVERSITY

1

The Importance of Being Different

FIRST OF ALL, WHEN you think about it, we're all stuck here on this planet while it hurtles through space in its orbit. If you imagine yourself free of gravity and floating off in the distance, you get a whole different perspective on us. I imagine us all looking exactly the same—like little ants, but full of self-importance. We're pretty good at dividing. And we're not bad at multiplying, either. (Sorry, I couldn't resist that. I am Ellen's mom, after all.)

How laughable we would seem from that far-off vantage point—self-obsessed busy-bodies divided by turf and custom and color and you name it. We're divided by everything from what we eat to whom we worship as God and what name we call Him/Her. We're not just divided by our religious differences: we've gone to war because of them; we've actually killed in the name of God. I'm certain that's not what He/She intended when we were first created and put on this good earth to live and thrive together.

When it comes to embracing diversity, I tend to think of myself as a relatively "average," "regular" person, not endowed with traits that would make me any more accepting than you or your neighbors. There wasn't anything in my upbringing that caused me to be more tolerant than the next person. If anything shaped that inclination, it is the fact that I became a mother. But I'm certainly not supermom. Rather, I'm probably more of an Everymom, with the same dream that most parents have for their kids—a live-and-let-live world where all the ants can celebrate individuality and diversity, yet still recognize each other as part of a larger family.

There's nothing new or radical about this image of ants. In fact, it's really just a spin on what is more commonly called the golden rule, something I was taught at the beginning of my education as Everygirl.

That part of my story starts in the depths of the Great Depression: on May 20, 1930, when I was born Betty Jane Pfeffer at home in a rented half of a double house on Dante Street in New Orleans, Louisiana. Despite the Depression and their own poverty, my parents—my father, William Dick Pfeffer, of German descent; and my mother, Mildred Morrill Pfeffer, of Irish descent—were happily anticipating my arrival and were planning for me to be the first of their three children to be born in a hospital. But I came too soon, and Mother gave birth at home, as she had with my sister Helen, seven years my senior, and my sister Audrey, five years my senior. So much for that plan. I've often wondered if it was my early entrance into the world that set the pattern of impulsiveness in my life, a pattern that has persisted to this day.

In any event, I am quite sure that being the third-born

and the baby of the family shaped my early personality. Where Helen, the eldest, was serious, intelligent, and always thoughtful, and Audrey in the middle was fun-loving and vivacious, I was known as the "littlest," and—with my thick golden curls and my apple-red cheeks—I was spoiled rotten, and notorious for never taking no for an answer. I was tenacious. Still am. I consider tenacity one of my great strengths and one of my great weaknesses.

My earliest memories are from about the age of four. What I remember most about myself was how irrepressibly curious I was about everything. By now we were living in a slightly larger rental, not far from where I was born, a raised half of a double on Apricot Street. This house had a tiny backyard with a dirt plot maybe three feet by six feet. To this day, I can still see myself planting nasturtium seeds there and—with time passing ever so slowly, as it does for the very young—watching the green stalks inch from the ground, the flowers eventually bursting into bloom.

Some years later, being an impulsive and curious child, when I saw an ad on a bus for cotton seeds, I wrote down the address and sent for them.

A month later, as we were sitting down to dinner one night, Helen and Audrey began to laugh. Mother and Daddy asked them what was so funny.

Audrey began, "Have you seen the backyard? She . . ."

"She? Who is she?" Mother said sternly. Mother thought it was extremely rude to refer to someone present as "she" or "her." Otherwise, Mother said, Audrey could have been referring to the cat—or the cat's grandmother. We were taught to refer to company present by name.

Audrey continued, "Betty Jane is growing cotton in the backyard."

That was correct. When the seeds arrived I had planted them on my own, per instructions, and I soon had a small but nice cotton crop.

Mother and Daddy must have thought it a little unusual. But they acted proud. That's how they were whenever I tried new things. The lesson was simple—it's OK to be curious. Over the years, this quality has endured and may be why I've always had quite a collection of hobbies and creative pursuits. And, even more relevant to the work I do now, being naturally curious has always made me open to meeting different kinds of people.

Of course, growing up in New Orleans—a real melting pot—meant that there were many kinds of people to meet. In later years, everyone started calling my hometown "the Big Easy," to contrast it with the hustle and bustle of the Big Apple and to emphasize its slow southern charm. As I recall, there was genuine ease in the way that the many ethnic groups—including French, Italian, German, Irish, Cajun, Creole, black, and white communities—lived together.

People had pride in their own culture and individuality, and pride in the city itself. New Orleans has a distinctive kind of beauty, with its streets lined by huge, moss-draped live oaks. When I was little we used to pretend the moss was silver fox fur and drape it over our shoulders. The muddy Mississippi is majestic, and the architecture of the French Quarter and the Garden District is truly distinct and wonderful.

The place was easier and the pace was easier. We *had* to take it slow and easy—it was so hot and humid most of the time. Goodness. Looking back, I don't know how we managed without air-conditioning, but we did. The house on Apricot Street had a sleeping porch as the last room, and every afternoon in the summer we had to take a nap, or at least lie down and rest. Afterward, we'd have a bath and put on fresh clothes and sit out on the front steps waiting for Daddy to come home from work.

Many evenings Mother would have a picnic supper prepared, and when Daddy got home we'd all go to Lake Pontchartrain for a swim. Then we'd drive to City Park and have our supper there, sometimes meeting other family members or friends. What I remember most about those picnics was Mother's iced tea, with lots of sugar, lemon, and ice—the best in the world.

Many years later, after my move to California, after my retirement, I took a poetry course and paid homage to those times with the following, one of my first efforts:

How did we survive with only
fans—electric and little
cardboard ones on sticks?

How did we survive the muggy south Louisiana summers—
summers that lasted half a year?

With lots of lemonade and iced tea
and cool baths and talcum powder.
And without complaining.

Back then, there didn't seem to be so much meanness in the world. Maybe it was the times I grew up in. Maybe we really were kinder and gentler.

Or maybe we were the same divisive ants that we seem to have become today. It's hard to know how much we have really changed. What I do know is that our current divisiveness does not become us. Instead of embracing those who are different from us as part of our human family, more and more we regard them with suspicion, fear, even hate. These divisions only weaken all of us. And what's more, I believe, they don't reflect what most commonsense, fair-minded people actually believe—that at our core, we're all the same; that no human is inferior and no human is superior.

So where does all the suspicion come from?

There is a song called "You've Got to Be Carefully Taught" from the musical *South Pacific*, which I have always remembered. The song says:

> You've got to be taught, before it's too late.
> Before you are six or seven or eight.
> To hate all the people your relatives hate.
> You've got to be carefully taught.

Isn't it true? Somewhere along the way, we were taught that being different was a bad and fearsome thing. Now it's got to be our job to teach a different lesson—that intolerance is unacceptable.

I got my first lesson about that from Mother when I was five years old.

Around the corner from our house was a little mom-and-pop grocery owned by Mr. and Mrs. Blanda, Italian-Americans and neighborhood acquaintances who had kids of about our ages. The family lived next door in rooms attached to the store. Every now and then, Mother would let me go to the store by myself for bread or some other item she needed. I'd always see Mrs. Blanda at the cash register in the front and Mr. Blanda in the back, where he ran the meat market.

One afternoon I was out playing when a few of my little friends dared me to run to the grocery store, put my head in the screen door, and yell out a certain derogatory name for people of Italian descent. It sounded like a reasonable dare to me. Obviously I was not a very bright child.

I took off, rounded the corner to the Blandas' store, threw open the screen door, and stuck my golden, curly head in, and yelled, "You old dagos!"

As I ran away, all I could think about was how impressed my little friends were going to be. Oh, and they were.

But my glory was short-lived. Mrs. Blanda did the right thing—she promptly went to Mother and told her what had happened. And very soon, I caught hell. Mother let me know that what I had done was shameful and stupid. The spanking wasn't the worst of it. The hardest part was having to go to the store and apologize.

I never forgot that lesson and never repeated a verbal act of intolerance. Mother taught me very young: Derogatory names are unacceptable. That is something we don't do.

MILDRED MORRILL PFEFFER was right sixty-three years ago, and she would be right today. If more and more parents made the conscious choice to teach their children to accept diversity, I can foresee a day when discrimination and prejudice will be made extinct.

Mother's lesson is not a sophisticated superprogressive notion. It's simple. It's what the Bible teaches us: Love thy neighbor.

And yet, these days, when it comes to loving our gay neighbors, we hear derision and hate from some people who claim to follow the Bible. They say things like, "I don't hate gay people; I hate their lifestyle." To me, that's only semantics. Hate is hate.

I will never forget a heartbreaking story I heard when I spoke to a university group in Ohio. After the speech there was a reception and, to my amazement, more than three hundred students lined up to have me sign their programs or have their picture taken with me. Then it was the turn of a young man who had waited patiently in line. He said simply, "I don't want an autograph and I don't want a picture. I want a hug." Of course, he got one. He explained, "My mom rejected me when I told her I was gay. Now, I'm HIV-positive, and she says I got what I deserve." Then he got another long, long hug.

What on earth could have made that mother so hateful? How could she have commited such an act of hatred toward her own child?

Others do not express their hatred so bluntly. They say, "You have the right to be gay, but I don't want to know about it." What they're saying is, "Stay in the closet." That message, in effect, was the one I saw being given to Ellen over the years that she was developing her career. Hide the truth, she was told, cover up, pretend you're someone else. What is it about being gay that is so threatening that others would have a whole segment of society live in hiding? It's the same thing as telling African-Americans to hide their blackness or telling ethnic and religious minorities not to be who they are. Can you imagine anybody telling the Blandas to deny their Italian heritage?

Of course, at the time when I was growing up, gays and lesbians were in the closet so much that I had no idea they even existed until I went off to college. And even then, my exposure was limited to innuendo and rumor. So although I was not predisposed to be prejudiced, I was totally ignorant. That's why, years later, Ellen wrote to me in her anguished letter, "I know you can't understand—you probably never will. . . . You were brought up totally different—lifestyle, generation, surroundings, people, environment."

Well, El was wrong in saying I would never understand. But she was right to recognize how those various aspects of my upbringing would make my process of understanding more difficult.

The Pfeffer household was almost textbook conservative—white, Christian, working-class, traditional all the way.

Daddy was the typical male role model who went on to become a working-class American success story. He was the son of a businessman who lost his hardware store to drink. Handsome and hardy, young Dick Pfeffer—he was known to everyone as Dick, never William—started out as a stenographer at Pan American Life Insurance Company and worked there forty-seven and a half years, ultimately rising through the ranks to become a vice president.

As if it were yesterday, I can still see Daddy sitting alone during the Depression years and later World War II at our big dining room table at night after dinner, with his record books and bills spread out before him, deciding how to make ends meet. I marvel to this day that with his salary stretched as far as it could go, he was able to raise three daughters and later send us all to college.

Daddy's girl that I was, I also remember doing my version of ballet in the living room while he was paying bills—to get his attention and to cheer him up, but also to avoid Mother's call from the kitchen, "Bets, it's your turn to help with the dishes."

Then I thought of another ruse: "But, Mother, I have to practice the piano."

What a scam artist I was! It generally worked—except for a time when Helen brought home some popular sheet music and I taught myself to play and sing a song called "It's a Sin to Tell a Lie." Mother was horrified. She didn't want me playing it because of the words "sin" and "lie."

While my father exemplified the male role of being the one and only breadwinner and head of the house, Mother was very much a woman of her time: a homemaker and caretaker, proficiently doing everything possible to economize and run the house on what was most certainly a meager budget. Somehow she managed to turn our limited food supplies into meals that, though not fancy, were ample and filling.

"Waste not, want not," was Mother's credo. Leftovers appeared in every imaginable form. And this idea that being wasteful was nothing short of criminal stayed with her the rest of her life.

In addition to all that stretching of food, Mother scrimped and saved, crimped and cut, and sewed all our clothes. Following her example, all three girls took up various forms of handiwork later on. But at the time, I hardly appreciated her efforts, especially since the clothes she made for Helen and Audrey became hand-me-downs for me.

We were like many families of our time, striving to better our lot, all of us playing our rather well-defined roles and doing our part to get ahead.

Home, family, security—this was the shelter in which I grew up, and I loved it more than anything. The worst day of my young life was having to leave that cocoon and go to kindergarten.

"But I don't want to go!" I protested daily to Mother, crying every time the topic was raised. "I want to stay home with you!"

When the day arrived, Mother saw no other recourse than to put me out on the front porch, go back inside, lock the door, and pray. Her prayers, apparently, were answered. After my terrible suffering, I adjusted well to grammar school. Then, at age twelve, when I had a chance to go to summer camp, I went through the whole process all over again.

By this point, after many long years of striving, we had finally been able to buy a house of our own at 9121 Nelson Street. Finding the right house for what we could afford hadn't been easy.

Since Helen and Audrey were in their late teens and busy

with their own activities, that left me to accompany Daddy and Mother to go look at the various houses, some of them large, some in nicer neighborhoods.

Daddy had been certified as a real estate appraiser, so whenever we went to see a house for sale he knew just what to look for. He would crawl under the house with an ice pick looking for termites while Mother and I stood outside and prayed that he wouldn't find any.

Number 9121 Nelson Street was not one of the bigger houses, and not in one of the better neighborhoods, but it had no termites and it turned out to be our house. It had a relatively big backyard with a productive fig tree and Daddy soon built a fish pond and a brick patio. Inside it had two bedrooms and one bath, for a family of five, and no air-conditioning—in New Orleans, yet! Even so, we were definitely moving up in the world. We were achieving the American dream: home ownership.

Again, the lessons I learned were not unusual. Through my family's example, I was taught that as long as we worked hard and had a positive attitude, all Americans could have the same chance at that dream.

Maybe that's why, today, I have such a hard time understanding those who don't support laws to protect the rights of gay citizens on the job and their right to live safely where they choose, without the fear of being fired or evicted simply because they're gay.

When people call these "special" rights, I have only to think of the segregated neighborhood half a block away from us on Nelson Street and the laws that became necessary to provide these very rights for our black citizens.

In fact, one reason we were able to afford our house was its proximity to this section where the black families lived. There were no visible boundaries, but it was as though we lived in separate cities. Their ramshackle houses made our little house and those around it seem palatial by contrast. Our black neighbors sat on their front porches and steps. Now and then, they passed by our houses. And yet it was as if they were invisible. We just didn't see them. I don't even know where their children went to school. That's how segregated we were.

Strangely, and sadly, I had forgotten this example of injustice until only recently. But now I remember that time when others were made invisible because of the color of their skin. It wasn't right then, and it isn't right now.

AS YOU MIGHT EXPECT, my sisters and I were raised with very traditional ideas about marriage and family. The message was that nice, pretty girls like us grew up and married nice young men who would provide and look out for them and their children. Just like Mother and Daddy.

Mildred Morrill—"Miss Millie" as Daddy called her—was only seventeen when she became Mrs. Dick Pfeffer, and he was only twenty-one. Imagine—a wife and mother while still a child herself, suddenly thrown into child-rearing and other wifely duties.

We never tired of hearing the story about our parents' romance. "Was it love at first sight?" I, the romantic, would ask Daddy.

"Bets!" Mother would quiet me before he could answer. That question was much too personal.

Audrey, always sunny, giggled. Helen gave me a knowing, thoughtful look as if to say of course it was love at first sight. How could it not be? Mother was very pretty with her pale Irish coloring and slim figure, even though she never seemed to realize how cute she really was.

Daddy was notoriously impatient—something I inherited in a big way—and he jumped in, "For crying out loud, do you want to hear the story or not? I was making . . ."

"Your father was making ninety dollars a month," Mother interrupted, "and he got a ten-dollar raise, thought he was rich, and proposed." She smiled, deferring to Daddy, the boss, as always, "Right, hon?"

"That's right, Miss Millie," he said.

Though Daddy always had the last word, he knew better than to argue or hurt Mother's sensitive feelings. That was how, in her own quiet, deferential way, she wielded a good deal of control in our family.

"After that," I concluded, "you lived happily ever after."

Their story to me was just like all the fairy tales that shaped my early consciousness. Like Cinderella and Prince Charming. Then, later on, I learned about love from the movies—all the different versions of Girl Meets Boy. I loved going to the movies. I grew up at our neighborhood theater, Ashton's. Once a week Mother and Daddy and I would walk the eight blocks there, sometimes stopping beforehand for a seafood dinner of delicious fried oysters and fried shrimp.

The stars I loved most were strong, sensitive young women like Jeanne Crain, Jane Powell, and Elizabeth Taylor; later on I liked Ida Lupino's acting and Anne Baxter in *The Razor's Edge.* Watching these heroines, I remember being completely carried away. On the way home with Mother and Daddy, I'd always walk half a block ahead of them, in my own world—pretending that I was that beautiful young girl on the screen with the storybook life.

I remember one of Ida Lupino's speeches in a heartbreaking farewell scene that stayed with me long into adulthood: "All of us are standing in the mud, but some of us are looking at the stars."

In our sheltered household and with all the love stories that filled my head from the books I read and those I saw in the movies or heard on radio, never once did I encounter the kind of love stories that have, in reality, been happening since the beginning of written history—Girl Meets Girl and Boy Meets Boy.

No wonder Ellen thought I would have trouble understanding her sexual orientation. In many ways, I really was brought up in the dark. Or, as my sister Helen's kids like to say, in the Dark Ages.

SO, HOW DID I get past all those damaging myths? Very slowly, unfortunately. But the point is that I did get past them. And the fact is that as human beings we all have the potential to grow and heal and evolve.

I recently heard an inspiring example from a young man in the South whom I'll call "Joe." Joe came out to a straight friend who was also a coworker. "I thought he knew," Joe told me. "He seemed to be dropping hints, you know." But the friend looked down and after a moment said, "My coach was right—you should all be put in a stadium and an atom bomb dropped on you." The friend said he no longer wanted

Joe to see his wife or children, and warned Joe not to tell the wife—who was pregnant—why, or "She might have a miscarriage." The inspiring part of the story is that over time the friend went from complete rejection to complete acceptance. The friendship has grown even closer and, yes, Joe is also close to his friend's wife and children—proving absolutely that love is always more powerful than hate, ignorance, and fear.

NOT LONG AGO, a caller to a radio show on which I was speaking asked if my Christian Science background had made me more readily accepting of diversity. My answer was that it did, to some extent. Christian Science teaches that God created man in his image and likeness. That makes each and every one of us God's perfect child—and that's the way we strive to see our fellow humans.

Our family journey into Christian Science was interesting. For most of my life, I always thought that it was Daddy, who was raised Protestant, who insisted on Christian Science and that Mother, raised Irish Catholic, just went along with him. As it turned out, although Daddy was attracted to Christian Science as a way to help his severe hay fever, Mother had another reason for breaking with the Catholic church—an argument with the priest over birth control. Mother wanted to use it. She had seen what having eight kids had done to her mother and had decided three were enough for her. Having me was the last straw!

Birth control? That was forbidden, the priest informed her. So she left the Catholic church. Mousy or not, Mother could sometimes put her foot down and leave it there.

Christian Science, as you may know, was founded by Mary Baker Eddy in the mid 1800s in New England as a system of healing based on prayer; she insisted that prayer was scientific. She thought the churches would embrace the idea. When they didn't, she started the Churches of Christ, Scientist. There are no ministers. Instead, there are practitioners who pray specifically for others when asked and charge a fee for doing so. In church on Sundays, a First and Second Reader conduct the services. There are also Wednesday night prayer meetings when those attending can stand and give their testimonies of healing.

Christian Science eschews all "materia medica" and stimulants such as alcohol and cigarettes. But Christian Scientists, as a rule, go to dentists and also have babies in hospitals, using obstetricians. I believe Mary Baker Eddy approved of having a broken bone set by a physician. People over the age of twenty who are attending church on a regular basis, and who wish to become members, go before a committee and are questioned about their knowledge and sincerity.

Through childhood and into my high school years we attended regularly but didn't join. We would call a practitioner for help, but we still used medicine and took vitamins—something devout, dedicated Christian Scientists don't do. At a later juncture, Mother joined the church, as did I in my college years. But Daddy—who smoked regularly and drank on occasion—never became a member.

In general, I received much good from my religious education. Because it stresses the good in all of us, Christian Science instilled a lasting, positive outlook in me. I am to this day an incurable optimist. And certainly, had I not grown up with faith in God and faith in prayer, I don't know how I would have survived the difficulties that were to come.

But I also learned a negative message from Christian Science: feelings don't count. Instead of acknowledging our feelings, whatever the problem was, we were taught to work it out, to solve it scientifically through prayer. In other words, when it came to negative emotions, the solution was: deny, deny, deny.

The following joke illustrates how this works:

Three men die and go to Hell, where they are met by the Devil, who asks each of them if they know why they got sent there.

The first man, a Catholic, says, "I cheated on my wife. I know it was wrong. That's why I'm here."

The second man, a Presbyterian, says, "I embezzled money from my employer. I know it was wrong. That's why I'm here."

The Devil turns to the third man and asks, "What are you doing here?"

And the third man, a Christian Scientist, says, "I'm not here."

Even without the input from Christian Science, Mother and Daddy were private people. Also, we grew up with far too many unnecessary secrets. This had to do with Mother's younger sister, our aunt Ethel. In an unusual turn of events, Aunt Ethel married Daddy's younger brother, Uncle Charlie. That made their daughter, Maisie, our double first cousin.

The same age as Audrey, she grew up as a virtual fourth sister to us.

Besides the fact that they married men who were brothers, Mother and Aunt Ethel's relationship was unusual in other respects, which dated back to their childhood. Ethel was the younger of the two—by one year—but Mother was smaller and less outgoing. Whenever the two went anywhere together, Grandmother dressed them as twins and put Ethel in charge, letting her carry the money and speak for both. I believe Mother must have resented this on some level, but rather than complain she dealt with her feelings indirectly.

Over time, this situation made Ethel perhaps bossier and Mother even more passive and sensitive. So Mother would do anything to avoid getting a lecture from her younger sister.

"Don't tell Aunt Ethel" was a constant refrain we heard from Mother, no matter what it referred to. Sometimes it involved Mother's hurt feelings about something that had been said or not said. This trait was so prevalent, I later picked it up and may have passed it on to Ellen.

Fortunately, we're both aware of it, recognize it, and work hard to overcome it. Ellen is much better at confronting—in a direct, fair manner—others who have been thoughtless. That has always been hard for me, but I'm getting there. On a positive note, being extrasensitive does make one especially compassionate to other people's feelings, something I think both Ellen and I very much are.

Daddy's temper and Mother's hurt feelings weren't the best mix. Sometimes, he could be cold and rather distant. And his opinions—so staunchly conservative that at one point he belonged to the John Birch Society—were firmly set.

The message? Opinions, like feelings, were best kept to oneself.

There was another way Mother had of brushing off any kind of disappointment, using a borrowed saying from her childhood: "Things can't be nice."

Whatever misfortune fell—from rain spoiling a picnic to getting jilted by a beau—Mother would sigh and say, "Things can't be nice." That expression explained away every unpleasant thing that ever happened to us.

Its author was a woman by the name of Mrs. Nungesser. Mother grew up next to the Nungessers. The Morrills and the Nungessers were good friends, and Mrs. Nungesser was looked up to as the matriarch of both families. The Nungessers had a son and a daughter. Their daughter, Marie, never married. I always laugh when I remember a comment Mrs. Nungesser made when she was about ninety-five years old and "Miss Marie" about sixty-five. Instead of concern for her daughter's future, Mrs. Nungesser said, "I'm old, but Marie has her whole life ahead of her."

All these messages that taught us not to speak about unpleasantness were compounded by the fact that in the South, at least in the 1930s and 1940s, such talk was thought impolite and improper, particularly for well-brought-up young ladies. "Don't talk personal," was how most people said it in New Orleans. And then there was the perennial, "Don't say anything if you can't say something nice," and the ever-popular, "What will people think?"

It would take me many years to recover from all that

worrying about what people were going to think and to realize some of the other negative messages I got in the process: Don't rock the boat; don't make a scene; don't be different; fit in; and, of course, just be normal.

CLEARLY, I CAME from a background which in no way prepared me to become a spokesperson. There was however, one exception—the training I received from my Aunt Tillie, Daddy's older sister. A remarkable woman, Tillie founded and ran, for many years, the Carrollton School of Elocution. Later, "elocution" became passé and the name was changed to the Carrollton School of Speech.

Aunt Tillie was short, just over five feet, and I always remember her in high heels. She was a human dynamo, teaching classes to high school students on Friday afternoons and to younger students on Saturday mornings. When she wasn't teaching she was typing and making copies of poems and readings for her classes. She also taught piano and managed to find time to give me lessons, in addition to special outings like plays and concerts.

Tillie's influence on our whole family was unmistakable. Even though New Orleanians have a distinctive accent—a sometimes strange blend of rural southern and urban East Coast—none of the Pfeffers or Morrills talked that way. In New Orleans, those people are called "Yats" because of how they ask the question"Where are you at?"—"Where're y'at?" There were to be no Yats in our family—at least, not once Aunt Tillie got hold of us.

Helen, Audrey, and I were each required to attend the Carrollton School of Speech. After all, Aunt Tillie let us go free. With no tuition, there was no question—we had to go. It was drudgery, especially on Friday afternoons and Saturdays, when I knew that my friends were out having fun while I was in speech school learning and reciting poems and studying mythology, Shakespeare, Longfellow, the arts, and other boring stuff.

At the time, I didn't realize how blessed I was that Aunt Tillie was so determined to have "Miss Betsen," as she called me, exposed to real culture. Nor did I have any idea that she was not only giving me a foundation for my later career as a speech pathologist, but also giving me the only background I had for the public speaking I do now.

Try as I might, speech school was one thing I couldn't beg my way out of. So I settled down and participated rather well. Those who didn't got a look from Aunt Tillie. That's all she had to do, and order was restored.

Although the school was in her basement, it was immaculate and thoroughly professional. I would take my seat with the rest of the girls and boys in class, and we would form a semicircle of folding chairs around Aunt Tillie's chair and table at the front. "Sit tall in your chairs," she would remind us, so we learned the importance of good posture and breathing. And when we stood up, her well-articulated instructions continued: "Shoulders back; chest up and out . . ." and so on. This is how we began every class—with deep-breathing exercises and vocalizing different vowel sounds. There were no nasal voices in our family!

We had poetry recitals in February and plays in June. Many of these plays were written by Tillie herself. The most memorable recital was the one when Cousin Maisie and Betty

Ann Nicholson were reciting a poem together and one of them got the giggles.

Soon that got the other one going.

Tap, tap, tap went Aunt Tillie's baton on her stand, waiting for them to calm down. That only made Maisie and Betty Ann laugh harder. Aunt Tillie had to ask them to leave the stage. They left in shame, but laughing all the way.

That was a strong lesson for me—keep a straight face no matter what. It comes in handy both in life and in public speaking.

In the summer, when we didn't have speech school, Aunt Tillie gave us a reading list and we had to read a certain number of books by September—an experience that fostered in me a love of reading from that time forward. Here's another poetic effort to pay tribute to those days:

The J. T. Nix Library

With my summer reading list I'd climb the stairs
And enter the wide open doors into the soft, humid air
Cooled gently by ceiling fans and wall fans.

I can still smell the pungent aroma of
Bindings and pages and glue.
I'd make my choices from the list—the so-called
Required reading that early on nurtured my love for
books—
Their smell, their words, and then as now, their magic
ability to take me away.

Aside from this early appreciation for the written word and the lessons I learned from Aunt Tillie about speaking, nothing in my background prepared me to be an activist. I never heard anyone in our family speak out or take a definite political stand and act on it. We pretty much lived quiet, private lives, summed up in all those old messages: Don't make waves and don't take an unpopular position. And, once again, don't be different.

FEW OF THOSE messages have changed much in our supposedly more progressive times, especially for teenagers. Today, as always, gay teens go through hell because they're different. My heart goes out to those kids. I remember my adolescence and how important it was to fit in.

I was a typical teenager, wanting so much to conform, to be just like all my friends. But deep down, because they were all Catholic and I went to the Christian Science church, I felt different. So I didn't follow Christian Science very much. Instead, I followed the crowd. We went everywhere together.

On Saturday mornings in cooler weather, I'd ride the streetcar downtown to meet my friends at our regular meeting place: under the clock at D. H. Holmes, a large department store that was a landmark everyone knew. The girls in my crowd acted and dressed alike. For school, it was dresses only. On our off-days our "uniform" was blue jeans, a boy's white dress shirt worn "out," and, of course, saddle oxfords or penny loafers. And only white socks.

After we'd all gathered, we managed to spend the entire morning window-shopping. (I can't imagine much of any other shopping going on.) Then we'd head over to White Castle and buy hamburgers, greasy little square things; take our food with us to the Orpheum, Loew's State, or Saenger; and eat while we watched the movie.

On Saturdays in warm weather, instead of meeting downtown, my girlfriends and I took buses and streetcars—as many transfers as it took—to the lakefront. It was a more modest time and we wore skirts over our shorts. If we swam, we changed into our suits in Krupp's bathroom. Krupp's was on the lakefront and sold cold drinks and sandwiches. We didn't really go to swim. We went to meet the boys in our crowd, boys who went to Fortier and Jesuit.

One afternoon, I caught the attention of one of the cutest boys, all because I laughed instead of getting mad. He was tall and wiry with Irish-American good looks and had quite a sense of humor. This day, acting like a smart aleck as always, he picked up my skirt—a full, gathered skirt, white with a pattern of large red flowers, rolled it up tightly, and threw it out into the lake. I watched as my skirt opened up and landed on the water like a big round flower. For some reason, it struck me as a very funny sight. When I laughed so spontaneously, he was completely surprised that I wasn't furious. And I will never forget the smile that broke out on his face and how, in that moment, I looked into his eyes and felt something stirring inside me that I had never really felt before. Major sparks!

Soon after that, he called and asked me out. We ended up going steady for a year or so. Was I in love with him? As an adult, I'm inclined to wonder what, at that age, I could have really known about such things. But at the time, experiencing that first love, I felt a passion that, in some respects, I wouldn't feel again. In any event, we were very serious. That is, until one day I flippantly mentioned that I might want to date someone else too and he made the honest mistake of giving me an ultimatum.

"Him or me," he said flatly.

I hate ultimatums. I always make the wrong choice—"Oh, yeah? Well, I'll show you." I really didn't care about the other boy. But, stubborn and impulsive, I shot back, "Him."

We broke up. He married young (as I was also about to do). In fact, he married the very next girl he went out with. Through my turbulent years ahead, I often wondered what had happened to that cute boy with the great sense of humor. Forty-eight years later, at my mother's funeral in 1993, I reconnected with him. There were still some sparks. We renewed our friendship and relationship and had plans to marry.

It would have made a very sweet story—girl next door and first boyfriend meeting up after all those years—a fairy-tale ending like the ones I grew up on. But it didn't take long for reality to set in. We were two very different people. He had never left New Orleans; I'd moved on a long time ago. Our worldviews had little in common. At first, this came out in subtle ways. But he was opinionated and closed-minded; also, he was an ardent debater who tried incessantly to convert me to his way of thinking.

When it came to our opposite stands on abortion, for example, he wouldn't even listen to me. He was vehemently pro-life. "Pro-life" is a term I resent. Every thinking, caring person is pro-life. How could we be any other way? But some of us vehemently believe that a woman's body shouldn't be a subject for legislation. We believe that abortion should be legal and safe for women who find it necessary to make that terrible choice.

He and I broke off our plans after encountering a bigger and more personal conflict. I was the proud mother of a daughter who is gay, while his son and daughter-in-law were vocally antigay, claiming something along the lines of gay people not being in sync with their family values.

"Family values" is another term I've come to resent. Unfortunately, this perfectly nice phrase has become far too politicized. Now, coming from a background where it's not polite to talk about personal matters, I generally believe that politics and religion are topics that should be avoided whenever possible. People feel too passionately about both. However, since I have delved into religion, I might as well go a bit further and delve into politics. Although I was raised in a Republican, conservative household and voted along those lines most of my life, I have not always agreed with the party platform or the candidates—especially in the last decade. In fact, it was in 1990 that I first voted for a Democrat—Ann Richards, for governor of Texas. A strong, articulate woman who, in my opinion, was the best suited to serve the state and its needs, she also appealed to me because of her tolerant stance on diversity.

In the meantime, watching the extreme right move the Republican party toward its stance of intolerance has run me off—and turned me off—as the right has done to many others who want to think for themselves. When the party becomes more moderate, I may return. I hope by then we'll have gotten beyond that exclusionary phrase "family values," with its narrow definition of "family" as only heterosexual married couples and their biological children. This excludes single parents, or couples without kids, or gay couples, or gay partners raising kids, or adoptive parents, or extended families without biological ties.

What defines a family? Well, definitely not political affiliation. For me, a family is simply a group of people related by blood or friendship, looking out for each other and loving each other, the older members helping the younger to grow and flourish and reach their potential—and vice versa. When I think of my family—the one I came from and the one I made—I see a pretty average American family, with good, basic, real family values. Given that definition, somehow I suspect that your family is a lot like mine.

In my family I also see a group of wonderful characters, unique individuals, all of us with the differences that make each so special. I only wish that I had learned to appreciate my own differences when I was younger. I am so grateful for Ellen's differences and for my ultimate ability to accept them. Instead of an ordinary daughter, I was blessed with an extra-ordinary one.

In 1979, my aunt Gladys Mercer Morrill, who had married Mother's oldest brother John, published *Of Old Places and Dear People*, a small volume of family genealogy. In her foreword, Aunt Gladys wrote:

> It was that remarkable woman, Helen Keller, who said that in the ancestry of every king can be found a slave, and

> in that of every slave, a king. A leveling thought, but true. Between those great differences in status is the vast army of men and women who are our ancestors—each a contribution to what we are today and each life a story in itself.

In other words, we're all related. We're all family. Thank God for our differences.

2

Motherhood

EVERYONE WANTED TO KNOW—who was the girl with the legs?

The newspapers were calling it a Cinderella story. The girl whose legs matched the legs of the girl in the picture was about to go to the ball.

It was the summer of 1948, and I was a coed at Louisiana State University in Baton Rouge. Having completed my freshman and sophomore years, I was attending summer school that session—not because I was filled with scholarly zeal but because I had to make up for bad grades. In my first go-around at college, I was into the social whirl and was not the least bit motivated to study.

I may have been a party girl, but even by the standards of the time I was as naive and unsophisticated as a person could be. Once at a party, a young man walked in on me in the bathroom. I thought I would die of embarrassment—literally. Another time, at another party, the belt on my dress broke, and instead of taking it in stride, I was mortified. What would people think?

Earlier, as teenagers do, I had experimented with smoking and drinking, though it's hard to imagine anybody serving me a drink then—I looked fifteen until I was well into my twenties. But by the summer of 1948, my serious college romance was with a Christian Scientist, and I dropped all those vices. A short time later I officially joined the church.

I'd love to say that not smoking or drinking meant that I was starting to think for myself, but I can't. In fact, I had gone to LSU in the first place only because both Helen and Audrey had gone there. Like them, I joined Phi Mu. Like them, I majored in speech and drama. That was natural, given our background studying with Aunt Tillie. Still, it might have been nice if I had explored other academic options, or even thought about what I really wanted to do when I grew up.

Instead, I kept busy with dating and sorority activities. I did dabble in radio at the LSU college station, with my own show, *Especially for the Ladies.* Also, as part of my speech and drama curriculum, I acted in school productions. This is significant for at least two reasons.

For one thing, this was the first time in my life, to my recollection, that I heard that someone I knew was gay. It came out in gossip between some of the girls in a drama class—a particular handsome, talented young man was said to be "that way." Upon overhearing this, I looked so confused that someone explained, "You know, he doesn't like girls." There was an obvious negative connotation. A short time later, it was whispered that a girl on campus was a lesbian, which sounded ominous, but I had no idea what it meant until someone explained that she liked other girls. Again, there was an underlying sense of taboo.

I didn't exactly think there was something wrong; rather, the idea was just unheard-of. It was like saying gays and lesbians came from another country or spoke a different language. This exposure left me as ignorant as before.

What a shame that homosexuals were kept so much in the closet in those days that a relatively well-educated eighteen-year-old, such as myself, had never known or met anyone who was gay. Imagine how much easier it would have been for me to deal with my daughter's coming out if I had been informed during my own growing up that there are plenty of gay people in the world—that there always have been, in all walks of life. As it was, not until 1978, thirty years later, would I meet and actually know a gay person, my daughter.

Once I became more knowledgeable, I realized that in fact there were other gay people in our family. One was my father's cousin, Elmer Schunke, whom Mother and Daddy chose to be my godfather. The family understood him to be a "confirmed bachelor." He lived in San Antonio and, as I recall, I met him only once, in 1989. At some point, I heard that he was gay. Nothing derogatory was said. It was simply a fact.

Similarly, I found out that Daddy's cousin Freddy was gay. And there were close friends of Helen's—two women who were more than likely a lesbian couple, though they were accepted just as longtime companions. I only regret not knowing about these friends and relatives sooner. It would have been helpful in my own process with Ellen if people had talked more openly about this.

The second interesting aspect of my involvement in speech and drama at LSU is that I got a chance to meet and act with a classmate who went on to become one of our nation's great actresses—Joanne Woodward.

Joanne and I used to try out for the same parts. No need to guess who always got the part. Joanne was impassioned about acting; I wasn't. To me, the stage was still a chore, a reminder of many childhood hours spent at the Carrollton School of Speech.

I have an indelible memory of standing in the wings with Joanne as we waited to go on in a play we were doing together. At this important moment, Joanne leans over and says to me, "Oh, I'm so nervous. I always get such stage fright." And I reply, cool as can be, "Oh, I never do."

This incident may prove that stage fright is a good thing. It gets you "up." In any event, the conversation stayed with me as I watched Joanne's career unfold over the years, including her performance in *The Three Faces of Eve*, for which she won an Academy Award.

Ellen knows this tidbit from my past, of course, and with her skewed view of things she likes to say that Paul Newman could have been her father.

My first taste of celebrity, though not as an actress, came that summer of 1948. It happened, mainly, because of my legs.

Bear in mind that the Dior look had just come in and hemlines had dropped, so legs were becoming an uncommon sight.

One hot July afternoon I was at my dormitory helping to paint signs for the impending LSU-Texas football game. Although the game wasn't until September, it would be the first time the LSU Tigers had played the Texas Longhorns, and so we started our preparations early. I was wearing shorts that day and had kicked my shoes off as I painted a game banner when a photographer for the campus paper took a flattering picture of me and my legs.

Suddenly, I was making front-page headlines throughout Louisiana and Texas. Here's how they reported it in *The Summer Texan*:

> It's too hot to be thinking about football but a picture in the *Summer Reveille* . . . published a couple of weeks ago was too enticing to pass up.
>
> It was a pert-looking lass, Miss Betty Pfeffer of New Orleans, painting a "Tigers Take Texas" sign." . . . The sign wasn't why we sighed—it was Betty.

And so, the article went on, editors of *The Texan* had sent a telegram inviting me to come; and the next thing I knew, I was being crowned the LSU "Ambassador." As the game approached, the papers continued to follow the story closely. The event and my role in it kept expanding until the day of the big event, and my itinerary included a meeting with Governor Jester and the president of the University of Texas, an interview on the local radio station, a reception at Austin's top hotel, and a presentation at halftime.

Once again, Aunt Tillie's lessons helped me to be poised and articulate. That game—won by Texas, by the way, though that did not spoil my fun a bit—was a highlight. I've often wondered what would have happened had I completed my degree at that time and stayed with my budding career as an ambassadress. Who knows? Maybe it might not have taken me five decades to become a national spokesperson for an important cause.

That may have been better for me, but would it have been better for Vance and Ellen? I don't think so. In fact, they may not have been here at all. And that's exactly why we can't second-guess the choices we make in our lives. After all, how else would I have had my career as Everymom?

As it turned out, in the fall of 1948, once the excitement cooled off and I got back to my regular routine, that was the direction my life was ready to take.

BY NOW, BOTH Helen and Audrey were married and had become mothers. Helen had given birth to her first baby, a boy, the first of three boys; and Audrey had a new baby girl, her first of three girls. I was greatly impressed by their leap into parenthood, and once again I wanted nothing more than to do just what they were doing—get married and have babies. After Audrey gave birth to Carol, I made the baby a darling little sunsuit (is there still such a thing?) and hand-painted butterflies and flowers on it. With every stitch, my desire for my own baby increased.

These were the factors, combined with a lack of any other real goals or direction for my future, that led me to accept a proposal of marriage. It had been a lovely college romance. I was Cinderella and he was my ever-so-handsome Prince Charming with shiny black hair and dark eyes and a beautiful smile—and he came from a prominent south Louisiana family. But it should have stayed just a romance, at least until I had finished my last two years of college. Instead, we married when I was still nineteen and he was just twenty-one. I was a spoiled youngest child and he was a spoiled only child. We didn't have a chance.

Almost from the start, I felt that he was sorry we had married—that he felt trapped. In the middle of our first argument, he just stopped talking and walked out the door. When he came back, hours later, and I asked in tears, "Where were you?" he said he had gone home to his parents' house. That happened a few more times. For my part, there were far too many weekends when I found excuses to go home and see my parents. Apparently, neither one of us was ready to leave the nest. Marriage is for grown-ups, after all. It didn't take long to see that ours was a disaster.

I'll never forget the day that Daddy and Mother came to pick me up and take me home. With very little to say, they walked me to their car—a new dark blue 1950 Studebaker. There wasn't much to pack. Perhaps in my twenty-year-old mind, I didn't want any reminders of my disappointment. This would not be the only time I left behind material items. Nonetheless, I was taking away with me a deep sense of failure.

At the same time, I was relieved to be going home—a place that I never wanted to leave, not for kindergarten or summer camp or college, not even for marriage. As Daddy drove us back to New Orleans, Mother at his side, I sat in the back and looked out the window, listening to the car radio, which, thankfully, made conversation unnecessary. Sitting there in silence, I hardly allowed myself to feel all the terrible dejection and sadness inside me. Instead, I tried to put on an indifferent face, as if this wasn't the end of the world. It was my version of "Things can't be nice," another negative lesson teaching me to bury serious emotions and passions.

Then a song came on that was popular at the time—"Because," a romantic song, often sung at weddings. It was then that Mother finally spoke.

"Oh, Bets," she said, "how can you listen to that and not cry?"

FLASH FORWARD: IN February of 1998, I gave a speech to a civic organization in Los Angeles that supports gay businesses. Afterward, as people thanked me, one man shook my hand and said, "Lucky that you're such an extrovert—makes your job easier, I'll bet." I loved that! An extrovert? I hadn't been blessed, or cursed, with that description before.

A few months later I was at the HRC event in Oklahoma City, and after my speech I got a chance to meet some of the wonderful people who were attending and hear their stories. I received another compliment from one of the local HRC members who told me, "You're so at ease with people, such a good listener, and you talk to them so easily."

What's funny about these reactions to the new me is that for most of my adult life, the old me was rather reserved. Of course, when I was young I wasn't reserved. But somewhere along the way I changed, probably after the end of that first marriage.

I kept a cheerful front and neatly tucked away feelings of

shame and disappointment. But inside I was shell-shocked, and what had been a fairly healthy level of self-confidence began to erode.

To their credit, Mother and Daddy took me in with open arms and were not in the least judgmental. Maybe they were just happy to have their baby back home. At any rate, the idea of getting my own apartment wasn't even considered. Also, divorce was rather uncommon and it never occurred to me, as a divorced woman, to return to school, so I went out and got a job and embarked on what, through the years, would be a variety of jobs as a secretary, administrative assistant, and employment counselor—not to mention many other full-time and part-time positions that would include getting my real estate license.

One of the first places where I went to apply for an office job was the California Company (now Chevron). When I walked into the personnel department, I spotted a familiar face—a young man named Elliott DeGeneres. I'd known him casually for years through a Christian Science young people's social group.

Elliott worked at the California Company as the editor of its company newspaper. He was tall and thin, and he had a habit of bending over a bit, as if he were uncomfortable with his height. Elliott didn't have the kind of dashing good looks that I had grown up expecting of a Prince Charming. But he did have the most beautiful blue eyes (which Ellen would inherit), set against dark hair and lit by a warm smile; and his personality instantly put me at ease.

We spoke briefly that day—I don't remember about what. I filled out an application and went home. That night, Elliott called to make the helpful suggestion that it would be easier for me to get a job there if I learned shorthand. We chatted about other things, leaving the door open for him to call later. A friendship began to grow.

As it turned out, I soon found employment at Hardware Mutuals Insurance Company, which made learning shorthand unnecessary. But in the meantime, my phone conversations with Elliott had led to our attending church together and, eventually, dating. He proved to have a great sense of humor and kept me laughing at his silly jokes and funny remarks. Once, while sitting in church, he whispered to me, pointing to the EXIT sign over the door, saying, "You know what that stands for? Elliott's Xylophone's In Tune." He delighted in complicated little jokes like that. Some of them were groaners—he was, and is, shamelessly corny. But some were quite clever.

A few years ago he sent Ellen a cartoon he'd drawn of geese sitting in church. The minister, also a goose, was saying, "Honk if you love Jesus." Elliot was good at playing up the obvious and the absurd, something Vance and Ellen herself would take to new heights.

While Elliott didn't sweep me off my feet, our courtship was a happy time in my life. The only other fellow I dated was so aggressive that he scared me. Elliott was such a contrast—kind, thoughtful, and respectful. Most of all, he made me feel safe. And probably, on a certain level, he was saving me from my feelings of failure over my short-lived first marriage. Deep down I may have felt that if I could succeed in my relationship with Elliott, I could redeem myself.

Was I in love with him? Not with the passion that I had felt about my first boyfriend in high school. Not with the romantic, storybook feelings I had when I got married the first time. But I was growing to love Elliott. He was a wonderful friend. Our tastes and interests were similar, and we enjoyed going to the symphony and to Broadway plays when they came to New Orleans.

Elliott was a wonderful person. He was of French descent on his father's side and English descent on his mother's, and he seemed to have a strong work ethic. With his deep rich voice, he had a background in radio announcing and, although he had not been to college, he had plans to attend night classes at Tulane. And I liked the fact that he was a devoted Christian Scientist. When Elliott proposed, I considered all these fine qualities and said yes.

We were married on November 7, 1952, in a little room at St. Luke's Methodist Church at 6:30 in the evening. Our wedding party consisted of us, Mother, Daddy, Elliott's mother Ruth, and "Auntie"—his mother's older sister. After the wedding, we drove home to Mother and Daddy's house on Nelson Street, where our families were waiting for us, and had a small but very warm and loving reception.

It was there, amidst the well-wishing and unwrapping of a few thoughtful, useful wedding presents from family members, that Elliott gave me a beautiful silver bracelet. It had an inscription on the back that read, "To the loveliest woman in the world."

Later that night, after the reception, we said our goodbyes. And, under the dark sky, we left in Elliott's big, old, blue, two-door DeSoto for a honeymoon in the Smoky Mountains in Tennessee.

Our first stop was a motel in Mississippi. When we left the next morning, the owner put a bumper sticker on our car that said: "We slept well at Hill's Motel." This was entirely true, because nothing else happened. That was somewhat upsetting, but I chalked it up to exhaustion and nerves. We had talked candidly about sex during our courtship and while Elliott was honest about the fact that he was still a virgin, he definitely let me know how much he was looking forward to the physical part of our relationship. I figured a good night's rest was all he needed.

When we checked into our motel in Gatlinburg, Tennessee, we were shown to the honeymoon suite. It had a big picture window overlooking a beautiful stream rushing over rocks and down through the mountains. We settled in for a while, and then I said demurely, "Elliott, I think I'll take a shower."

"Good enough," he replied and picked up his drawing pad, telling me he was going to head outside and draw a picture of the brook.

I finished my shower and, in my lacy new lingerie, waited with great expectation for him to come back inside. As I remember it, he never did. I just gave up, dressed, and we played tennis. In fact, the marriage wasn't consummated on the honeymoon at all. At one opportune moment, Elliott announced that he really had to get a letter off to his mother.

"Really?" I asked.

"Of course," he explained. "She's at Auntie's. You know she won't stay by herself. A letter will make her feel good."

Naturally, our lack of intimacy made me feel bewildered and let down, almost panicky. I had to wonder, in my efforts to be "safe" and respectable, what kind of turn was my life taking? When we got home and still nothing had happened, I remember thinking, "I could get an annulment." But of course I didn't want to admit that I had made another mistake, so I did not act on that impulse. Thank goodness!

Within another week or so, Elliott overcame whatever the hindrance had been and we consummated our marriage. Nonetheless, this was not the passion that I had dreamed of, and sex was never a frequent occurrence in our marriage.

Where was Dr. Ruth when I needed her? Nowhere to be found back in the prim and proper 1950s.

Sadly, my sex education at that point was equivalent to zero. I couldn't talk about my concerns with Elliott, not with my expertise at avoiding confrontation. I eventually came to believe Elliott was so spiritual that material and physical needs just weren't very important to him; he simply wasn't a very sexual person. After all, to serious Christian Scientists like us, sex is considered a material desire, and we are taught to try and overcome those.

I didn't even talk about any of this with Mother or Helen or Audrey—we all had too much training in not talking about personal things.

Mother couldn't even handle the words "sin" and "lie." Hearing the word "sex" would have made her faint.

SEX WAS ONE problem. There was also a second problem, which contributed to the first—Elliott's mother, who lived with us. When we began our married life, I moved into their already established tiny apartment. At first, the notion of living as newlyweds with an in-law did not seem unreasonable. I assumed we would move out once we had the means, within a few months, perhaps.

Wrong. What I didn't know yet was how dependent Ruth DeGeneres was on her only child. Elliott didn't just support her financially; he took her everywhere she went. Mom, as I called her, rarely left the house, and never without us. As Elliott had reminded me on our honeymoon, she truly refused to be alone. So whenever we went out, we had to make arrangements to drop her off at a friend's or relative's and pick her up again on our way home.

From the beginning, our lack of privacy bothered me. And then Ruth had a tendency to make offhand critical remarks. Not a good mix with my extrasensitive side. But I tried to understand how difficult her life had been and why she was so dependent on Elliott. I knew they had survived a turbulent home life and that her alcoholic husband had eventually abandoned wife and son. So I couldn't bring myself to complain about Mom or our cramped quarters. Instead, in my optimistic way, I tried to look on the bright side and see all the good in her.

"Oh, Mom," I would tell her whenever she dressed up to go to church, "your hair looks lovely." A very neat person, she usually presented a nice appearance, and she did have wonderful curly gray hair, which she cut herself.

"You think so?" she'd say, proud to remind me that people used to tell her she looked like the actress Billie Burke.

And then there was her excellent cooking, which was her contribution to the household, since Elliott and I both worked full-time.

On the other hand, if she happened to need an ingredient that wasn't in the cupboard, she wouldn't walk around the corner and pick it up herself. She'd call us to pick it up on our way home from work. That wasn't so bad, but it had better be the brand she asked for or we'd hear about it all evening.

I didn't know how much my patience was being tested until Mardi Gras, the first that Elliott and I had celebrated together. He and I really enjoyed putting together costumes for masquerades. At one party before we were married, we went as a prizefighter and trainer—he wore a robe with "The Horizontal Kid" printed on the back and I wore a turtleneck sweater and slacks and carried a bucket, towel, and sponge.

On Mardi Gras day, we really got into the spirit. Elliott dressed as a cowboy and I went as Bugs Bunny, in a costume I bought at a local five-and-ten, complete with big tall ears, a face mask, and bunch of carrots.

We set off in a happy, carefree mood—Elliott driving, with me at his side and Ruth in back. We wanted to arrive in plenty of time to find a parking place as close as possible to St. Charles Avenue, where the Rex Parade would pass by. Apparently, so did the rest of New Orleans.

There was no parking space to be found.

"I told you we should have left earlier," Mom said angrily.

"Well, you were right," I agreed, diplomatically.

Elliott drove a block further, calmly assuring us that he'd find a space.

Mom wasn't assured. And with each block we drove away from the Avenue, she became angrier, finally accusing us both of not finding a parking space on purpose, just to upset her and make her walk. She wasn't used to walking; she was used to being dropped off.

By the time we parked, though it was only a walk of five or six blocks, her ill-humor had all but ruined the day for me. Thank goodness for that silly, smiling Bugs Bunny mask because behind it my eyes were brimming with tears.

When I think of my life then, I see myself as wearing a mask most of the time—keeping my feelings to myself while staying busy and playing the happy, cheerful role that was expected of me.

Work took up most of our time. Elliott would soon get started in the life insurance business, and I was still working full-time at Hardware Mutuals. Aside from work, our lives centered on the church. It wasn't long before we decided to take an intensive two-week course of religious instruction, a step most serious Christian Scientists take. There are church-qualified teachers all over the United States, and our class was given in Houston, Texas. Some teachers, such as the one we had, recommend abstaining not only from alcohol and tobacco but also from any stimulant containing caffeine, such as coffee, tea, and cola drinks. We followed the recommendations precisely. Prayer took precedence in our lives, with Bible study every day without fail.

• • •

ON SEPTEMBER 2, 1954, at Touro Infirmary in New Orleans, my prayers were of gratitude when, to my great joy, I gave birth to Vance Elliott DeGeneres—the most beautiful, perfect little being I had ever laid eyes on. There is no feeling that even comes close to the awe and adoration a mother feels when she first holds her newborn. I was in love.

It had not been an easy birth, and my labor had been long. But at seven pounds eight ounces, Vance was healthy and fine. As was I. Over the next day, my family and friends excitedly stopped in to admire him. At one point when I was alone in my room with my mother-in-law, the nurse brought Vance to me for a feeding—only he was more interested in sleeping than eating.

"We'll just wake him up," the nurse said, as if returning later wasn't convenient for her schedule; and she proceeded to do just that, by thumping her finger on the bottom of Vance's tiny foot.

She might as well have slapped me hard across the face. I said nothing, but tears sprang to my eyes.

Seeing me upset, the nurse laughed and said, "That doesn't hurt him." And she did it again.

Now openly crying, I said, "Could you please leave?"

Ruth looked appalled. "I don't know what's wrong," she said to the nurse. "She's not usually like this. She's really easy to get along with."

The two of them gave me disapproving nods, seemingly unaware that I thought my baby was being hurt.

Thankfully, I survived that trauma and soon we proudly brought Vance home to our little apartment. Now we were a family of four living with just one bedroom. I was still trying to nurse—the healthy, natural way—but he cried a lot. Being a new, nervous mother, I worried about disturbing the neighbors. And then there was the day that a friend of Mom's came to visit while I was nursing, and the friend saw fit to scoff loudly, "Well, how does it feel to be a cow?"

That did it for me. I put him on the bottle after that.

Aside from those upsetting incidents, with the onset of young motherhood I found a happiness I had never known—a sense and meaning to my life that seemed to have been lacking before. Vance was a very beautiful, good-natured baby and toddler. Early on, he had a keen ear for music and seemed to have a genuine sense of humor. Naturally, I thought his every utterance was brilliant. There was a catchphrase in those years when Elliott and I were voting for Eisenhower, the Republican presidential candidate: "I Like Ike." Little Vance's version was, "Ike, Ike, Ike." We thought that was adorable.

I immersed myself in taking care of Vance and in part-time self-employment which included being an Avon Lady and an encyclopedia salesperson. Later, I did part-time office work for a wholesale grocer. Between church and my usual array of hobbies (oil painting, knitting, and sewing—at that time) I was busy and thriving.

THOUGH THEY WERE not acknowledged, my marital problems hadn't gone away. Our sex life had yet to improve and Mom—or Mumsy, as the kids would call her—was still very much on the scene.

Elliott seemed to be in denial. And I enabled that denial

by not talking about it. In Christian Science we worked quietly, talking only to a practitioner, while waiting for things to "work out." I don't remember talking about this to anyone else or even admitting that things weren't perfect. Whenever I had feelings of doubt, I avoided them, resolving to stick it out with Elliott and to pray more sincerely for some improvement.

That came soon when, thanks to help from Mother and Daddy, we were able to buy our first house—a two-bedroom, one-bath house in Metairie, a suburb of New Orleans. Elliott and I still didn't have much privacy, but at least we had a bit more space in which not to have it.

Later, Mother and Daddy helped us afford an add-on. As it happened, home improvement was one of my budding interests and something in which I would become expert, given our frequent moves. In 1955, I entered a nationwide essay contest sponsored by the National Home Improvement Council. There were more than 80,000 contestants, who were asked to write an essay on "Why Americans Want to Improve Their Homes." To my surprise, my essay won, and I received a prize of one hundred dollars. A picture of me and another local winner, along with Mayor deLesseps S. Morrison, appeared in the New Orleans paper, the *Times Picayune*.

That encouraged me to try my hand at writing, and soon I was contributing local-color stories to the *Christian Science Monitor* on subjects as diverse as pet care, family vacations, and a day at Mardi Gras with my four-year-old son dressed as a cowboy and my one-year-old daughter, my miracle child, dressed as a bunny.

Ellen was indeed a miracle. I had to beg for a second child. Elliott thought one child, whom we dearly loved, was sufficient. Nothing if not tenacious, I didn't give up. I thank God every day that I persevered, and so does Elliott.

When we first found out that I was pregnant, we decided to tell Mother, Daddy, and Mom at the same time. A few nights later, at dinner over at my parents' house, we announced the happy news. My parents were thrilled. Mom tried to act pleased, but I could tell in her voice that something was wrong.

We found out what it was in the car on the way home.

"No advance warning?" she said, livid. "How could you just surprise me like that?" And she went on.

The next day, still seeming out of sorts, she got busy helping with the housework. When she figured out some gadget that wasn't working properly, I offered, "I think you're very smart."

"Well, I don't think you are," she shot back.

This wasn't the best way to begin this pregnancy that I so wanted. But I was too happy to let her get me down for long.

Of course, once Ellen bounced into our world, Mumsy adored her, just as she did her first grandchild. Vance and El were the light of her life.

Though we told Vance that he was going to have a brother or sister, we gave him no explanation about the pregnancy or where the baby would come from. Then one day, close to my due date, when I asked him to do something that he didn't want to do, his answer was, "No, Mrs. Fat Tummy." Did we think he wouldn't notice?

I was so huge, in fact, that Elliott's mother later said she didn't know how I could go outside.

Vance had come early, but Ellen was two weeks late. Finally, one Sunday morning after a big breakfast, the pains started and my water broke. When we got to the hospital—Ochsner Foundation Hospital in Jefferson Parish—the nurses weren't happy to hear about the amount of food I had eaten.

In the meantime, hearing the news, Mother and Daddy rushed to the hospital to be with us. But Elliott met them downstairs and asked them to wait there until he called them. Mother later told me Elliott's coat pockets were bulging with Christian Science literature. We did pray without ceasing.

And so God answered that day, January 26, 1958, when Ellen Lee DeGeneres was born. She weighed a whopping nine pounds, thirteen ounces. The birth was not difficult. They held her up immediately for me to see, and I just had an impression of a beautiful little blob of fatness. Later, when relatives gathered to look through the glass at the babies in the nursery, they overheard a man point to Ellen and say, "Look at that one—he's going to be a football player."

Mom corrected him indignantly, "That's a girl."

Ellen was a placid, happy baby from the start—and a pretty, chubby, cuddly, blond little toddler whose piercing blue eyes always seemed older than their years. They could twinkle mischievously one moment and fill with sensitive tears the next. As a little girl, she adored two things above all else: her baby dolls and her big brother, Vance.

As she shed her baby fat, Ellen stretched into a thin, lanky tomboyish, active, fun-loving girl, fairly athletic (like Vance, who was extremely athletic). I encouraged her to take ballet, but she wasn't a bit interested. Still, that man was wrong about football—she wasn't interested in that either.

Many years later, a good while after she came out to me as a lesbian, Ellen still couldn't understand that I'd had no inkling beforehand. She would point to pictures of herself in ties and short pixie haircuts, saying, tongue in cheek, "No, of course not, there were no clues."

I do recall one funny incident of confusion when El was about six and we went for a weekend to Gulfport, Mississippi. We stayed at the very nice Edgewater Hotel—a stay which I had won for us in some sort of Hammond organ contest. El had short straight hair and bangs at that time. Though she did wear dresses, while on vacation she mostly wore shorts and T-shirts. One morning while Elliott was in the elevator with Vance and Ellen, a hotel guest asked, "Is that a little boy or a little girl?"

In a huff, Elliott replied, "That's a little girl." Then, as the elevator reached its destination, without missing a beat, he turned to Ellen and said, "Come on, Albert," as they got out. Just more of her dad's instant humor.

ELLIOTT AND I felt blessed to have two very good, very sweet children. Aside from the present, this era—when Vance and Ellen were babies and growing up—was the happiest time of my life. Motherhood really seems to have been my calling.

The responsibilities of being a parent are great. As our guide, we relied on prayer for almost everything. The children never had any vaccinations or medicine. We took great care to dress them properly in cold weather. If it turned cool during the day, I would rush to school with sweaters for them. Also, I think we had the world's first hair-dryer—a real dinosaur. In winter, we would dry their hair so they wouldn't catch colds. I still have that hair-dryer. Isn't it funny, the things we hang on to?

Vance and Ellen both enjoyed Sunday school and learning Bible stories and prayers. There's a nice children's prayer they said every night:

Father-Mother God, loving me,
Guard me when I sleep,
Guide my little feet,
Up to Thee.

I still have the message Ellen scrawled not long after learning to print: "God is Love." Once Vance was playing outside with his friends and fell but didn't hurt himself. One of his friends said, "Oh, he's on God's side." I don't know where that came from, unless they heard their parents talk about how important prayer was in our lives. Even though today the three of us are no longer affiliated with Christian Science, we've taken the best, most positive aspects and incorporated them into our lives.

I do believe that giving children an early spiritual foundation is a very positive thing—particularly the message that God loves them unconditionally, just as their parents do. There are other important messages to teach your children.

Most important, I think, is to let them know that they can do anything that they truly want to do in life.

That was one of the greatest gifts Mother gave me, always saying, "Bets, you can do anything"—with each sweater I made, each picture I painted, each needlepoint I sewed, each course I took.

It's important to teach your kids that they have not only the ability and the right to achieve their dreams but the ability and the right to achieve the love they desire. And as they seek what they want, it's important to teach them that they need to be responsible, responsible for themselves—that they can and should be assertive, which does not mean aggressive.

Though Mother gave me the positive message that I could do anything, she didn't help me become assertive. Hearing her say all too often, "You shouldn't feel that way," I learned that my feelings didn't count. That was a lesson I didn't want to pass on to my children.

Children need to be respected, I learned. If you give them respect—not yelling at them or ignoring them—they learn to respect.

I learned daily in my journey into motherhood. I learned that it's important to be consistent as a parent, and that parents as partners should do their best to present a united front. I learned that it's important for a child to see parents expressing real love and affection for each other. Some of these things happened in our home, and some didn't, but I believe they represent the ideal situation.

I learned as I went along, through trial and error. Knowing what I know now, I'd love to have another crack at certain things. Since that's not possible, I continue, as I did along the way, to do the best I can. If there is one thing I would have done differently, it has to do with communication. The DeGeneres family simply did not excel in soul-baring.

One thing I fortunately did do, when the children were little, was spend time with them. Dinah Shore, who had a TV show then, sang a song about a child asking his mother to come out and play with him. His mother was too busy and said "later," but later never seemed to come. That message got through to me, and I did enjoy my children when they were little. Maybe that's why I have such happy memories of this time. Maybe that's why we stayed so close in spite of later traumatic events which could have forced us apart.

MOST PARENTS WOULD probably agree with what I've just said. We all want the best for our kids. We want a world that is safe and full of opportunities for them to flourish. We want them to succeed in their chosen careers and to grow up to find loving life partners. We all do the best we can to impart those values, and we all make some mistakes. In these respects, I doubt that most families are very different from the DeGeneres family.

And yet, to my shock, I have found that there are people who say that the principles of loving and nurturing your child don't apply in the case of a child who happens to be gay. During a call-in radio interview I did recently, the lines were lit up with people calling to thank Ellen and to thank me. Then a caller came on who identified herself as a mother and began by saying, "I want to tell Betty that I respect her unconditional love for her daughter, I think it's wonderful that she supports her . . . unconditionally . . ."

There was a pause and I mouthed to the people with me at the radio station: ". . . But . . ."

This woman was more formal than that, though. She said, "However . . . ," and then continued in a harsher tone, "I wanted to share with you that Ellen's choice to be gay is . . ." There was another pause. I wanted to stop her there and object, but I waited as she went on, saying, ". . . it's not my choice and so I am very concerned about this proactive movement infiltrating children and teens. The word of God on this issue is clear." She added, "I'm not prepared to give you a sermon," even though the implication was that she would be happy to cite chapter and verse.

"Well," I responded, "I understand exactly where you're coming from and what you want to say. And I don't want to debate with you or change your mind. You feel strongly and I appreciate that." I could have ended there, but when I thought of the gay sons and daughters living in her community, I felt the need to continue: "Being gay is not a choice. No one can be recruited. Absolutely not. In a lot of high schools today, there are gay-straight alliances and they're made up of both gay and straight teenagers who support and accept each other. They're not swapping back and forth. They are who they are."

This mother really had a lot of conflict. She began again, saying, "I am against anyone causing pain to anyone else's life because of whatever they choose to be . . ."

"Good," I replied.

"However . . ." she said again. "My plumb line is the word of God. It's not me, it's not my choice, it's what God has given us. And in the word of God, it is clear, it goes from Leviticus, Luke, Romans, Revelation—all the way through—on this lifestyle which comes from our innate humanness when we take our eyes off God. And I'm not hearing enough on this from people who are Christians and believers."

I countered, "Lots and lots of gay men and women are Christians and believers." That brought the discussion to an end. After the caller signed off, I added another observation saying, "The Bible—or rather, the interpretation of the Bible—has been used through the years for whatever purposes certain groups have had. Scripture was used to condone slavery. It was used to keep women from having the vote. And now it is being used vociferously for this purpose."

As I continued to think about this exchange, I found it mind-boggling that those who profess to be biblical experts seem to have skipped Jesus's admonitions: "Judge not . . ." and "Let him who is without sin among you cast the first stone."

It also seemed unchristian to commend another mother for loving her child unconditionally and then add "however." "Unconditional" means no "buts," doesn't it?

It's true that until Ellen came out to me, I was totally ignorant about homosexuality. Even so, I can't imagine for one second that there would have been a "but" connected to loving her.

Knowing what I now know about how hard it is to find

another person with whom you are compatible and passionate and with whom you can make a happy life, I can't imagine begrudging your daughter or son that kind of love because it happens to be with a member of the same sex.

I can't imagine that this basic right with which we are born should ever be denied to any person. We love who we love.

3

The Paper Doll Family

THE 1950S HAD ENDED, and a new decade was dawning. When I look back at the headlines of the 1960s—reporting major cultural, social, and political changes—it's strange to recall how insulated I was from everything.

In 1961, for example, as the civil rights movement began to gather steam, a group known as the "Freedom Riders"—blacks and whites together championing the cause of freedom—left from Washington, D.C., on an integrated bus tour of the South. Their bus was burned, and the riders were badly beaten. At the time that was happening, I was practically oblivious. Certainly, I read the news, but protected as I was in the cocoon of normal, day-to-day family life, it had little impact. Later, as the Reverend Martin Luther King, Jr., came to the fore, I recall being impressed by his impassioned speeches. But I didn't yet recognize that his struggle was also mine. Little could I imagine that decades later, I would join the ongoing struggle for equal rights for all and come to speak in the same forum as Dr. King's widow, the inspiring Coretta Scott King.

The women's movement of the later 1960s and 1970s must have bypassed Metairie, Louisiana. At least it bypassed me, and I wouldn't catch up until 1990. (Maybe all that bra-burning turned me off at first.)

Similarly, I didn't feel compelled to join up with the antiwar movement as the United States deepened its involvement in Vietnam. Like many other Americans at the time, I believed at first that we were there for a good cause, to protect democracy. But as the war dragged on and so many lives were being lost, I prayed with my fellow citizens for an end to the war. Thank God that end came before the day in the mid-1970s that Vance told me he had joined the Marines.

Being a typical all-American nuclear family—as families like ours were called in those days—the DeGeneres household did not go untouched by trends in music, art, and popular culture. From the moment the Beatles emerged on the scene, Vance and Ellen were caught up in Beatlemania, and later they were caught up in Motown and other rock music. Television was another staple. We all enjoyed watching variety shows like *The Ed Sullivan Show*, Steve Allen, and Jack Paar, as well as game shows such as *What's My Line?*

Vance and Ellen watched everything—any excuse not to do homework. Elliott and I tried to limit the amount of TV they watched, but Mumsy had the set on all the time and, as small as our house was, there wasn't much we could do to keep the kids away from it. Little did we realize that they were studying for their future professions.

It's strange that in such a turbulent, eventful decade, our family life was outwardly so uneventful. About the most exciting thing that ever happened to us was a trip we took in 1963, when Vance was eight and Ellen five. Elliott had gone to work selling life insurance for Pan American (the same company where Daddy was about to be promoted to vice president), and having done well, he had earned a trip to the sales convention in San Francisco. Then I was asked to address the convention on what it means to be the wife of an insurance salesman.

The four of us—without Mumsy—left New Orleans on the Sunset Limited, thrilled to be going on this wonderful adventure to glamorous California. Our first stop was going to be Los Angeles. We had a sleeping car on the train with an upper and lower bunk, and we soaked up all the new sights, thoroughly enjoying the changing scenery along the way.

Ellen gazed out the window with wonderment, clutching her doll in one hand and in the other her favorite blanket, which she took everywhere and which was now little more than a scrap. Vance made witty commentary. Somewhere in the West, we passed a herd of goats grazing and he said, "The mama goat's saying, 'Kids, eat your greens.' " Pretty clever.

In Los Angeles, we were starry-eyed tourists. On a bus tour in the Hollywood Hills, we were shown a helicopter pad above a house that was said to be Frank Sinatra's. We went to a studio lot where they were filming *Gilligan's Island* and the director was saying, "Back up the shark one more time." At that same studio, I said something embarrassing as we were going into the commissary and I saw Jerry Van Dyke walking out. "Oh, look," I said, "there's Dick Van Dyke's brother." Not good for Jerry's ego, I'm sure.

The highlight of the trip was a day at Disneyland. We stayed at a motel right across the street so we could get an early start. The four of us were awestruck and delighted by everything we did and saw.

One sight that impressed me was a young woman and her children who were being given the VIP treatment. They had an escort and were chauffeured around in a Disneyesque golf cart, and they didn't have to wait in lines. Who in the world are they to be so lucky? I wondered.

Ironically, just a few years ago, we could have been that lucky. But we never went back. The visit in 1963 was our one and only trip.

There are a few other ironies about this visit. One is my recollection of being in an amphitheater enjoying an authentic-looking Native American dance. At the end, the participants invited the children in the audience to get up and join in the dance with them. I looked around, spotting the kids who jumped from their seats to be part of the fun. Not my children. They were too bashful.

"Go on, Vance, you're a good dancer," I said, urging him to take Ellen too. Nothing doing. I gave Elliott a look, as if to say, "Do something." He only shrugged. I gave up, realizing that I was the one who really wanted to be having all that freedom and fun. How interesting that my two who were too bashful would end up entertaining the world, in music, TV, movies, and stand-up.

It was also interesting, later on, to hear Ellen tell an

interviewer that one of her reasons for wanting to be famous was that as a little girl she had watched her parents being impressed by celebrity and thought that was a way to win our approval. Hearing that bothered me, because we did try to give both Ellen and Vance the message that they had our unconditional love and approval no matter what. Nonetheless, upon reflection, I could see that Elliott and I were starstruck—in our own ways.

San Francisco was wonderful too. My speech at the convention was very well received. When I stood to address hundreds of life insurance salesmen and their wives, it was a foretaste of public speaking experiences that wouldn't come for another thirty-four years. I was very proud of Elliott's hard work and liked commending him publicly for an asset which I described as a saving grace in any household:

> —A sense of humor. This happens to be my husband's long suit, and many times where a situation wasn't really funny at all, we ended up laughing. When he first started and was getting home late, very weary from many appointments but not too many sales, he would say, "Well, Betty, the hours are long, but the pay is small!" (After this comes a wonderful imitation of crying which I won't attempt here.)

It's not easy to imagine how I could so sincerely extol the virtues of selling life insurance. But I did, saying that it could at times be "deeply satisfying."

We did more family sight-seeing, but it was hard for San Francisco to compete with all the heady stuff we'd experienced in Los Angeles. No wonder all four of us would eventually end up in southern California.

The train ride home was enjoyable as well, even though we were much more low-key, knowing that it was taking us back to our humdrum everyday lives. When we got home, we hadn't even unpacked our bags before Ellen began to sob, "My blanket, Mama, my blanket." She had left that old scrap on the train. We tried to locate it but couldn't. She braved the loss well. Even at that age, she was starting to have a sense of the dramatic.

Meanwhile, other truly dramatic changes were in the works.

IT WAS A cold, rainy morning with a sharp wind blowing off Lake Pontchartrain. The children were at school and Elliott was at work. I was getting ready to leave for one of my part-time jobs, which then included substitute teaching and selling encyclopedias—whatever I could do to help swell our limited finances.

I went to let Mumsy know I was leaving when I found her dressed and preparing to leave herself. Ruth never went anywhere by herself.

"Mom, where are you going?" I asked in alarm.

Angry and upset, she told me, "I'm going to walk to the lake."

We lived about three miles from Lake Pontchartrain, separated from it by fields and swamps. Not to mention that this was a woman who had never walked across the street and half a block to our little neighborhood grocery.

She insisted further, "I'm walking to the lake, I said." Mumsy was talking incoherently. Things weren't right, she said; she couldn't get them straight.

I acted as if I thought she was joking and managed to talk her out of it. If this had been an isolated incident, I would have been able to brush it aside. It was, however, only one in a series of bad days. Without a medical diagnosis, we'll never know exactly what the problem was, but she wasn't getting better and her mental condition only went downhill.

On top of my concern was the resentment that had built up over the ten years that she had lived with us. It's true that she was contributing a lot to the household by doing most of the cooking. But, as helpful as this was, it did nothing to improve my culinary skills or teach Vance and Ellen even rudimentary skills in the kitchen. Mom truly did have good days when she was industrious, often sewing clothes for the kids and even making slipcovers for our furniture. She paid great attention to detail and did wonderful work. In fact, before Elliott and I were married, she made slipcovers for other people and earned a little money that way.

I felt sorry for Mumsy. After a sheltered childhood, she married a man who turned out to be a hopeless alcoholic, and that wounded her deeply. This was probably the trauma from which most of her mental problems stemmed. But, although I was sympathetic, her behavior confused me and I didn't know what to do about it.

In spite of her dependence on us, in the past she had managed to keep in touch with her few friends. That stopped, and soon she was calling her practitioner every day. Again, there wasn't much privacy, and we had only one telephone in the house, so whatever was being said was audible to all.

Everything came to a head one day when I noticed that my mother-in-law was even more nervous and restless than usual, going to her room to read the Bible and *Science and Health,* then getting up and walking back and forth from her room to the kitchen. Vance and Ellen were both out playing, fortunately. When they were this young, I tried to keep them from thinking anything was "wrong" with Mumsy. But no matter how much you pretend that everything is normal, children have a way of picking these things up.

I started to worry even more when she went in to take a bath. I could hear her crying and muttering to herself.

"Are you all right, Mom?" I called through the door.

"I'm all right," she replied, somewhat dubiously. When she came out she asked if I'd drive her to see the practitioner.

We lived way out in Metairie and had to go into town, almost to the Garden District on St. Charles Avenue. Calling Vance and Ellen in from playing with their friends was probably an unwelcome interruption. But to their credit neither complained. I was lucky because both Vance and El were really well-behaved. This at least simplified my life. We drove the thirty-minute route quietly, as if everything was routine.

The practitioner lived in an apartment building above a drugstore. While Mom was with her, Vance, Ellen and I had ice cream cones and wandered around the drugstore. By the time we were heading home again, I could see that the practitioner had succeeded in calming Mom down. But these incidents were wearing me down.

Somehow, no matter how incoherent she had been all day long, when Elliott got home in the evening she was completely lucid. Such was the case that night. What was different on this occasion was that once Mom was in her room and Vance and Ellen were asleep, I finally snapped.

Elliott and I were in the kitchen, and I sat down on the green-speckled linoleum tile, leaning back against the wall, and started crying uncontrollably. Between my sobs, I managed to say, "I can't stand it anymore . . ."

Mom came out of her room to see what was wrong, and we sent her back in a hurry.

It was shortly after this that Elliott found her a little garden apartment nearby.

The day we helped her move, Mom made it very clear she was not a bit happy about being on her own for the first time in her life. Looking with disdain at the new place and then with reproach at us, she said, "I never thought I'd come to this."

But it worked out well. She fixed up her apartment with attractive slipcovers for her furniture and blooming African violets. We visited back and forth a lot. The forced independence actually seemed to improve her state of mind.

Even though our household seemed to heave a collective sigh of relief, I believe the damage to our marriage was irreparable. Before this, Elliott and I had never had enough privacy for the healthy intimacy a married couple needs. Ours had been an almost completely sexless marriage, except for having two children. By the time we got privacy, our habits of relating were deeply ingrained and it was hard for both of us to know where to begin to change them.

Nonetheless, without other major eruptions, life returned to normal and we continued with our regular routine for most of the 1960s.

NORMAL—THAT WAS the DeGeneres family. At least, we did a good job of keeping up that appearance. In her book *True North*, Jill Ker Conway mentions a "pretense of normality" in many families, referring to unhealthy denial. This term would aptly describe our family.

The way the pretense of normality worked in the DeGeneres household cannot be seen in what happened or what was said. It was everything that went undone and unsaid. We joked and laughed a lot. Just as I had said at the insurance convention, this was Elliott's strong suit, and because of all our struggles with money and work, I valued his sense of humor on a day-to-day basis. In retrospect, I value it also because from the time they were little both Vance and Ellen developed their own distinctive sense of humor.

On the other hand, Elliot's constant joking became wearing. Sometimes it would have been healthy to have a serious talk, an argument, even a tantrum. I wanted to be real, but it would take me years to learn how. Somehow Ellen did better at getting past the pretense of normality, seeing things as they really were in all their complexity and being able to talk about them. Vance didn't do so well at that, and he emerged from our version of *Happy Days* as an extremely private person.

My son and I talked recently about his memories of growing up in a household in which problems or differences of opinions weren't faced, acknowledged, or talked out. He felt that this was because it was more important to have the appearance of a harmonious family. That was a buzzword in our house—"harmonious"—but the illusion of harmony left at least some of us seething underneath.

El has said she remembers us as being like a TV family—the Daddy, Mommy, Sister, and Brother. And, like a TV family, not quite real.

Not everything about our normality was pretended. Our two children really were well-adjusted, easygoing kids, well-liked socially and involved in many extracurricular activities. In Metairie we were members of the Green Acres Community Club—thanks, once again, to my parents—where we all enjoyed the swimming pool and tennis courts. Vance and Ellen started playing tennis there, and both did very well.

Vance's big interest was music. As a little boy, he took piano lessons from Elliott's cousin Dorothy, and he took clarinet in elementary school. The night his class at Bridgedale School gave a program, Elliott and I watched proudly as Vance and another boy played a lovely little clarinet duet. Vance's clarinet occasionally made that high squeaky sound that clarinets make when you blow into them wrong. And Vance held the clarinet out and looked at it as if to say, "What is wrong with this thing?" We found it very cute and touching.

Since I continued to enjoy playing the piano, I thought I'd expand my musical repertoire and bought a guitar for myself. I didn't learn much more than the most basic chords, but Vance took to it immediately. He stuck with the clarinet, playing it in the junior high school band, and went on to master the guitar in the rock bands he started to form in these years.

When he was in junior high, Vance joined a band called Lick. The other members of the band were in senior high, so Vance thought he was really something.

I could tell how proud he was by the way he strutted into the kitchen one evening after work when I was in the middle of preparing a quick dinner. I was still trying to get caught up on my culinary skills, which had been neglected all those years when Mumsy did the cooking for us. In spite of my almost full-time work schedule, I was determined to become a good cook, for the sake of my shortchanged but patient family. At first, I fed them far too many "quick and easy" meals from recipes in my two cooking Bibles, *The Joy of Cooking* and *Better Homes and Gardens Cookbook.*

One of our mainstays was some sort of shortcut ragout. And then there was something called Lazy Day Casserole that Vance recalls as a favorite and Ellen remembers too, though not exactly fondly. If you lack kitchen experience and need an idea for a quick, filling, inexpensive supper, you might want to try it:

2 cans pork and beans
2 cans Vienna sausage
1 jar applesauce

Put the ingredients in a pot. Heat, stirring.

For a gourmet touch, I suggest adding a soupçon of yellow mustard. (A couple of years ago some publisher proposed that I write a cookbook called *What Ellen Ate.* Ellen's comment was, "Well, that will be short.")

Vance was usually the only one who cheered when I made Lazy Day Casserole. Once dinner was ready, I asked him to round up Ellen and Elliott. That meant calling out, "Supper!" Ellen was there in a flash. Vance excitedly told her what was on the menu.

"Lazy Day Casserole?" El said, hiding her distaste. "That's so funny. I *was* feeling kind of lazy today."

Vance cracked up while I chuckled, serving everyone. Elliott had yet to appear. "Where's Dad?" I asked the two of them.

"He went to the bathroom," Vance replied.

El corrected her brother matter-of-factly. "Vance, you know Dad doesn't 'go to the bathroom'—he washes up!"

Vance said something to Ellen about her being a smartmouth.

Elliott arrived just in time to create harmony with his big news: "I saw a tie I really liked today at Godchaux's."

Now it was Vance's turn to be a smartmouth. He asked his father, "So did you go to Maison Blanche and D. H. Holmes and Rubenstein's too—to see if there was one you liked better?"

We all smiled at this harmless teasing. It was true. Never let it be said that Elliott was impulsive—except, perhaps, when it came to his sense of humor, which was totally spontaneous.

I remember when we brought home our new Yorkie

puppy and were wondering what to name him. Without missing a beat, Elliott dubbed the little guy Spot. That way, he said, "When he's bad we can say, 'Out, out damned Spot.' "

Spot was another one who really loved Lazy Day Casserole. Since he was always begging for scraps and Ellen's plate was always licked curiously clean, I figured that one out pretty easily.

Ellen was definitely an animal lover from the time she was very little. She was forever bringing home lost or wounded animals to add to the family of pets we already had, which consisted of an assortment of cats and dogs, usually one at a time, but sometimes overlapping.

Before Spot, we had a dog that was Vance's favorite, a mutt who had been abandoned at our swim-tennis club in Green Acres. Everybody fed him, and at the end of the summer someone had to take him home. We were the lucky family. We named him Happy, and he had ten happy years with us. We also had a parakeet who said a few words and phrases. The parakeet flew out of a carelessly opened screen door, never to be seen again.

Added to these family pets were Ellen's personal pets. At various points, she had fish, mice, a horned toad, baby birds she rescued, a snake that ate live mice (but not her pet mice), and a Burmese cat which she loved although it was a bit too high-strung. The cat had a habit of jumping up on people unexpectedly, holding on with her claws. She died in an unsuccessful spaying operation, and Ellen mourned her for quite a while.

Then Ellen had a chipmunk; it was cute and tiny, and she

enjoyed holding and playing with it. One day she thought some fresh air would be a good idea, so she opened her window—and the chipmunk was never seen again. We had a neighbor, a fundamentalist, who had just arrived home from church when all this was happening and she prayed loud and long with Ellen for the Lord to bring back that little chipmunk. I don't know who didn't hear that prayer—the Lord or the chipmunk.

In future years, Ellen would combine her love for animals and her offbeat sense of humor in some great stand-up bits. I'm convinced that if she hadn't eventually gone on to find her niche in comedy and acting, she would have done well in some sort of veterinarian work.

WE JOKED ABOUT Elliott and his deliberations over buying one tie, but the issue actually went a lot deeper for me. This was especially true now that we were again living uptown, where we had moved because Elliott had become a First Reader and felt he needed to be closer to church.

After spending every weekend looking at houses to buy, I found these deliberations frustrating. Always, the right house was either just out of reach financially, or not in an area or neighborhood we wanted, or not near the schools we wanted for the children.

I can remember many of those houses well. One of them had only two bedrooms but had a little guest house in the backyard. Vance really wanted us to buy that one. He would have felt like he had his own little kingdom with that guest house. The house was Spanish-style with a red tile roof, two stone lions on either side of the front walk, and wonderful

Spanish tiles in the bathroom and kitchen. Not too many years ago, on a visit back to New Orleans, I drove down that street, and the house was gone. It had been bought as a teardown and replaced with a two-story house—much too big for the lot.

In the end, we sold our home in Green Acres and, instead of buying a new one, rented a small house uptown on Audubon Street—from a church member—until it was sold. This was only the first of several moves. We continued house-hunting, dreaming of better days, but we never really took the leap and seriously considered buying one.

We seemed stuck in our working-class struggle, and I wanted better—for my kids, for me, and for Elliot. Just a house of our own, more creature comforts, family vacations—nothing extravagant. I wanted to go back and finish school. Elliott surely wanted all those things for us and himself too. But moving up in the world often requires taking risks. And that he was either unequipped or unwilling to do.

Looking back, I realize how much resentment I was accumulating about this inertia, especially when Elliott turned down better job opportunities because it would have taken us too far away from First Church, which as far as he was concerned was the only Christian Science church. But acknowledging these issues, unfortunately, would have meant confronting many of the things I was in denial about. That's the key to the pretense of normality: once you admit that even one thing isn't as hunky-dory as you'd like, the whole house of cards starts to come crashing down.

It almost happened one day when I hurried home to tell Elliott about an opportunity for Ellen to go to camp. It was going to cost us nothing. I had a part-time secretarial job in the physical education department of Newcomb College, a part of Tulane University. Through friends at work, I was offered a job as secretary for six weeks at a summer camp in northern Alabama. El could attend while I was there, free of charge. I couldn't wait to tell Elliott the good news.

"Absolutely not," he said. "I didn't marry you to live like a bachelor."

That got me. There were many times—either with the kids or with bosses and coworkers—when Elliott didn't put his foot down soon enough. When he finally did, as in this case, it seemed totally inappropriate. But instead of confronting him then and there, I steamed privately and let it go.

Another time that I came close to a confrontation was when I arrived home from work to find the front door open and nobody in the house. When I got into the living room, I noticed that the TV was gone. For some reason, even though I knew that Elliott was at work, I called out for him, just in case he happened to have come home with a sudden desire to move the TV.

When it finally dawned on me that someone had broken into our house and stolen the television, as well as jewelry, our camera, and a lot of change that we kept in an ornamental can, I became very upset. I called the police, I called Elliott, I called Daddy—in that order. And the first person on the scene was my father. The police came later. Elliott waited to deal with it until he got home.

(An interesting footnote to our burglary is that to this day Ellen has kept that old can which the burglars emptied of our change—a reminder of a different time and place.)

And when it came time to repair the broken door, it was Daddy who was able and ready and helped me take care of it. My husband wasn't really handy. Nor was he a take-charge kind of guy. So what? I rationalized. Daddy was—and he liked being relied upon.

None of this was explosive. But the next event would definitely inflame me. We'd moved—again. This time we rented an upper duplex on South Robertson Street in the same general area.

I was now serving as Clerk of the church, a paid position. One day while I was at work and Vance was off with his friends, Ellen was out playing with her friends on a swing in a yard across the street and crashed into a low jagged wall, slicing her knee open.

As I later pieced the story together, a woman in a house overlooking the yard happened to be at her window and Ellen saw her mouth, "Oh, my God." She and her husband came running while someone hurried to tell Elliott. After a bit, he came over—calmly—standing apart from Ellen and the crowd around her.

"Come on, El," he called, gesturing to her to come with him. "You're OK, honey. Let's go home." When he saw she couldn't walk he picked her up and carried her across the street. At that point, Dr. Buck, our neighbor, had been alerted and had his car door open, ready to take her to the hospital for stitches.

Elliott refused his offer, assuring him that Ellen was just fine, taking her into the house, wrapping her knee with a rag, and drawing a happy face on it.

When I got home and heard the story, I ran downstairs

to Dr. Buck and asked if he could still help. He did clean the wound very well and pulled it together as best he could. El's scar is barely visible now, but for a long time she had a big scar and a story to tell.

I disagreed strongly with Elliott's handling of this accident. I was starting to see, for the first time in our marriage, the genuine difference of opinion that we had about practicing the teachings of Mary Baker Eddy.

TWO OTHER THINGS happened that made me seriously question, and ultimately leave, Christian Science. Earlier, I had come down with a very painful ear infection and could not seem to get relief. I went to one of our neighbors, Dr. Burch, and asked him for a prescription, which he gave me. It worked—fast!—and it made me rethink those years of abstaining from doctors and all medical treatment.

Not much later, on February 3, 1970, to be exact, came the kind of phone call you most dread. I received it while at my job as Clerk at the church. Helen and Mother were calling to tell me that Daddy had been admitted to the hospital. The details of what had happened were sketchy at first.

Daddy was sixty-nine at the time, and although he was a youthful sixty-nine as far as I was concerned, he hadn't really been himself since his retirement four years earlier. After forty-seven and a half years working for Pan American Life Insurance, this stage of life was hard on him. He had really defined himself by his position. I guess we all had. When I was a little girl someone asked me if I was Catholic or Protestant. I said, "Neither, we're Pan American."

The last few times I had seen him, Daddy seemed almost at loose ends, and in spite of his appearance of health, unbeknownst to us he suffered from high blood pressure—which was not helped by his smoking habit.

Mother later told me she had been fixing lunch and called Daddy when it was ready. When he didn't come in, she went to look for him and found him lying on the bed in the guest bedroom. He told her his chest and his left arm hurt. Clueless as we were about these things, Mother still had the presence of mind to insist that he get in the car. She immediately drove down the block to their doctor's house. The doctor came out to look at Daddy and said, "Oh, it's probably the flu. Take him to the hospital and I'll meet you there later."

As directed, Mother drove to a very small hospital in Metairie where Daddy was admitted to a double room. It took Mother and Helen—who arrived quickly—forever to find me at church. Of course, I rushed as never before to the hospital, only to find that the doctor still had not arrived. Daddy was perspiring heavily—not a clue to us, but it certainly should have been a clue to somebody—and I wiped his brow and face for him.

There are many "if only's" that would haunt me for years. I've always wondered what that doctor could have been thinking of. The flu? Did he really believe what he said?

Not realizing what should have been obvious—that my father had suffered a heart attack—we decided it would be best for us to leave so he could rest. As Mother and Helen walked out of the room, I paused, staying behind momentarily to make sure he was resting comfortably. And at that very moment, Daddy died. It happened so quickly. One minute he was here and then, within seconds, he was gone. I called desperately to the nurse who was attending to the man in the next bed. She came at once and called for more help. Everyone got busy doing CPR, but it was too late.

In the months and years following his death, Mother, Helen, Audrey, and I speculated that if Daddy had been given better immediate care, he would still be with us. We always ended these musings the same way—agreeing that if it meant he would be an invalid, then this was all for the best. Since we all knew well that patience was not Daddy's long suit, we couldn't even imagine him coping with that.

Although up until this point I hadn't realized it, my father had been my true anchor—the strong person in my life who had made so much of his own life, embodying the role of protector and provider for the family that loved him so. When Daddy died, my world, as I knew it, fell apart.

Even worse, I could find no spiritual comfort. While other religions have helpful ways of dealing with loss—like the Catholic wake or the Jewish days of mourning—Christian Science basically ignores the entire subject of death, referring to it as a transition to a happier state but not taking into account the natural, normal grieving process.

In leaving Christian Science, I was not alone among the Pfeffers. Daddy had never joined and after he died Mother soon went back to the Catholic church, which gave her lots of support and put her back in the company of many longtime friends. Having married men who weren't Christian Scientists, Helen and Audrey both had drifted away years before.

When I left the Christian Science church, it never occurred to me not to go to another church. Though I would later come to feel that an organized religion isn't necessary for a full spiritual life, at that time church was important to me. It was a way to enrich my life and to soften the rough edges of everyday existence. I shopped around and very soon found that I was comfortable at the Episcopal church. Since Christian Science shuns ritual and pageantry, I had been missing that for a long time. I enjoyed the ritual of communion, and kneeling for certain prayers. Vance and Ellen came with me a few times, but it didn't hold the same appeal for them. They continued to go to the Christian Science church with Elliott for a few more years.

It's hard to conceive of anything that would have given me comfort in those first days and months after Daddy died. Without knowing it, I was going through a mourning process that has several stages. According to Elisabeth Kübler-Ross, who has written extensively about death and grief, these stages follow a natural course: from denial to anger to bargaining to sadness and, finally, to acceptance.

AFTER THE FIRST shock and my own denial wore off, anger set in, slowly and covertly. Meanwhile, the DeGeneres household reverted to its old harmonious mode, making an even greater effort to pretend that everything was fine. Ellen later made the observation that we had become a paper doll family, with everyone going through the motions. We didn't even qualify as a TV family anymore.

One of the last family vacations we took together was around this time. We drove down for a long weekend to

Fort Walton Beach, Florida, in our new-to-us Mercury Cougar—a sporty model with a black hardtop and turquoise body. Since Vance was learning to drive, he was at the wheel with Elliott at his side. Ellen and I were in the back. We must have thought it would be safe for Vance to practice on the long stretches of highway along the Florida Gulf Coast. And it was, until he decided that he had time to pass a car before oncoming traffic arrived.

Even the ever-calm Elliott was screaming, "Vance, get back in your lane!"

I chimed in, "Hurry, Vance, hurry!"

And Ellen was just screaming.

Vance passed the car and got back into his lane in the nick of time.

This was more excitement than any of us were used to. We probably would have done well to scream a bit more often. Instead, we went back to our pretense of normality.

Thirteen-year-old El was the one who saw through it. I think she knew before I did that her parents' marriage was ending. Vance was less aware; he was busy finishing up high school and working as a DJ, and he was starting to spend time traveling on the road with his band. On the other hand, as he himself would be inclined to comment, even if he had been around more, we simply didn't talk about what was really going on. There were always jokes, but there was no talk about anything meaningful or substantive. If that one aspect of our marriage had been different, maybe Elliott and I would have stayed together.

Oh, yes, there was another move. We were now renting a lovely lower duplex in Lake Vista that a church member owned. When we moved there, Elliott and I bought a beautiful walnut dining table. I remember that table and exactly where it was, but I don't remember happy times around it. I believe it was too late for that.

Once I made the decision that I could no longer, in good conscience, embrace Christian Science, Elliott and I lost one of our strongest bonds. It made matters worse that he was resentful about my new affiliation with the Episcopal church. I had stifled so many years of frustration that when, at long last, Elliott had begun to show more of an interest in sex, that too seemed to be too late. Also, there was a catch: he thought I should be the one to buy the prophylactics. Horrors. Back then, condoms weren't at the check-out counter. You had to ask the pharmacist for them—that was much too personal for me.

And, of course, because Elliot refused even to mention the possibility of more babies—which I would have loved—without some form of birth control sex was out of the question.

My anger was such that even though there was no cursing in the DeGeneres household, one day I used the word "crap." Elliott was horrified. He must have known that I was at a boiling point, but as usual he was in denial.

So, on my own, without any discussion, I began to take steps to leave our marriage. One day when Ellen and I were walking, I spotted a FOR RENT sign outside a nearby apartment complex. Scared but resolved, I told her of my decision to find a place to live.

Young as she was, she was well aware of my feeling of desperation. "This will be fun," El said, in an instinctive effort to cheer me up, and then went on to describe all the adventures Vance, she, and I would have as bachelor and bachelorettes. Not to mention that it would be a nice change for her pet snake.

As planned, I contacted the apartment owner, saw the apartment, and arranged to move in.

One of the saddest moments in my life was telling Elliott that I wanted this separation. It was after work, just the two of us. I arrived home a short while after him, came inside and told him, simply, softly, "Elliott, I'm moving out."

He said nothing. But I could see in his eyes, as they filled with tears, how devastated he was. A few minutes later, Vance came home, realizing instantly that something was wrong.

Speaking with difficulty, Elliott explained, "Your mother's leaving me."

Vance's eyes filled up with tears too. It was heartbreaking. Nothing more was said. In my mind, I desperately wanted Elliott to beg me not to go. He never did, not then and not in the two years that followed, before our divorce was final. Had he come after me at any point in that time, my resolve would surely have weakened.

When I left Elliott and our shell of a marriage, I left behind the security of the status quo—the only life I had known for eighteen years. As a kind of metaphor, I also left behind that beautiful walnut dining table, as well as an irreplaceable antique pine secretary, and an antique cypress coffee table. This continued to be a habit of mine—leaving material things behind, not wanting reminders of my failure.

Sometimes one clear-cut event precipitates the end of a

marriage. In this case, though there was no specific last straw, I finally caved in under the weight of layers of resentment, inaction, and wrongs that had built up over the years. The moment I chose to leave, I began to shed those layers.

In the death of our marriage there would remain many "if-only's." The top of my list: if only we had developed a way of talking about our issues. In another place and time, we might have gotten help that could have saved us as a couple. These "if-only's" are part of the bargaining stage of grief. They can never change that which has died.

There is no blame here. I was just as much a part of the "Don't talk about it" conspiracy.

The great irony of the pretense of normality is that it is so commonplace. We have an idea that everybody else is "normal," and we keep our concerns secret, in the hope that we can pretend them away. When we finally admit them, it turns out that a lot of other people have the same secrets. In the end, nobody is normal—or at least nobody is your idea of "normal."

Do I regret leaving Elliott? Yes. Looking back, with that perfect 20/20 hindsight, I have wondered if I should have waited until Vance and Ellen had both finished high school. But whenever I've talked about it with them over the years, the consensus is always the same: I couldn't have waited another day. The wonder is that I waited as long as I did. At that point, my life was in turmoil, and I took whatever steps I felt necessary to bring some sense and meaning into it.

But, as it turned out, feeling the need for sense and meaning doesn't mean it will suddenly happen. For me, this was to be a long journey, and I was just beginning.

It was a terribly hard time for everyone. As I moved out of the bargaining stage and into a stage of sadness, I was so depressed that years later Ellen would recall this period as her most vivid childhood memory. She particularly remembered trying to cheer me up and make me happy by getting me to laugh. It was not an easy task, but El rose to the challenge by doing imitations of me. I'd laugh so hard I'd cry. Then she'd do imitations of that and I'd laugh even harder. If there was a silver lining, it might have been that her gift was being discovered and shaped through our family sadness.

And the other good news was that we were no longer a paper doll family. Our pretense was over.

For some families, when a son or daughter comes out to them, it shatters all their myths about who they think they are. In our case, the myths were already shattered.

4

Atlanta, Texas

YOU COULD NEVER HAVE called me a "gay divorcée"—a term which was popular when I was growing up but probably means something very different today. Even so, at age forty I came out of my eighteen years of marriage ripe for the picking. Attention from the opposite sex was not in short supply. Although I missed all the big movements of the 1960s and 1970s, the sexual revolution hadn't totally passed me by.

It was flattering to have a busy dance card, and my squashed self-confidence got a boost as I adapted to my single lifestyle. A feeling of independence is not the worst thing in the world. I still had an entrenched idea that ultimately I needed a man to take care of me, but for the time being I seemed to be managing surprisingly well.

The kids and I had moved into that little two-bedroom apartment in Lake Vista with just enough of our furniture to fill the small rooms. Vance had one bedroom, while Ellen and I shared the other, along with—yes, of course—her snake that ate live mice.

Elliott also got a one-bedroom apartment in the area so the children could see him often. After an initial period of difficulty and discomfort, he and I developed a cordial manner of talking to each other about matters having to do with the kids. Fortunately, he had a support system with friends in the church.

To a certain extent, Mother was my support system. Ellen was very much so. There had always been a special bond between us, and now we grew even closer. I know that mother-daughter relationships can often become strained when daughters go through adolescence, but that was not the case with us. If I hadn't be going through a divorce, this might have been different. As it was, our difficulties strengthened our bond.

Another move came a short while later—to a townhouse in a Metarie complex. And another came soon after that—to a larger apartment in the same complex.

By now Vance was hitting the road with a band which would take him out of town on tour for several months to the area around Charleston, South Carolina. So El and I often spent our leisure hours as a twosome, enjoying each other's company. As she blossomed into her girl-next-door good looks, she was well-liked by boys, and she would tell me about her crushes—mainly on famous rock stars. We went shopping together for clothes—something she was becoming more interested in as a teenager—and we would go out to eat together. One of our favorite indulgences was to stop at the one and only Camellia Grill at Carrollton and St. Charles to share a small slice of their sinfully rich cheesecake. Whenever we arrived, there was one waiter who always greeted Ellen by saying, "Hi, star." Apparently, he knew something we didn't—yet.

The cheesecake was so rich that we only needed one piece. We would sit talking about this and that and Ellen would soon have me laughing with some unusual, funny observation. She would later tell the interviewer Judd Rose on his *PrimeTime Live* profile of her that the divorce and our constant moves were very hard on her—she was always having to adjust to a new group of kids, always feeling a little different.

When he asked if the kids were mean to her, Ellen joked, "Oh, no, they just poked at me and called me big-head; nothing too bad." So El's humor helped her cope as much as it helped me. Like all kids, she wanted to be liked. And that she was—by everyone. I know that my friends all enjoyed her a lot, though it was somewhat unusual for a thirteen-year-old to be so interesting to adults.

Ellen was precocious in other ways. In her efforts to cheer me up, she not only used jokes but found other, very sensitive, ways of being thoughtful. I was working at the time for Ella Brennan of restaurant fame, first as a secretary and later in reservations. On my birthday, unbeknownst to me, El called up the management to say, "It's my mom's birthday, so please be extra nice to her all day, please."

And when I got home, Ellen bestowed upon me an autographed picture of herself. Glimmers of things to come!

"DEAR MOM—GOD, I'm finally here," began the first letter I ever received from Ellen, postmarked August 10, 1972, from the Colorado Rockies where she attended Christian Science summer camp for a week at age fourteen.

This was the first time we had ever been separated from each other, and her letters reflect that. They also show what a flair for the dramatic she was starting to show, even then. I had to laugh at some of her spelling and grammar, not to mention her experimental language. She continued:

> You should see all the people. There all real nice and precious guys. The first night of course I was a baby and got homesick. But today I met so many people. And everyone has a different accent, I'm starting to catch one. Today I rode all day long (horses). I got a lot of sun. God Damn, the scenery is gorgeous it doesn't even look real. I drank some water from a running creak. It was so good! The nights and mornings are freezing but it feels good for a change. Well gotta go they just rang the bell. We're all supposed to meet down by the pool and trampoline and then go to the dance. Well by. But now, I'm really having a good time.
>
> Love,
>
> Ellen
>
> Tell Vance Hi.

We were soon happily reunited. And all in all, at least for a short while longer, life wasn't so terrible. But after two years of not being married and an unhappy relationship or two, I changed my tune. The novelty of the dating scene and being a working single parent had definitely worn off. As Mrs. Nungesser used to say, "Things can't be nice."

It was in this frame of mind that I met a man and fell

hook, line, and . . . well, you know the rest. It was one of those accidental meetings; we lived in the same apartment complex. Of course, being so enamored, I thought it was fate when he caught my eye from across the pool one Sunday afternoon not long after Ellen and I had gone down for a swim. It would have been hard not to notice him, since he was staring at me unabashedly. Well, I was in a two-piece bathing suit and quite slim and tan. He obviously liked what he saw, and in a few minutes someone we both knew was introducing us. That was it. He pursued me vigorously, and I didn't run. I loved him, as the saying goes, "not wisely but too well."

Mindful of past mistakes, I took it as a good sign that he was nothing like Elliott in any way. For that matter, he was nothing like any man I'd dated. In style, he was a cowboy—short on culture but long on charm, with his West Texas twang and his earthy, macho good looks. The word "spiritual" probably wasn't even in his vocabulary, but with our powerful physical attraction, that didn't bother me much at first.

When we met and for the next seventeen years that we were together, this man had a first, last, and middle name. At present, because of later events, he has been reduced in my memory to an initial: B. I would have erased that too, but I have kept it for the purposes of this book, at least as a way to refer to him. He would play a central role in the next few tumultuous chapters of my life and of Ellen's.

What an idiot I was. Unfortunately, it has been my lot in life to be a late bloomer. As with those nasturtium seeds I planted in childhood, which seemed to take forever to grow, it has taken me a long, long time to get things right. Life was always giving me lessons, but how much was I learning? Apparently not enough—and not fast enough.

Once again with B. I was jumping too quickly into a relationship, all because I was so eager to be in a "real" marriage, to be safe—as if that would make me whole. If only I had been more eager to stand on my own to find wholeness and safety. I had a lot yet to learn. And one of the big lessons in being my own person was learning how to trust my instincts.

There were clues even at the beginning that my new Romeo wasn't all I envisioned. I ignored them. The knowledge that B. was a salesman—in fact, that at one time he had been a used car salesman—should have told me something. When he took me to his hometown on a visit and introduced me to his old friends—similar types, also in sales—I remember having a flash of insight that he and his friends weren't the basic, warm sort of people to whom I could relate. But as was my habit, I rationalized that uneasy feeling away.

Instead I listened to my libido, which directed me to his very male appeal, his attractive appearance, and his healthy sexual appetite. I liked his gregarious personality, his take-charge attitude, and his practical know-how about car and house repairs and gardening. With B. it was always, "Betty, honey," and he could never tell me often enough how cute I was.

And he was a character. I remember when we were in Dallas and went to Sakowitz, a very upscale store, on opening day. B. and I were sitting near the escalators on the first floor, and Bob Sakowitz was near us talking frantically on a walkie-talkie to someone on the third floor about escalator problems. B. looked at him and in his flat West Texas way said, "Beats hollerin', don't it?"

Then there was a time, when we first started dating, that I agreed to meet him on the City Park Golf Course, a flat, wide-open expanse. When I got there, I looked out and saw groups of golfers as far as the eye could see. Then I saw, in the distance, a hat flying high up in the air like a Frisbee—his way of showing me where he was.

B. was direct and outspoken; actually, he was crude, though I misinterpreted that as refreshingly forthright. Like me, he was divorced. He had three kids from a former marriage, and he seemed to be a strong father figure to them; seeing that, I thought he might offer Ellen a bit of needed discipline. And when he proposed, asking me to move with him to a tiny dot on the map in East Texas, some eight hours northwest of New Orleans, the change of environment seemed just what the doctor ordered.

The area of Metairie we were living in at the time was known as "Fat City." It consisted of apartment complexes, shopping areas, and nightclubs—not the best neighborhood for a young girl to grow up in. The high school, Grace King, was good, but on weekends and some school nights Ellen and her friends were somehow gaining entrance to a local disco, and at fifteen she was too young for that. Some of her friends were older and worked part-time at the mall. Ellen told me about one friend who was stealing jewelry. All this worried me, and I was only too glad to get her out of there.

• • •

THE IMAGE IS etched forever in my mind: fifteen-year-old Ellen, a lovely girl—slender and rather tall—with her shiny shoulder-length blond hair, standing alone in front of her high school, shrouded in the morning fog.

It was the first week of April, 1974, a few weeks after I'd remarried, and I was leaving New Orleans early that morning for East Texas. It had been decided that Ellen would stay with her dad until June so she could finish her sophomore year at Grace King. We would see each other in a few weeks, for Easter, but we had never been separated for even that long.

The school was across the street and down the block from our apartment, and Ellen and I walked together, just the two of us. We hugged and kissed and said our temporary good-byes. She went on alone, turning back and waving through the fog, then walking slowly and sadly with her head down, then turning and waving again—playing it for all it was worth. A bit of the actress was emerging already. She was so dramatic, my Ellen.

Just before she disappeared from view, she paused as if to say something.

I thought of Ida Lupino's great farewell speech: "All of us are standing in the mud, but some of us are looking at the stars."

But Ellen's farewell moment took place in total silence. Then she vanished into the fog.

I walked back to our apartment and locked up. Then, with two cars loaded—B.'s and mine—we headed off for Atlanta, Texas, population 6,000.

• • •

I LOVED THE novelty of East Texas right away. The quiet, easy pace of small-town life was a new experience for me, and I relished it. The countryside was beautiful, with rolling hills and tall pines—a sight for sore eyes after all the years I had spent in a city below sea level with not a hill in sight. In New Orleans, we had to drive across Lake Pontchartrain, to Slidell and Covington, to see forests of pines. But they didn't grow to the size and extent of the pine trees in East Texas. I suppose I was just ready for a change of scenery.

Atlanta's little two-square block downtown didn't have a building over two stories. And I was especially taken with all the pickup trucks. In New Orleans, it seemed that only plumbers and electricians drove pickups. Here, practically every other vehicle was a pickup. The sight of women driving pickups was also a novelty. I thought it was all very quaint.

Downtown consisted of a drugstore, a greasy-spoon café, and a few miscellaneous shops. My first visit downtown made the priorities of my new community pretty clear. I had already noticed more churches per capita in this tiny town than in any place I'd ever been. When I walked into shops, people knew immediately that I was new in town. One shopkeeper asked, "Do you have a church home?"

"Yes, I do," I replied, never having heard that expression before, "but I can't find it." So far I'd spotted only various other Protestant denominations and one small Catholic church.

The woman wasn't sure where the Episcopal church was,

but she seemed to think there was one. Finally, I met someone who gave me directions: go up a certain street to the end, turn left, go to the end of the next street, turn left up the hill and into a little open field. And there it was, a darling little white frame church with bright-red doors that opened into a simple interior of natural wood pews.

I turned out to be a welcome addition, not only joining the congregation but playing the small organ during services for many months.

Then one Sunday morning I arrived with other church members to find our much loved church in smoldering ashes. It was a terrible shock for all of us. All that wood and the secluded location had made it entirely too easy for an arsonist to torch and destroy our place of worship. As is often the case, the perpetrator of the crime was never found and the motive remained unknown.

Afterward, our priest and his wife opened their home for Sunday eucharist. Very soon the congregation purchased a house and a lot on a busier, well-traveled street. Services were held in that house until a beautiful A-frame church was built.

We joined the Atlanta Country Club, which had a challenging nine-hole course. At that point, any course would have been challenging to me. Never having played, I was taking lessons and receiving lots of advice from everyone with whom we golfed. It didn't take long for us to make new friends and get involved in lots of club activities—golf tournaments, dances, and barbecues.

B. and I lived in an apartment and later found a small

house for rent. As always, when I went out job hunting I had no trouble finding secretarial positions. I started with the Southwestern Electric Power Company, later worked as a legal secretary, and then got a job with a local glove manufacturing company.

El flew up for Easter vacation, and we had a great visit. We toured the high school and were both impressed with what we saw and heard. We played tennis on the local public courts in a lovely, tree-shaded park. Being together again was wonderful, and I looked forward to her coming back for good as soon as her school year was over.

I was sure the change would be as welcome to Ellen as it was to me. And, again, I was eager to get her to this small friendly town (very Baptist and very dry), away from the bad influence of her fast crowd in the big city. We drove down to New Orleans in June and came back with Ellen and all her belongings. She, too, made friends right away. As for protecting her from the bad influence of her friends in Metairie, here was what Ellen said later (November 9, 1993) in an interview with *Gambit*, a New Orleans weekly:

> I was hanging out with people who were older, staying out late, and I think that was one of the reasons my mother thought it would be good to move to Atlanta, Texas. . . . We lived in a dry county, which meant that teenagers would drive 45 miles for beer. And when you got there you didn't want to get just a six-pack, since you'd driven all that far, so you got a case. So we'd go out in the middle of a big field and build a bonfire and drink beer. At that time, the

height of aspirations was to get your name in iridescent letters on the back of your boyfriend's pickup truck. You can see why the day after graduation from high school, I headed back to New Orleans.

Of course, I didn't know anything about those bonfire and beer sessions. At first, I also didn't know that Ellen felt out of place in Atlanta. She seemed to adjust right away.

Everyone who met Ellen was immediately impressed by her. That's what I heard from a friend I met at the high school track, just behind the house we were renting, where we used to walk and jog. This was Paul Garfield, a marathon runner, about my age, who had moved with his family to Atlanta from Boston. Paul told me how Ellen used to jog with him and talk the whole time and not even be winded. He, on the other hand, had all he could do just to answer and keep running.

The Garfields were one of two Jewish families in all of Atlanta, Texas. I recall finding out, after the fact, that their kids had to endure a couple of anti-Semitic incidents at school. Clearly this town was not one to easily embrace diversity. Nor was it a place where a teenager like Ellen might easily come to terms with her sexuality.

When El started high school in the fall, her junior year, she was very popular. Naturally—she was the new girl in town, and there weren't too many of those. But although she was well-liked, the only joining she did was to play on the high school tennis team. Football was very big; the whole town went to see the Atlanta Rabbits on Friday nights. The high school girls were either in the band, cheerleading, or in the Maroon Jackets—a pep squad. Ellen chose none of the above, and perhaps she marched to a different drummer from then on.

When we moved to East Texas, El went through a sudden weight gain. She had been a rather tall, skinny little girl, but all that changed in Atlanta. Ellen's tendency to put on a few extra pounds during times of stress would continue until her coming out episode in 1997. It was only then, with her newfound liberation, that her extra weight dropped away from her effortlessly. Amazing.

In high school, El had the usual dates and boyfriends. Yes, one beau did put her name in iridescent letters on the back of his pickup, "right above the gun rack," as Ellen would later quip. In her senior year, there was even a promise ring with a tiny diamond chip from a nice-looking boy. They went steady for several months. Then there was the time a couple who were dating arranged a blind date for her. Ellen was all dressed and ready to go when there was a knock at the door. She opened the door and saw the boy standing there.

He said, "Ellen?"

And she pointed down the block, saying, "No, she lives two houses over."

After he went back to the car, the other couple assured him that he had the right house. So back he came. This time, laughing sheepishly, she went with him. More glimmers.

NOT LONG AFTER we had settled into our rented house, we found a house for sale that, fortunately, we could afford.

Unfortunately, the reason we could afford it was that it had been half destroyed in a fire. But we bought it anyway and rebuilt it from top to bottom. Ellen and I cleaned off bricks and nailed decking and rolled tarpaper on the roof. The three of us did everything ourselves, backbreaking work after our jobs and on weekends.

One of the things that appealed to me about B., I thought, was how handy he was. He was a real take-charge guy, sometimes too much in charge. In fact, on some days B.'s main contribution to the work was to direct traffic. Friends stopped by one day while I was precariously perched on the roof, nailing down tar paper over knotholes to keep the rain out, while my husband was safe and secure inside the house, shouting orders. Our friends looked at me quizzically—what's wrong with this picture?—but I shrugged it off.

B.'s take-charge approach with Ellen was not so easy to shrug off. Ellen was used to her father, who was so kind and gentle that he was absolutely permissive. B. was bossy. Not all the time, but there were a couple of instances of his stepping in and insisting that she do something his way. This was not the positive exposure to discipline that I'd hoped for; instead, he came across as harsh and mean-spirited.

There was one incident when B. became very unhappy with the way Ellen was cleaning an old toilet in the house. I heard them disagreeing just at the point that he was showing her how to do it. "Like this," he said gruffly, putting his hand down in it and scrubbing. "Put some elbow grease in it. Do it right, if you're gonna do it."

El glared and said nothing, absolutely refusing to put her hand into a toilet.

He started to yell; she started to cry. I stepped in and managed to defuse the situation, saying that I wouldn't do it either. Ellen wiped her tears, but I could see the conflict in her face. On the one hand, she was furious with the man I had chosen to be my husband; on the other hand, she loved me and wanted me to be happy with him.

And there I was, in the middle, trying to placate the two of them. Even though my instincts told me the problem wasn't going to go away, I did manage, again, to shrug it off—for the time being.

JUST BEFORE MY remarriage and my move to East Texas, I'd had a complete physical to be sure I was in good shape. And, so far as we knew, I was. However, in early 1975 I discovered a small lump in my right breast. A doctor friend of ours in Atlanta referred me to a physician-surgeon in Texarkana, Texas, a larger town just twenty-five miles away. I liked Dr. Dawson very much, and I liked the fact that he was conservative. He wanted to wait and see if the lump changed or went away at different times of the month.

Then, during a visit to New Orleans, I went back to my gynecologist, Dr. Bradburn, who had delivered Vance and Ellen. He ordered a thermography test and had the results sent to Dr. Dawson. The consensus was that this was a benign mass. A biopsy was scheduled for March 26, 1975, at Wadley Hospital in Texarkana. Early that morning, as I left the house with B., Ellen followed us, pleading with me to let her come to the hospital with us.

"El," I reassured her with a hug, "it's only for a biopsy. The doctor feels certain it's benign. You don't need to miss school for this. I'll be home this evening."

Late in the day, I awoke from the anesthesia with one breast removed. My right chest was completely bandaged. A modified radical mastectomy had been performed. In those first hours and days, I vacillated among many emotions—horror, shock, fear, anger, disappointment. How could this have been done to me? Because, I was told, while I was anesthetized my husband had given permission for the procedure. A part of me recognized that he made that decision with my best interests at heart; emotionally, however, I felt totally betrayed to not have been consulted.

Years later I sent for a copy of the four-page medical record of my operation. In it, Dr. Dawson stated his procedure for the biopsy and then said, "To our surprise and chagrin the report was malignant disease." I appreciated his concern and care, but no one was more surprised and chagrined than I was. Because of my background in Christian Science, I was woefully ignorant of all things medical. That was bad enough. The fact that I was not given any advance preparation felt like an even greater violation.

Though I had persuaded Ellen not to come the first day, she was there with me constantly the next two days. B. was in and out, but El hardly left my side. We had seen each other through a lot of loss already. But this was different. We had no experience whatsoever with illness. Now there was the horrifying specter of cancer. Just as horrible, she had to see me in a hospital—something completely foreign to both of us. To see me lying in that bed, dejected and shocked, must have been terrifying for Ellen. And yet she remained strong and calm, attending to my every need. Only much later would she break down and say, "When you had that operation, I could have died."

When the doctor said I could go down the hall and actually enjoy a bath, it was El who helped me in and out of the tub and sat by me, worrying that I was in pain.

El wasn't present, thankfully, when the doctor came in to remove the bandage. I was horrified to see what a complete job had been done. I don't know what I had expected, but I cried, "You didn't even leave the nipple!" I believe that today a lumpectomy would have been done. At that time, it wasn't so common.

Dr. Dawson explained calmly, "This was the safest way to go—to be sure we got it all." Otherwise, he said, if there were any cancer cells left, they could turn up anywhere else in the body.

I was sure that my womanhood, as I knew it, was over. B. and I were still newlyweds, and all my dormant sensuality had been reawakened with him. Now I worried that he would be repulsed by my appearance. Later that day, with Ellen and B. in the room, I blurted out to him, "You can have a divorce if you want one."

His response? He shrugged, muttering, "Aw, hell, I don't care. As long as I can still turn you on in other places." That was B.'s poorly worded attempt to reassure me. It wouldn't have been so offensive if Ellen hadn't been sitting right next to me.

Stony-faced, she said nothing. Later, she told me that she was the one who was repulsed—by his crudeness and insensitivity.

As devastated as I was, I made up my mind to do everything in my power not to be victimized by what had happened to me. And I think I adjusted quickly and well, though B. was really clueless about how to offer emotional support. Even less helpful were his occasional comments, through the years, that the lump probably hadn't been malignant. That was what finally motivated me, after many years, to send for the medical report.

B.'s lack of support to some extent was my own fault. I had scheduled what was supposed to have been just a biopsy over the three-day Easter weekend and had planned on going right back to work, but when things went differently I should have changed my plans and stayed home longer to recuperate. Instead, I did my normal "I can handle it" routine: came home from the hospital on Monday, stayed in bed on Tuesday, and went back to work on Wednesday, with cut-up panty hose in my bra. That in itself was awful. No one had told me about a prosthesis or anything special to wear. Only later, during a trip to Dallas after a saleswoman in a lingerie department had made the suggestion, was I fitted for a prosthesis.

At that time and in that place, there was no informative visit while I was in the hospital and no support group for me to join to cope with this loss.

I wasn't able to move my arm very much at first, so when I was at work, from time to time I would go to a doorway in the back of the office and practice walking my fingers up the door frame until eventually I could get shoulder-high. Besides golf and jogging, for several years I had been doing yoga. So when I could once again swing a golf club and once again do a headstand, I really felt I was all the way back. Those pursuits, my usual handiwork projects, a budding interest in calligraphy (which I later taught), night classes to complete my bachelor's degree at East Texas State College in Texarkana and, of course, my secretarial job—all these kept me busy and involved.

Then there was the completion of our house. Painstaking and slow though it was, once it was done the house was really a lovely home. Perhaps I cherished it especially because so much of our joint labor had gone into it. After we finally moved in, I threw myself into cooking, entertaining friends, and caring for our very own home—a regular Martha Stewart before any of us had ever heard of her.

Besides Ellen's unbelievably wonderful support in the wake of my mastectomy, I received loving letters and calls from Mother—Noni, as the kids called her—and Helen and her gang in Pass Christian, as well as Audrey and Bob and the girls, who were living now in Baytown, Texas, just east of Houston. I believe that the art of letter-writing was not lost on any of the Pfeffer women, and these were years in which my sisters and I became much closer in spite of our geographical distance.

Mother kept in constant contact with me on the phone. "Hon," she said one day, "I think I should tell Aunt Ethel, don't you?"

After all those years of "Don't tell Aunt Ethel," this was a change. But I agreed that, yes, she should be told.

So Mother called her sister and began, "I have something to tell you about Betty . . ." to which Aunt Ethel quickly said, "Oh, what? I'll go downstairs and tell Maisie . . ." and further mentioned that, as it happened, at that moment my cousin Maisie was having her weekly gathering of several friends—most of whom I knew from high school.

Not wanting "all those people" knowing our business, Mother backtracked and said, "Oh, never mind. I'll tell you some other time." She never said another word about it.

Decades passed. A few years ago I asked Maisie if she knew I had a mastectomy and she said, "Yes, Betty, I do know."

And Aunt Ethel had known too. All those years, and they had never said a word.

Clearly, once a family gets into a secretive pattern, it becomes hard to break.

OF COURSE, VANCE was very upset to hear that anything could possibly be amiss for his typically together mother, and he called and wrote as often as he could. Vance's calls and letters were full of exciting tales of his musical endeavors and travels. Always his number one fan, Ellen listened intently to these reports.

It may have been during this time, while Ellen was still in high school, that she started to have some ideas of pursuing a musical path, like Vance. She was naturally musical, with a nice singing voice, and was already starting to write poetry and songs. Interestingly, she would later have several comedy bits that were music-related.

Unlike Vance, who performed as a musician and had

acted in plays in school, up until this time El hadn't done any kind of acting or performing. In fact, some of the kids who remember her from high school have recalled that, though popular and friendly, she could also be somewhat shy. Certainly she was nothing like the many comedians who have histories of being class clowns. But she was funny. In those years, whenever I was angry with her about something and was trying to correct her, she would imitate my facial expressions until my anger gave way to laughter. Her humor was growing more spontaneous and more sophisticated.

As it turned out, Vance ventured into comedy before Ellen did. By 1976, he had started writing sketches which were so well received that he and his partners decided to take the plunge and go to New York City. Eventually the act made it onto *Saturday Night Live*; Vance was the notorious "Mr. Hands," the archenemy of "Mr. Bill." Oh, no, Mr. Bill!

I was proud of my two extremely creative kids. Of course, I do remember being less than happy when Vance chose not to get a college degree but to dive directly into music and then comedy. I'd hoped that when I returned to finish my college education, I would be setting a good example. But it was his choice to determine his own path. Multitalented and a creative person to his very soul, this was who he was. I would no sooner have tried to talk him out of being who he is than I would try to talk Ellen out of being who she is.

On the other hand, I was completely shocked by a phone call I got from Vance in the middle of 1977. He was living in New Orleans, after having returned from fast-paced New York, and was developing television ideas for local productions. Up until this point, I had been hearing about his high hopes for a sketch comedy pilot he had written called *Cuisine Deluxe*. He worked on it for months, and everything was ready to shoot in a local TV studio that he had arranged to get for only one night; everything had to be torn down the next day. In a stroke of bad timing, there was a power blackout and everything was ruined. This may have brought on Vance's complete about-face, of which he informed me that day with his phone call.

"Mom," he said, "I joined the Marines."

I waited to see if there was a punch line coming. When I understood that he was completely serious, tears came to my eyes. I asked him, "Vance—why?"

Because, he explained, it was the best way to get the kind of discipline that he felt he needed and that he hadn't received in his growing-up years.

"Oh?" I said, still baffled. Talk about getting hit from left field. I don't think it would have shocked me any more if he had called to say he had been abducted by aliens. Added to my shock was fear and a feeling of helplessness. The Vietnam war had ended only a few years before and was fresh in everyone's memory. Vance in combat? In the Marines?

"What did your dad say?" I asked, grabbing for something, anything, to change the reality of what was happening.

Vance said that Elliott, being an ex-Navy man, told him he wished he had joined the Navy. But it didn't really matter what we said, since he'd already gone through the whole enlistment process. He was in the Marines.

When I asked Vance if maybe this was because his last few projects hadn't worked out well for him, he replied, "I guess so, Mom. It's just time for a big change in my life." He was fully determined.

I wasn't happy about it, I told him honestly. But I certainly respected his decision and his conviction. This was something he had to do on his own journey into manhood. All I could do was give him my love and encouragement and pray that he would find what he was looking for.

WHEN ELLEN GRADUATED from high school in June of 1976, I doubt that she knew what she was looking for or had any idea where her destiny would take her. But I think that she had already decided that it was absolutely going to take her somewhere, that she was going to be somebody. Apparently she also knew that it wasn't going to happen in Atlanta, Texas.

One night, through tears of pride, I watched her graduate from high school. The very next day, she moved back to New Orleans.

Elliott came up to Atlanta for the graduation ceremonies, bringing with him his new wife, Virginia. We had them over for breakfast the next morning. Then they loaded their car with all her things and off she went—out of my life.

The effect on me was devastating. We missed each other terribly.

In the beginning, Ellen had a hard time finding what she

wanted to do with her life. Mother generously offered to pay for her tuition, but after just under a month at the University of New Orleans, Ellen could see that college wasn't the right path for her.

Living with her father, stepmother, and two young stepsisters wasn't the same as living at home with me. In our conversations and letters, I could sense that Ellen was going through the difficult process of cutting the proverbial cord. Then, again, this process of leaving home was complicated by the fact that after all our moves, "home" wasn't so much a physical location but really wherever I was.

This was why Ellen made three different attempts to move back to Atlanta—to be with me—only to flee the smallness of the place within weeks. Once she even tried going to work at the glove factory where I was working. She lasted a few days, if that.

After she left for the last time, I wrote the following, which was later published in a literary magazine at Louisiana State University–Shreveport, where I would eventually transfer to finish my bachelor's degree:

To Ellen

A rosebud is perfection, but
to try to keep it so by tying it in place
with silken ribbons would destroy it.
and we would never know the full-blown
beauty of the mature rose.
It grows when it is time.

We tried to stay together.
So many false moves—but
It was wrong for me and wrong for you.
It was time for mother-daughter to let go.
It was time for us to grow.

Not many months after I wrote that poem, and about a year after Vance had shocked me with his announcement that he had joined the Marines, I found myself on the beach in Pass Christian, Mississippi, hearing an even more shocking announcement from Ellen—"Mom, I'm gay."

As she cried and I hugged her, a hailstorm of conflicting emotions continued to pummel me from every direction. There was my shock and disbelief, yes, together with my fear that was very much on the same level as my feelings when Vance enlisted. As it must be for all mothers, the prospect of either one of my kids being hurt was unbearable. And with this revelation from Ellen, I was probably even more scared, mainly because of my ignorance. How could I protect her from the unknown?

Since I couldn't, my irrational impulse was somehow to convince her that this wasn't really who she was. And so, when I asked, "Maybe this is just a phase?" Ellen took it to mean that I was ashamed of her.

It took El almost twenty years to tell me that. Thankfully, she said that I never made her feel rejected or unloved. But nonetheless, my denial and my worry were conveyed to her as shame.

Ashamed? Hearing that made me feel awful, especially

after twenty years. By that time, it had been so OK with me for so long that I had almost forgotten about the difficult process I had gone through. Of course I was never ashamed of Ellen. But after hearing what she remembered, I started to think hard about that time, the feelings I did have, and just how I had gotten to the point of total acceptance.

Looking back, I saw that for me, as for many people, the steps toward understanding could be compared to some of the ones I went through when I was bereaved—the stages described earlier as denial, anger, bargaining, sadness, and then, finally, acceptance. The process of coming to terms with my daughter's sexuality may not have been that clear-cut, but it was definitely a process of growth. And I did experience a sense of loss.

What exactly that loss was, I didn't yet know at the time when the first shock waves were hitting me. But as El and I walked back from the beach with our secret and into Helen's house, I knew then and there that we were not the same people anymore. We said nothing. I wondered if anyone could tell that we had both been crying, but no questions were asked.

Not much was said on the drive back to New Orleans. When we dropped Ellen off at her father's house, I gave her what I hoped was another strong, affirming hug. "I'll call you," I promised, letting her know without words that we had more to talk about. El nodded in agreement.

Watching her go into the house, I was able to fathom a part of my loss. She wan't my little girl anymore. Just as I had written in that poem. It had been time for her to grow and find herself, and discovering her own sexuality was very much a part of that growth. But I had never pictured her with another woman. In my mind was a picture of her with a strong man—and her smiling face in the newspaper's engagement section.

When El and I talked a few nights later and I mentioned my disappointment about the engagement picture, I immediately felt foolish. It began to dawn on me that my feeling of loss was not so much about Ellen as it was for myself. These were my own losses about which I had been in denial, my own disappointments, and the ideas I had about her having the fairy-tale life with a Prince Charming of her own—a life I hadn't succeeded in making for myself.

What really got to me in Ellen's letter, which arrived shortly after that phone call was her comment: "I'm very happy and I'm sorry you can't approve—I know you can't understand—you probably never will."

At this point B., never known as Mr. Sensitive, figured out that something was upsetting me. "C'mon, Betty, honey," he said, in that drawl of his, "tell me what's eatin' you up."

With all the effort it took me to finally stammer, "El . . . Ellen told me she's . . . she's gay," he must have been expecting earth-shattering news. But this revelation was no big deal to him.

"Aw, hell," he said, "is that all?"

B.'s reaction made me feel a bit better—that is, until a month later, when we were home visiting and B., without asking me, decided to take it upon himself to betray what I considered a strict confidence and tell Mother. B. just brought it up, announced it over dinner, as casually as if he'd just asked Mother to pass the salt.

I froze in my seat and glared at B. Mother looked momentarily shocked, but that passed quickly. She turned to me, patted my hand, and reassured me that she loved us all. Mother didn't seem to be bothered much by the news. What a relief! A few months earlier, I recalled, B. had volunteered some other information that upset her a lot. He really had a big mouth.

That earlier night, when we were relaxing at Mother's, he blurted out, "You know, Betty really enjoys sleepin' in the nude."

Mother was horrified. "Bets," she exclaimed, "you weren't raised that way!"

Well, there wasn't much room for change in her household.

B. really went too far when we were driving one day. He was at the wheel, I was in front with him, and Ellen was in the backseat. I was asking about her friends—questions about the places they were going, what kinds of things they were doing for fun.

B., crudely direct as ever, asked Ellen, "What do you do for sex? What exactly do two girls do together?"

"I don't want to talk about that with you," Ellen replied with a look of disbelief. The subject was changed, but the atmosphere was uncomfortable and awkward.

That incident—which reminded me of my own ignorance about homosexuality—may have prompted me to head to the local public library. Helen visited around this time and, after I broke down and shared the secret about Ellen, I told her how much the books I was reading were helping.

Helen was shocked, but more than anything, she wanted

to reassure me that this news didn't change her high, loving opinion of Ellen. Then she confessed how little she knew about homosexuality. "What do the books say?" she asked.

"Do you know," I told her, "according to historical and anthropological experts homosexuals have been part of our human race from the time that we evolved as a species, typically 3 percent to 10 percent of the population? And in different cultures they have been much more widely accepted than in ours."

This made sense to her, scholarly as she is. "As I think about it," Helen said, "I've read before that lots of famous and successful people have been gay."

It was also a relief, I told her, to read that homosexuality is not a mental or physical disease, shortcoming, or deviance. Five years earlier, in 1973, the board of trustees of the American Psychiatric Association had voted to remove homosexuality from its list of mental disorders, asserting that being gay or lesbian is normal and healthy.

When I conveyed this information to Helen twenty years ago, it was relatively new. Today, very few medical or psychological experts would disagree. This is not to say that some misguided psychiatrists and psychologists, because of their personal religious beliefs, may not approach therapy from a standpoint of trying to "change," "cure," or "fix" a gay man or woman. And because of society's negative messages, some men and women struggling with their sexual orientation may attempt to fit into the role society says they must play. However, this rarely works, especially over a long period of time. We love whom we love. We are who we are.

Just as was true two decades ago, there are still those who

argue that there is something wrong with being homosexual, that it is an aberration from the norm—the norm being heterosexuality, of course. I have since learned that this is only a social value judgment. For a gay or lesbian person, the norm is being attracted to, and having romantic feelings for, another person of the same sex. Gays and lesbians may have lots of friends of the opposite sex but feel nothing at all romantically toward them. That doesn't make homosexuals wrong and heterosexuals right.

Helen remembered our conversation more specifically than I did, reminding me not long ago how grateful I was for those books. So, to anyone struggling to come to terms with the news about a gay family member, I highly recommend taking this important step—whether you choose your local library, a bookstore, or an Internet search. There is nothing blissful about ignorance.

During the year that followed Ellen's coming out to me, the secret was gradually shared with other family members. Before long, as in so many families, it was known but unspoken. So far as we knew, everyone in our family was comfortable with the knowledge that Ellen is gay. Vance, of course, loved his sister and was not in the least bothered. In fact, they later joked about wanting to date the same girls. Audrey, like Helen, was terrific, as were their kids; and Noni, who loved her granddaughter and only wanted her to be happy, continued to be surprisingly comfortable, even with Ellen's girlfriends.

The person who really seemed to have trouble with Ellen's news was Elliott. Because of their ignorance, he and his wife asked her to move out, saying she would be a bad influence on her young stepsisters. When she called to tell me about it, I could hear the terrible hurt in her voice.

"El," I said, trying hard to convince her that she wasn't being rejected by her father, "your Dad loves you."

"I know," she said, but she couldn't help adding, "That's why he's kicking me out of the house." She went on to say, though, that he was taking out a loan to help her get started in her own apartment. It was a very painful time for Ellen. To her credit, however, she did not reject her father in return.

In interviews years later, Elliott would reflect upon his reaction as one of ignorance, saying he was ashamed for having done that to her. For El and her dad, it wasn't too late. But for some parents who reject their kids and later feel remorseful, it is.

On a recent Mother's Day HRC trip to New Orleans, I heard such a story from one gay man. "When I came out," he said, "my brothers and sisters refused to let me have any contact with Mom." He went on to describe how his siblings put their elderly mother in a nursing home in a different state and then divided her house and belongings among themselves. They told their mother she was not to speak to him because he was gay and would abandon her—that he couldn't care for her because of his "persuasion."

In fact, the siblings and their children never came to see her again—no birthdays, no Mother's Days, nothing. He said that for the first year, she would hang up on him when he called. After about a year, she finally called him, and then they began to communicate. Just before she died, she told a nurse to tell her son, "I love him and I'm sorry."

Heartbreaking. Then I heard the opposite kind of story—a story of understanding and acceptance. This was from a woman in Wisconsin, a mother of six whose seventeen-year-old son just came out to them. She said, "I'm so glad he still has a year at home so we can make him know what a great person he is."

That mother has a lesson for us all: don't waste precious time. I wish I had realized that sooner. Unfortunately, although I was combating my ignorance, it took me a while to get beyond my fears.

The books and articles I was reading gave me concrete knowledge with which I was able to emerge from my denial. This was reality, a truth that I wasn't going to pretend away. I began to understand that there was nothing wrong with being gay; but still, why did Ellen have to be that way? In other words, whose fault was it?

Well, if Ellen is being exactly who she is supposed to be, how can it be anybody's fault? She has also achieved major success in Hollywood. Is that my fault, or her dad's?

In talking to El at this time, I may well have asked the question that parents often ask next: Why do you think this happened? From my vantage point now, I know that this is a ludicrous question. Being gay or lesbian isn't something that happens, like an accident. As Ellen later said, it's as much a part of her as the color of her eyes or her skin.

I may have asked a follow-up question: Was it caused by any of the experiences you've had? This is the same sort of futile effort to find a cause for something that just *is*. Our experiences throughout life shape our character, but they don't make us straight or gay. Just like heterosexuals, all the gay people in this world were brought up under different conditions, some optimal, some dysfunctional.

Thank goodness, I got beyond the need to find myself or someone else or some cause to be at fault. Still, though, I had other questions, like the dreadfully old-fashioned question: "But who'll take care of you if you don't get married?"

"You," Ellen teased, letting me know that she wasn't worried about needing a man for that reason, so why should I be?

I'm happy to say that this question is now outdated. Women are such an established presence in the workplace that there is no longer any need to have a "good provider."

"And what about children?" I asked, voicing another fear—that being gay meant she would be childless. This too is an old-fashioned notion. At that time, having children wasn't a priority for El. These days, she has many options. I have met numerous gay and lesbian couples who are having or adopting children. In all these cases, the children are beautifully cared for and the parents have put a lot of thought and care into making this momentous decision.

I still had to ask one more time, "Maybe you just haven't met the right young man?"

"Didn't we have this conversation before?" Ellen retorted. But shortly thereafter, she obviously decided to give the heterosexual world one last chance and started dating Jeff. When she described him to me, over the phone, she said he was a very nice-looking young man, friendly and talented. My hopes soared. He sounded like everything a young woman could want—it would seem.

"Ellen," I suggested during a phone call, "why don't you

invite Jeff to spend Christmas day with us in Pass Christian? We'd all love to meet him."

"That's a nice idea," she said and arranged for him to come with us to Helen's.

He was just as she'd described him, even nicer-looking, and very articulate. I enjoyed talking to him on the drive over from New Orleans. In my mind, I was starting to visualize Ellen's picture in the engagement section all over again.

The family was very impressed with Jeff. He brought his guitar, and during the day he played and sang some very humorous songs that had us all laughing.

At one point, I glanced at El. She was laughing along with us. But as a woman, I could sense that she wasn't smitten. They were really only friends. I faced up to the truth that I was the one who wished it could be more than that. I wanted her life to be easier and felt it could be if she were "like everyone else." But she wasn't. In time, I would come to appreciate and admire her for not being like everyone else and for her strength, courage, and honesty in being exactly who she is supposed to be.

The right young man wasn't going to "save" Ellen. She didn't need saving. What a breakthrough that realization was for me! And so that Christmas day of 1978 marked a turning point in my journey to acceptance. From then on, my world began to open up and expand as I started meeting El's wonderful, loving circle of friends. I was touched by their camaraderie and their support for each other.

A friend named Liz became a family favorite. Often, when I'd been in town visiting, El brought Liz—or Ms. Lizard as

Ellen called her—to Mother's house. Liz was "in" with Noni right away because at that time she was working for Pan American! Ellen brought Liz to the Halloween street dances that Mother and her neighbors had every year. Everyone contributed by bringing food and drinks and there was always a DJ and lots of dancing in the street.

On a trip back to New Orleans recently, I saw Liz and she reminded me of Grandma, one of Noni's friends, a cute little Cajun lady in her nineties.

"Man," Liz said, "she could cut a mean rug."

We remembered the year that she and Ellen arrived just as Grandma was "gettin' down with the music." Ellen loved it and rushed out to join her in the wildest dance of the night—to a highly appreciative audience.

As I opened my mind and my heart to El's friends, and then, as time went on, I met her special girlfriends, I beheld only good and only love. Ellen was happy and was on the road to achieving her goals in life. What more could I ask for? I loved my daughter as much as I ever had—maybe more, because she needed my love more.

El had once said that I probably would never completely understand. I'm happy to say she was wrong about that. I'm even happier that she was willing to give me time—to learn, to reason, to see. That's all I needed.

I know some of you reading this may be just beginning your own process and you may feel troubled and resistant, even angry and frustrated. You, like parents with whom I have talked, may be wondering how long it's going to take—what exactly will put you over the top to feeling okay. I can only tell you, from my own experience, that in this gradual, painstaking way I finally arrived at a new place—a place of complete acceptance where I could celebrate Ellen for who she is.

It was a new day. The clouds of confusion and ignorance had passed. I saw that those three words, "Mom, I'm gay," which had once seemed such a burden, were just the opposite.

As I now know, when El came out at age twenty, she gave me the greatest gift I have ever received—her total honesty. The seeds were planted then for the person I could be and wanted to be—independent, strong, honest. I wasn't there yet. Over the next few years, as Ellen began stepping into the world of stand-up, I would very slowly be taking steps to learn how to stand up on my own.

For that reason, and many more to come, I consider my daughter my best teacher and my best friend.

PART II

1978–1997

God couldn't be everywhere, so therefore he invented mothers.

—PROVERB

This is a fairy tale story—life isn't this pretty.

ELLEN DEGENERES,
AGE TWENTY-THREE,
DESCRIBING THE GOOD LIFE

5

The Importance of Being Honest

LOS ANGELES, APRIL 30, 1997

IT WAS JUST AFTER 7:30 P.M. that Wednesday night when a limousine delivered us to the Creative Artists Agency building in Beverly Hills, where a party, already under way, was celebrating the television star Ellen DeGeneres; her eponymous TV series, which was now in its fourth season; and the airing of what was being called—with a code name—the very special, very controversial "Puppy Episode."

As we pulled up in front of CAA, I looked out at the large white modern building with its curving lines, and thought to myself that, for many in the entertainment industry, this agency—with its roster of famous, powerful clients—represented the height of show business success.

Ellen had definitely come a long way from Atlanta, Texas. And so had I, for that matter.

I stepped out of the limo first, followed by a radiant-looking Ellen, and her beloved, the likewise radiant Anne Heche. Photographers snapped away and reporters pelted Ellen with questions. Remarkably composed, she smiled for the cameras, made a few humorous remarks, and then, Anne at her side, made her way into the lobby. Nearly bursting with excitement, pride, and nerves, I followed quickly behind the two of them, feeling rather like a mother of the bride.

Indeed, the event that was to take place in under less than an hour was not so different from a wedding or any other important life passage that parents have occasion to witness in their children's lives. No, Ellen's character, Ellen Morgan, was not getting a new puppy. What was about to happen was the coming out of both the TV character Ellen Morgan and the real person Ellen DeGeneres, to millions of viewers around the world. It was certainly like a wedding in the sense that it was a cause for celebration—not only for all of us at that party at CAA and all of us who are a part of Ellen's immediate and extended family, but for millions of gay men and women and their families all across America, for whom this was a historic night.

In fact, once I joined the party in the large, airy, modern space, where champagne flowed and waiters circulated with trays of delicious hors d'oeuvres, the big buzz was about the "Ellen parties" taking place all over the country. These were like gatherings for the Super Bowl or the Oscars, it seemed, or for something even bigger.

"Can you believe it, Mom?" said Vance as I met him in the crowded lobby and gave him an exuberant hug.

It was enough to make any mother weep for joy. But then again, no matter how positive our anticipation was, there was no way to predict the reaction to the show itself. I hoped and prayed that viewers would feel the way I had felt a month earlier when I sat at rehearsals and watched the episode being shot: delighted, thrilled, entertained, touched, moved, proud. At the same time, I knew that what Ellen had made the terribly hard decision to do was not without severe risk. Already, controversy was bubbling. Could America really accept that the lead of a mainstream situation comedy, a regular girl next door, was gay?

For almost a year, plans had been in motion. Everything about the episode was supposed to be top secret. In the summer of 1996, after Ellen made the decision, she had the writers over to her house and told them about it. They were immediately very excited, knowing it would be a history-making event. One of the writers, however, had some trepidation—that was Vance, who was on the writing staff that year. If Ellen hadn't been his sister, he might not have worried. But as a protective older brother, he couldn't dismiss the negative possibilities.

And the negativity started right away with leaks to the press which could have derailed the whole episode. We will never know who leaked the story. Certainly no one we knew has admitted it. The first fallout I felt was over a planned trip for Ellen and me to DisneyWorld for the grand opening of a film called *Ellen's Energy Exhibit*, with Bill Nye, the science guy; it was set to be a permanent part of Epcot. Disney, which owns ABC, *Ellen*'s network, was flying us out. Never having been there, I was looking forward to seeing the park and the energy exhibit. But when news of the coming out episode was leaked, the powers that be at Disney decided it might be better if Ellen didn't show up. We were disinvited.

That was bad enough, but then something horrifying happened. On the last day of shooting the episode, no sooner had the show ended than the assistant director got a call telling her to clear everyone out of the building. Disney security officers were soon on the set, escorting everyone out in an orderly way. There had been a bomb threat.

Safety was our top concern, but there were other serious consequences to consider. These included warnings by knowledgeable people in the industry that coming out of the closet would ruin or significantly harm Ellen's career, not to mention the damage it might do her private life and even unrepeatable worst-case scenarios. Of course, we didn't know that Ellen would become even more famous afterward and her love life would blossom as the most fulfilling and happy that it's ever been—and we would all share in her journey and would soon see our lives transformed for the better in ways we hadn't even dreamed of.

Yes, there would be a backlash. It was a risk that went with the decision—that the network and the studio would back down, withdraw their support, and eventually cancel the series. But even if that had been a certainty beforehand, it wouldn't have changed Ellen's decision. Nor would it have changed my feelings about her decision.

Ellen didn't make her choice on the basis of what she had to lose and what she had to gain. For her, it was a decision based on the importance of being honest, so that she wouldn't have to lie anymore about who she was and whom she loved. Of course, she could have kept up her pretense of normality, creating a straight persona for the public to see while being openly gay and accepted within her own private circle of family and friends. But I don't think Ellen had forgotten that twenty-year-old girl in Pass Christian, Mississippi, who cried and reached out to her mother for understanding. And she knew that there were other young women and men out there going through similar experiences of self-discovery. When Ellen saw that she, as a mainstream, accepted positive image of success, was in a position to make a difference for those kids and for other gays and lesbians in all walks of life, she knew it was worth all the risks.

Amid everything we did and did not know, I doubt that any of us knew how monumental this event was going to be. I didn't know—at least not when I took my seat close to the front in the auditorium, which by 8:25 P.M. had filled to overflowing as we gathered together to watch the show. I will never forget how, just before the lights dimmed, I turned around to see Ellen and Anne sitting together in the middle of a row near the back of the auditorium. The self-assured grace on both their faces was so beautiful that I couldn't help whipping out my camera and snapping a picture of the two of them. In that moment, with all the fears and what-if's running through my head, the magnitude of what was going on finally struck me. And it hit me that my daughter—who never wanted to be an activist, whose only true desire in life was to make people laugh—was the bravest person I knew. She was laying herself on the line, risking all for the truth.

BEFORE I TELL you how this exciting saga unfolds, I should probably backtrack and recount exactly how we got to this great moment.

Fortunately, rather than having to rely on memory alone,

I've been able to document the years through a wealth of family correspondence. Even though I've let lots of material things go, I have always held on to personal and sentimental items such as correspondence or gifts that were made for me. At the end of one note Ellen sent me during the very early years of her career, she wrote, "Please keep these letters. It's the only form of diary or log that I'm keeping so I can look back—so either you or I can write a book someday."

Me and my curls—age two.

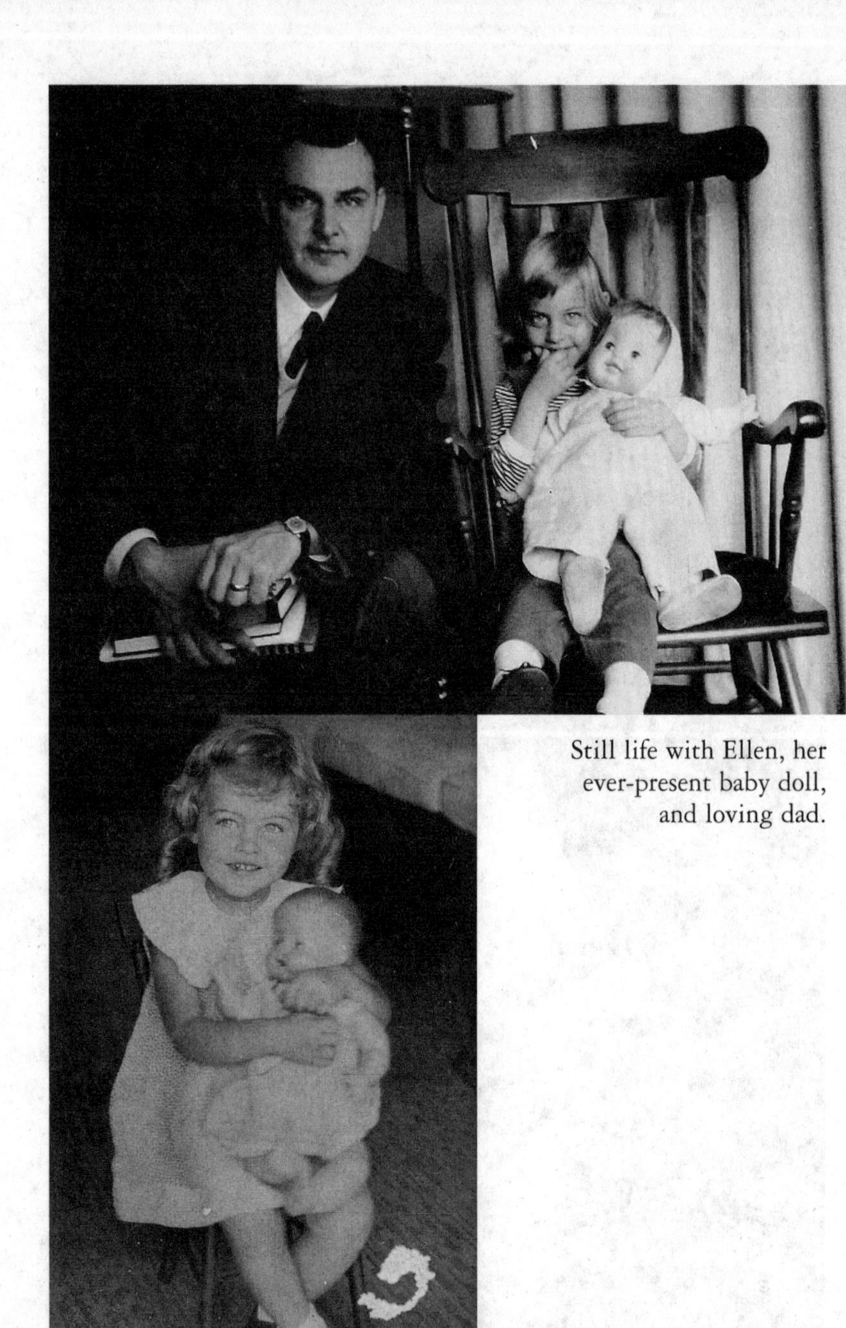

Still life with Ellen, her ever-present baby doll, and loving dad.

Like mother, like daughter. I liked my doll a lot, too.

High school picture of
Betty Jane Pfeffer—
a glamour-girl wannabe.

Three sisters in 1948:
Betty, Helen, and Audrey—
still three girls next door.

In 1946, the three of us at Audrey's wedding. Helen was the maid of honor and I was the bridesmaid, already dreaming of being next.

Audrey, Betty, Mother, and Daddy.

Public speaking, then and now: a 1963 Pan American Life Insurance Convention in San Francisco . . .

. . . and in 1998 as the Human Rights Campaign's national spokesperson.

Here I am with Vance. Look at the fifties fashions!

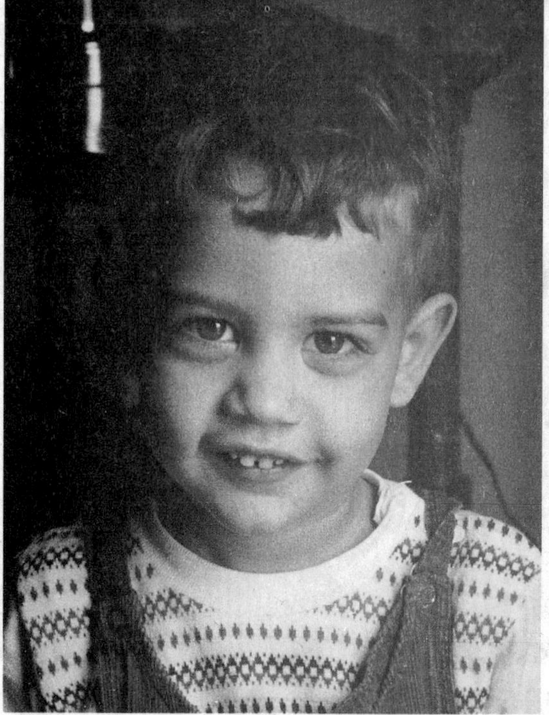

Young Vance, my precious firstborn.

Ellen at her first birthday—a star in the making.

Little Ellen in her PJs—laughing from the start.

El with Mumsie—an early paparazzi shot!

Ellen in rain gear . . . She'll kill me!

Ellen with her beloved big brother, Vance.

My two innovative kids, clowning around in a makeshift RV.

With Ellen and Vance, around 1963, reflecting the stress we weren't talking about.

Here's Ellen—the emerging comedienne—on the beach in Pass Christian.

Thirteen-year-old Ellen autographed this picture for me, an omen of things to come. What did she know?

Ellen would later look at this photo and comment, "Oh, no, there were no clues."

The three sisters—
Helen, Audrey,
Betty—circa 1994
on a trip to an
Elderhostel, making
the most of our
time together.

Ellen and me
together at
the Emmys.
Who's prouder?

Vance and me enjoying a typical L.A. day.

With my two daughters
—all dressed up and
heading off to a premiere.

Ellen and I visited Cedars-Sinai's Teen Line,
where teenage volunteers answer a hotline for troubled teens.

A group of young activists give me a warm welcome.

At one of my first HRC dinners with Dr. Joycelyn Elders.

In London with Sir Ian McKellen.

On a trip to Bermuda—a woman on her own and liking it just fine.

6

I Love You, Mom; I Love You, El

At age twenty, Ellen shared her secret with me, and gradually it was shared with other family members and close, trusted friends. But to the outer world—coworkers, employers, landlords, casual acquaintances, and later, as she became famous, the public—she still had a secret, one which would last almost twenty years.

Because I shared in that twenty-year secret, I became, in a sense, Ellen's co-conspirator. At first, I'm sure I must have worried about the wrong people "finding out." In time, I became adept at avoiding and evading questions from my friends and coworkers, questions about whether she had a boyfriend or whether it would be all right to introduce her to a nice young man. I learned to be careful about my choice of words when I referred to Ellen's romantic partners, describing them as "friends" or "roommates" or discreetly not mentioning them at all. Once an associate at work asked me point-blank, "Is Ellen gay?" Somehow, I managed not to answer. I probably shrugged it off with a laugh, saying something along the lines of "Well, that's awfully personal!"

Having to keep any kind of secret can become a terrible burden. But, on the other hand, given my years of early training with Mother's warnings—"Don't tell Aunt Ethel"—I really know how to keep secrets. It wasn't my place to share this information about my daughter. That had to be Ellen's choice.

So, along with everything else we had survived together, perhaps the secret brought us even closer. Whatever we did or did not share with the outer world, with each other we became very honest and open. El found ways to let me know she loves me a lot just because she does. And I let her know that not only do I love her with all my heart, I also admire her. The life she lived in her growing-up years was not smooth or seamless. And yet, she emerged from adolescence with unusual strength and courage that may have had something to do with her being tough enough to stick it out in a field as difficult as show business.

Of course, in 1978 Ellen's aspirations were far from being that lofty. Most of her letters and our conversations dealt with the more mundane aspects of day-to-day survival. In early fall of that year, I remember calling her to ask how she was doing with her latest job as a placement counselor in an employment agency, Snellings & Snellings.

"Everything's wonderful!" she answered proudly, allowing herself to brag a little. "You know, on the board up in our office there's this chart with everyone's name and whenever one of us makes a placement we put the amount of the fee up under our name. My list is the longest, and I'm number one in our office now—I have $3,800.78 up so far this month!"

"El, that's great," I said, happy to hear her so upbeat.

Ellen went on: "My boss came in the other day—the lady that owns all the Snelling and Snellings in New Orleans—and she said, 'Boy you're a hot one, kid!' Then my other boss at the downtown office called and said, 'Oh, the superstar!' I acted cool about it and then she told me that no one has ever made that much in the amount of time I've been there."

I congratulated Ellen on her hard work, and we talked more about the new apartment that she was sharing with a roommate. Her report was glowing. A few days later, she wrote a letter indicating that reality was setting in:

> . . . Got the first bill today. Phone bill—It's $44. It was $42 just for the installment plus the regular bill! Oh well, now it gets rough. And we went to the grocery store last night and spent $21. I'm getting a tiny bit scared—but we'll make it. The apartment's fine, roaches everywhere.
>
> Nothing else really is going on—except I want a TV. And my car!! I walk 2 miles home every day from work—but it's pretty nice—except when it rains! So far I've been lucky—I've just gotten wet from sweat! . . .

Ellen's job as an employment counselor lasted a couple of months longer; then it was on to a position as a salesclerk at Dixie Art Supplies. During the short while she was there, she was very enthusiastic about it. In the meantime, I had given her an old lemon-yellow Chevy Vega of mine and an allowance for gas, which eased up the amount of walking and bus-riding she had to do. Still, with food, rent, phone, and utilities, she had to make do with very little. When she needed clothes, she went shopping at secondhand stores—if she could afford even that. In one letter, Ellen described how cool the weather was getting. She jokingly asked if I might knit her some clothes, everything from sweaters and scarves to pants and shoes.

While Ellen's creative aspirations had not yet come to the forefront, Vance DeGeneres was already making a name for himself. As it turned out, Vance's two years in the Marine Corps would prove to be beneficial to his whole career. He found the discipline he felt had been lacking and actually did well under the rigors of military life. In fact, when he finished boot camp in San Diego he had been selected as Honor Man.

While he was in the Marines, stationed in Yuma, Arizona, Vance was able to get training as a broadcast journalist and even a part-time position as a weekend sports anchor on KYEL-TV.

During one phone call to Vance, I confided my concerns about Ellen's struggles at her jobs. Without thinking, I must have said something like, "I feel guilty for not encouraging Ellen more to stick with college. With both of you, Vance, I guess I just didn't put my foot down enough." His situation was now different, I acknowledged, because of the job training he was getting in the Marines. But Ellen worried me. A week later he wrote me a long letter—a rare feat for him. He stressed some of the following points:

> Ellen is very bright and will do alright. There is nothing for you to feel guilty about. It's ridiculous to feel like that. I think Ellen and I are just crazy and nothing can be done about that. So, just accept the fact that your children are neurotic and be happy with the fact that we're not mass murderers or People's Temple members. Ellen will do fine, believe me. She gets along very well with people and I'm certain that she'll get a job offer before the year 2000.

Well, we all know that Vance was right about the last part.

When his two years were up and he returned to New Orleans, Vance got a job as a DJ at station WQUE, where he had worked part-time in high school. With his deep, resonant voice and quick wit, he was a hit. At the same time, he connected with other musicians and the lead singer Barbara Menendez to form The Cold, one of the hottest bands to come out of New Orleans in the early 1980s. Vance DeGeneres was a local star and rising fast.

Before long, the bug had bitten Ellen. Having a well-connected brother wasn't going to hurt. Through Vance's girlfriend, Marcia Kavanaugh, our New Orleans NBC anchor and a member of the local Gridiron Club—the press and broadcasting organization—El was able to land a small singing part in its annual musical satire. That year the show was a musical spoof of *The Tonight Show*—another glimmer of things to come.

Though this was an inauspicious stage debut, Ellen was thrilled, telling me on the phone, "I can't wait! It'll be lots of fun and good exposure, too."

Exposure for what wasn't exactly clear yet. But obviously the humdrum nature of her various other "day jobs" was starting to get to Ellen. The list was continuing to grow as El tried her hand in a multitude of positions—waitress, bartender, house painter, car washer, clothing store clerk, a stint doing singing telegrams, law firm gofer, and a job as a gardener that lasted all of three hours (to name only a few).

For a creative person like Ellen, not having an outlet in her work must have taken its toll over time. Some of her day jobs became downright degrading to her. But on an up note, I would say that many of these jobs probably gave El her best training for comedy.

One of her well-worn stories was about the time she was selling vacuum cleaners and working hard to get customers to buy the top-of-the-line cleaner, which cost about a hundred dollars more than the next less expensive model. They were really identical except that the top model had a light in front. One day when Ellen was pitching that cleaner, a woman asked the obvious question, "Why do I need a vacuum with a light on it?"

El thought fast and said, "That's so you can vacuum at night and not wake people up by turning the lights on."

The woman must have had a sense of humor. She took the higher-priced model.

ON MAY 20, 1980, I celebrated my fiftieth birthday by buying myself a violin. B. shook his head, poured himself a drink made of bourbon, water, and Seven-Up that he called a "pres" (short for Presbyterian), and said, "Have you lost your mind?"

Of course I hadn't lost my mind. I simply was interested in learning to play the violin. The fact that this concept was so foreign to B. should have been a clue that he neither understood nor supported me in being who I was. Shortly after that, we were on a business trip to Chattanooga, Tennessee, and I read that their philharmonic orchestra was playing there. I had to beg B. to take me.

"Eileen Farrell is the soloist," I said, trying to entice him.

"Isn't that the old gal used to be married to Frank Sinatra?" he asked.

"No," I said, "that was Mia Farrow."

At first B. flatly refused to go. But I wanted to go so badly and was so nervous about driving myself on the icy, snowy roads that he grudgingly agreed to take me—on the condition that he could leave at any time if he didn't like it. Miraculously, the first violinist, a young red-haired man, was a virtuoso. He played so passionately from the feet up that B. was mesmerized and we stayed through the whole program. Predictably, though, this did not fuel in B. any sudden interest for things cultural.

Oh, well, I rationalized, thinking about my years with Elliott, sharing a love for classical music wasn't a prerequisite for a successful marriage. And off I went on my own to take violin lessons, becoming proficient enough after a while to play in the Texarkana Civic Orchestra.

I wasn't aware of it at the time, but after much reexamination of this period in my life I can see that pursuits like the violin were my attempts to address the lack of real fulfillment in my day-to-day existence. All things considered, my world in Atlanta was small, narrow, and not very exciting. The world that Vance and Ellen inhabited was the exact opposite. Perhaps for that reason, I had most of my excitement vicariously, through hearing about their personal and professional ups and downs.

The importance of hearing from them as often as possible inspired a brainstorm one day: I sent both kids a stack of preaddressed, prestamped envelopes. That way, I figured, we could stay in frequent contact and save money on phone calls. With Vance, who was not a dutiful letter writer, I went even further, writing him a note and making a dotted line across the page with the words, "Cut here." That was where he should write his response. Then I would begin his letter for him by writing, "Dearest Darling Mom." He had no excuse for not writing back!

Ellen didn't require as much coaxing. She loved our system and wrote frequently. She didn't fail to let me know she thought my idea was ingenious, saying to me during one phone conversation, "Mom, did you know you have a daughter who wants to be just like her mother? Except for the violin lessons, maybe."

No matter how dreary the day was, El knew how to brighten it for me. I loved her response when I asked about her latest stint—she was working double shifts selling season subscriptions to plays at Saenger Theatre.

"Well," she began with typical optimism, "it's exhausting but the people are great, so that keeps it fun. " And then, sounding very worldly, she added, "Oh, you know, theater people—they're all alike."

But it was quickly becoming evident that Ellen didn't want to be behind the scenes, hanging out with theater people and selling subscriptions; she wanted to be out front, center stage. And somehow, the idea of doing a stand-up act was born. Exactly when the idea occurred is hard to pinpoint, but I do know that sometime between August 4 and September 9, 1980, El performed in a benefit at a Catholic girls' high school and was a hit.

This first success led her to develop an act and to start appearing regularly at a Friday night coffeehouse on the campus of the University of New Orleans. She received some encouraging comments and even a mention in the *Times Picayune.* Ellen cut it out and sent it to me, noting, "And here's my first newspaper clipping—save it so we can compare the size to the Vegas billboard."

After I received that note, I drove down to New Orleans and, for the first time, went to see Ellen perform. I went with my cousin Maisie and her husband, Armand. The three of us sat at a table right in front of the stage. Nearby were Elliott and Virginia, along with some old friends I knew from church.

In those days, when she was just starting out, Ellen used a lot of props in her act. (She later learned that it's better to let the audience imagine the props.) When she strode out to center stage, she had a long branch of ivy sticking out of her sleeve. That got a couple of chuckles, as she said, "I just got out of the hospital and they forgot to take out the IV." (Groan.)

El continued from there, warming everyone up with that winning twinkle in her eye. All in all, she was wonderful. I'm not sure what I had expected; perhaps I thought this was just going to be another one of Ellen's passing interests. But after ten minutes of watching her, I was very impressed. This felt different somehow.

Since I've never been a big fan of jokes, I was pleased to see that Ellen didn't tell jokes; instead she told funny stories and played off real or imagined situations. Her delivery, even then, was crisp—with her deadpan, fresh-faced, girl-next-door expression, she made the absurd even more laughable. My only complaint was that a young man seated at the next table kept talking during her act. Today, I would shush him. Then, I just fumed silently.

After the performance, Ellen came out and sat with us, accepting a round of congratulations and praise. After all the others had their say, it was my turn. First, I gave her a big hug and told her how great she was. And then I added, "El, I'll help you in any way I can." I knew this was it. She was really on to something.

10-13-80

Dear Mother,

I just hung up the phone from talking to you but I forgot to ask you a favor. REMEMBER at the coffee house you told me you'd help me in any way you could, even financially!? Well—I desperately need a cassette player (a pretty good one). But rather than ask you for $300 or $400 to buy a system—I'll only ask you to buy a good one in Atlanta (you said they're cheaper there). You could get the best portable

> one they have for around $30 or $40. I need one to study my tapes and would repay you with a brand new BMW and/or a condominium in Dallas one day. What a deal, huh? or send a check for $500 and in return get a trip around the world one day—or $1,000 and I'll buy you Dallas—or—
>
> Take Care of Your Cute Self,
> I Love You, Your Daughter

I opted to buy her the cassette player in Atlanta. Lucky me that Ellen would later reward me with all that she offered and more—except for buying me Dallas, that is.

Ellen's struggles were far from over. Her next letter came during one of her low points—after the old Chevy Vega broke down and her latest job had gone bust. Comedy wasn't paying the bills—nor was anything else, for that matter. She wrote in November of 1980:

> I've been looking in the paper for a job every day, but there's nothing available. I want to work near my house, too. I'm so sick of having to take the bus anywhere I want to go. I'm praying my song will sell—I need the money so badly. I've been poor all my life.

Work and lack of money had her down, and I gathered that she was also really yearning for someone special in her life. When I asked in my letter if she had met anyone recently, she wrote back:

> I haven't been going to "those bars" lately. Simply because I'm bored, bored with the same people every time you

walk in, bored with all the games, and bored with watching everyone deteriorating themselves with drugs & alcohol.

This weekend I went to see "The Cold" both Friday and Saturday night—They were fabulous! There were a lot of jerks there too!

Two weeks after that low, Ellen's fortunes changed significantly when she auditioned for Clyde's Comedy Corner in the French Quarter, the hottest comedy club in New Orleans at the time. The people at the club were impressed enough to give her a regular Monday night spot—for pay. Not only that, she wrote, but a man named Marty Bensen, a VIP in the comedy business who had caught her act, had told her, "You're a natural. You're real funny. I think you're gonna do it."

And thus Ellen entered the world of professional stand-up with her weekly set at Clyde's Comedy Corner and a grand sum of something like $15 a night when she started, though she worked up to as much as $25 a night. El didn't have to wait long before she was offered a position emceeing the shows. This six-month stint as an emcee gave her a real comedy education. She got a chance not only to observe more seasoned performers but also to hone her own talent for improvisation as she announced the other acts. El was brilliant when she had to react spontaneously to hecklers and loudmouths. Sometimes she could silence a drunk with just a look.

From early on, Ellen took an adamant stand against using dirty language or obscene subject matter in her act. Her reason? "My mother's in the audience," she used to say, even when I wasn't. Many people in the comedy world believe you have to be "blue" to get a laugh, but I think Ellen DeGeneres made them think twice about that.

By the following summer, she was starting to do small out-of-town engagements, including an appearance at the Dallas Comedy Corner. In a breathless phone call, she let me know how exciting this was. "They love me," she began. "It's going great, fabulous, wonderful! What can I say? I've never done so well." She went on to describe Dallas and how much fun it was being somewhere new and different. "And the people here. Everyone is real rich and real good-looking. We rode around in a limousine all day today!"

Things were looking up. Around this time, I had been hearing about Ellen's new girlfriend Kat. Before long, El moved in with Kat. When I heard the news, I eagerly made plans to meet the new love in Ellen's life as soon as I got a break from school.

WHILE ELLEN'S CAREER was beginning to take off, the one who was really riding high in 1981 was Vance, who was now playing bass guitar for The Cold. With his matinee-idol looks, he was gracing the pages of magazines like *People* and the covers of local music magazines. The band was sensational, one of the forerunners of the New Wave sound of the 1980s. And the lead singer, Barbara Menendez, was phenomenal. I always say that she was Madonna before there ever was a Madonna—very sexy, very talented, and a commanding presence onstage. They recorded a few albums, with some promising singles that they were hoping would take them on to national recognition.

Everything appeared to be going well for all of us. But then, in what exact order I can't remember, came a series of disappointments and difficulties.

For Vance, the problem was that although The Cold was one of the hottest bands to come out of New Orleans, it somehow didn't quite get out of New Orleans. The big chill probably came about when Barbara—so much a part of the band's success—got married and became pregnant. Vance and some of the other band members regrouped later as the Backbeats and continued to lead the way in the New Orleans New Wave sound, but never with the same magic as The Cold.

Then Ellen suffered a devastating personal loss. One evening, while driving somewhere, El passed an auto accident and saw that there had been a fatality. Later that night, she learned that the person who died was Kat, her girlfriend. This had been her first serious relationship, and it was the first time she had gone through the death of anyone close to her age. Just as I had grappled with the fact of our mortality when my father died, Ellen now questioned everything she had learned in her spiritual upbringing. If God was good and if God was love, how could He allow such things to happen?

Gradually, as she began to get some perspective on her loss, she developed a hypothetical dialogue with God about all sorts of questions. This was to be the basis for her "phone call to God"—a bit that would later impress Johnny Carson.

The amazing part of this story is that even in her despair,

after she had moved out of the apartment she shared with Kat and into the flea-ridden, roach-infested apartment where she wrote the bit, she knew that she would one day do it for Johnny on *The Tonight Show.*

It went something like this:

Hi, God. It's Ellen.

(a beat, waiting for a response)

DeGeneres . . . ?

(listening to the response)

What's so funny?

(listening)

Oh, yeah, it does sound sort of like that. No, no one's said that before. (a beat) *Oh, so, I was just wondering why some things are down here. . . . No, not Charo . . . I mean, Jesus Christ . . . No, not him, we're still talking about that . . . I'm just wondering why there are fleas here.*

(listening to the response)

Oh? No . . . I didn't realize there were so many people employed by the flea collar industry. . . . And flea spray too. . . . I didn't think about that either.

In later years, Ellen talked candidly in interviews about how she came to write this monologue that earned her so much attention—though not with total candor. Because of her secret, when Ellen talked about the car accident she had to refer to Kat as a friend rather than a partner or lover. It hurt her, I'm sure, to have to diminish the importance of that relationship. This was another burden of having to be in the closet.

Unbeknownst to me until 1981, Ellen had been keeping another secret, about two ordeals she had suffered with B. when she was in high school. Had I been in a happy, healthy marriage, she may have chosen never to tell me. As it was, on one visit I told her that B. and I weren't getting along well, but the last thing I wanted was another marital failure. I confided in Ellen that I just didn't have the resolve to leave and live on my own.

Ellen's face showed her disappointment. "You deserve better, Mother," she said.

"El," I said, "he has his good qualities. And we love our home." And besides, I added, "Whatever his faults, I know he loves me a lot."

That's when Ellen shook her head, sighed, and told me what had happened one day not long after my mastectomy, when she was seventeen years old. The words didn't come easily. She began, "He asked to feel my breast. You were taking a shower."

She stopped. I looked at her incredulously. What was she saying?

Ellen went on. "He said you were worried about your other breast and he wanted to feel mine to see if yours was like mine."

I felt sick to my stomach. What a horrible experience for her! How could she say no? She was only seventeen at that time, and she was used to confiding in me about everything. But for five years she had said nothing.

Now I spoke with effort, asking, "Why didn't you tell me this before?"

Ellen started to cry, "After what you'd been through, I couldn't hurt you like that . . . and then . . ." Her voice trailed off.

"Something else?" I asked.

El looked around helplessly, as if wishing she didn't have to tell me. Then she nodded. There was something else, she said, a lot worse, that happened about a year later. One week-end when I had to fly down to New Orleans because Mother was ill, B. gave Ellen a ride home from the movies and made a pass at her. Still crying, El said, "I pushed him away. He let it go but when we got home, inside the house, he tried again." She paused, composing herself.

I was furious, confused, and bewildered. "And then what happened?" I asked with dread.

"I ran into my room and locked the door. I was terrified. When he tried to force it open, I climbed out the window." She spent that night at a friend's house.

"Oh, Ellen, I'm so sorry," I said, hugging her. "I'm so sorry."

The pain of what she had gone through tore me up. It hurt even more to know that she had carried the burden of her secret, unable to tell anyone, and it touched me beyond words that she had done so because her concern for me and my well-being was so great.

It is as painful for me to write about this today as it was to hear about it almost two decades ago. Of course, I was angry and disgusted with B. But more than anything, I blamed myself. Most of all, I blamed myself for being so oblivious. "I should have known," I kept saying. "I should have known."

I thought back to El's senior year when she suddenly wanted to drop out of school and return to New Orleans. Absolutely not, I had said, putting my foot down and insisting that she graduate. It made no sense to me at the time. Now I understood why she was so anxious to get away.

In all honesty, I would rather not have included these events in my story of myself as Everymom. That probably comes from my old tendency for denial, for a pretense of normality in which such things just do not happen. Well, they did and they do. And, after some deliberation, I chose to talk about them in this context in the hope that some other mother—or any reader—who might be in denial will pay attention to instinct and act on it. This is not just about loving and protecting your child; it's also about loving yourself. Unfortunately, I still hadn't learned the second lesson.

Rather than talk to B. on the telephone about these events, I decided to drive home and confront him in person. I prayed the whole way there that it wasn't true, that there was some logical explanation. When I got to the house that night and marched inside, B. was still up. Before I could get a word out, he started saying, "Betty, honey, I missed you."

"Ellen told me what you did," I interrupted, furious.

A look of confusion came over his face. "What are you talking about?"

I repeated the story of how he had felt her breast. B. listened, nodded, and shook his head in dismay. Top-notch salesman that he was, he poured it on, using all his skills on me. "I'm sorry about that," he admitted. "It was poor judgment. I was just so worried about you."

"If you were so concerned," I pointed out, "why couldn't you have asked your own daughter?" He and his daughter—who lived not too far away—were very close. "Why didn't you check it out with her?"

B. shrugged. "I wasn't thinkin', I told you. It was wrong."

I let that go. But then I brought up the other incident, repeating to him what Ellen had described. As he listened, B. gazed at me sadly, with an expression of hurt and surprise.

"I don't understand how she could've said that," he muttered. "That's not how it happened, Betty, I swear . . ." He appeared to be struggling, wanting to confess something but then saying nothing.

"What?" I demanded to know.

"It was the other way around. Ellen came on to me," he said quietly. "She made a pass at me."

When I accused him of lying, he said Ellen was making it up so that I would leave him. Then B. turned it on some more, begging me not to leave—not to give up on our love and our home and our life together, which we had worked so hard to build.

When I called Ellen the next day and told her everything he had said, all I could hear on the other end was her breathing. She was crushed, aghast, and uncomprehending to think that I would even consider his side of the story.

My heart and mind felt ripped into pieces. Caught between my impulsive side which told me to leave immediately and my tenacious side which told me to stay on board even if the ship was sinking, I was, in effect, paralyzed. I could never really trust B. again, that I knew. But I hadn't stopped loving him—not yet, or not enough to acknowledge a third failure. Nor did I have the fortitude to leave and brave another period of adjustment while I made a new life—again! I regret to this moment that I did not leave then. It is my greatest regret.

It's hard to see how my relationship with Ellen survived. She had a difficult time understanding how I could stay with B., and rightfully so. Thankfully, it is her nature to forgive. Forgiving myself, though—that has been another story.

The irony is that in spite of the difficulties, or maybe because of them, during this period of hardship Ellen and I became even closer than we already were. This raises another important point about love and acceptance. It works both ways. We parents need it from you kids just as much, even when you don't understand everything we're going through.

OW, OW, OW! That's what I was feeling emotionally and physically when I came down with what I thought was just a really bad stomachache. What an underestimation.

The next morning I was being wheeled off to emergency surgery because gallstones, which I didn't know I had, had punctured my duodenum. After the surgery an infection set in which required another operation and a longer hospital stay than the mastectomy. Ow! again.

All my life, I had never had any illnesses. How odd that I should go through two life-threatening illnesses within the first five years of my marriage. El has since said that she feels there was a direct correlation between the inner turmoil and undercurrents of my life and the physical manifestation of disease. I would have to agree.

As before when I was feeling awful, Ellen managed to make me smile with the following message, which she sent to the hospital:

Dearest Most Precious Mother of Mine,
So you thought you had a tummy ache,
But you were wrong for goodness sake,
And now you're in the hospital
With tubes in your nose—
You're not happy at all.
You've got Aunt Helen worried sick
And Aunt Audrey—then there's Dick,
'course there's Vance and his
    whole band—The Cold,
And me and all the people I told,
There's Noni in Metairie,
Worried as she can be,
What in the world are you thinking of—
Don't you understand that you're
    Too well loved—
Now you get yourself well
    And go back home
'cause I don't have time to worry about you.
I've got problems of my own!

In my usual fashion, I wasn't out of commission for long. Soon I was back at work, school, and my array of hobbies and projects. One creative project I undertook as a surprise for Ellen was a song I wrote that described her entire history of jobs, set to the tune of "Holiday for Strings," played and sung on tape with my own violin accompaniment. Delighted, El wrote back:

> Mother, I can't thank you enough for all of your support, financially and emotionally! You are really keeping me going—keeping me alive and giving me hope. I always tell you how neat you are. But have I ever told you—you have a beautiful singing voice? You should've done something with it. I don't know what—but something. No, no, no, you're just bursting with talent. You can act, sing, dance?—well, play violin, play tennis, play piano, play golf, jog, teach calligraphy, paint, write, cook, sew, knit, macramé, drive, speak French, and still have time for me—Mom, you're incredible!! I think I'll keep you.

Reading these letters now, I feel very humble about my daughter's deep love for me and her gift for expressing it. Of course she knew I had all the love in the world for her and would give her all the moral support I ever could. Maybe having a number one cheerleader in her corner helped give her the courage to stick out the rough-and-tumble days in her early career.

In any event, in October of 1981 Ellen made a major, gutsy move—all the way, on her own, to San Francisco, California, where the comedy scene was really starting to boom. El wrote excitedly:

> Union Street is incredible, it's like a fantasy. There are gorgeous men—gorgeous women—fabulously dressed. Every-

> one is so rich. I can't even tell you. You'll see when you come for a visit. I'll take you there and you'll say—This is a fairy tale story—life isn't this pretty.

Starting to work clubs like the Punchline and the Other Café, she was getting an enthusiastic response. But going from being a medium fish in a medium pond to being a little fish in a big pond wasn't an easy transition. And so it was back to a day job as a salesclerk. When I asked her on the phone how that was going, she admitted, "Boring. My mind wanders. I just want to be a star—now! I hate waiting."

"Hang in there," I told her, my usual refrain.

In some letters, though she didn't say it, I detected a note of homesickness for friends and family, including her big brother:

> I called Vance the other day. We had a nice little chat. Dad had called me earlier and I asked Vance if he thought Dad was getting senile (is that how you spell it?). He said I don't know, why? I said because he sounds old and he kept telling me everything 5 times. Vance said, Oh, he's always done that. He's always done that. Yea, he's always done that. He's hilarious. Hey Mom—you have a real neat son.

Ellen was right. I do have a real neat son, one whom I really missed in those years when he was out on the road with his various bands. Until one of my visits to New

Orleans, when Vance picked me up at the airport, I don't think I realized how popular his playing with The Cold had made him, especially with all the young girls, or groupies, as they're called. Well, at the airport, I was met by Vance in the middle of a swarm of fans asking for his autograph. He had to push his way through the crowd to let me know he was there.

During all this time, he had never been able to make it up for a visit until finally his band the Backbeats played a gig in Shreveport and brought him close enough that I was able to go watch him play and then have him ride back to Atlanta with me. It meant so much for him to finally see our home. The visit was sweet but short; the next day I drove him back to Shreveport and he was off again.

A little while later, by popular demand, The Cold reunited. Again they came very close to breaking into the national music scene. But again the right combination of hit records and, perhaps, strong management just wasn't there. Vance then formed a band which had a cult following for a while. I remember when he told me what they were calling this band.

"Tell me what you think," he said excitedly, "We're calling ourselves The Petries."

"The Petries?" I asked, a little tentatively.

"Sure, in honor of Dick Van Dyke and Mary Tyler Moore," he explained.

I told him it was a wonderful name. As I said before, my kids were always hooked on TV.

• • •

CHANGE WAS IN the wind for all of us. By the summer of 1982, El had returned to New Orleans after deciding that things just weren't happening for her in San Francisco. Going it on her own was very lonely, she had told me not long before coming back. "And it's scary too," she said. "Sometimes I wonder what it's all for—if it's worth it."

In New Orleans, Ellen headed back to the local comedy circuit. Sadly, her original launching pad, Clyde's Comedy Corner, had closed, so she supplemented her income as a gofer in a law firm—where she would remain for almost a year. It was to be her longest-held day job, but also her last.

In March of 1983, still there, she sent me a quick note on the law firm's stationery:

FROM THE DESK OF
CINDY BRANTLEY

DEAR MOTHER,
I GOT TO THINKING, HEY I'VE GOT TIME, I'M SITTING AT THE PHONES, I OUGHT TO WRITE MY MOTHER A LETTER

P

THERE. I FEEL MUCH BETTER NOW
I Love You, Ellen Lee
or
CINDY

BARHAM & CHURCHILL
NEW ORLEANS, LOUISIANA

She never ceased to crack me up.

Driving along the Louisiana interstate, I thought of that "P" and started to laugh again. I needed to laugh. Once again, my marriage was in trouble and I was making another attempt to leave B. It was the same issue—the incident with Ellen.

Though I was a master at denial, I could never quite erase my concern. Obviously, I knew deep inside that something very wrong had happened and I couldn't rest; I couldn't leave it alone. He shrugged me off most of the time, but each time we did discuss the subject, he would slightly change his story or some little detail.

That was the clincher, I realized as I drove and watched the now familiar scenery pass me by, the giveaway that we couldn't continue sweeping this under the rug forever. It was there, and sooner or later I would have to deal with it.

Hoping to make it sooner, I moved back to New Orleans and got an apartment with my favorite daughter Ellen Lee.

Because I wanted to avoid a scene with B., I told him the separation was only temporary, figuring that I would work up to telling him it was permanent once I was settled in. I even got a secretarial job and was just starting to look into enrolling in school—to finish my bachelor's degree, finally—when I was notified by LSU Shreveport that I had been given a scholarship to complete my undergraduate degree there. I had only a year to go and Shreveport also had an excellent master's program in speech pathology.

When El came home from a long day's work at the law firm, she found me pacing the floor of our living room. This was, incidentally, a cozy, nicely decorated apartment. Ellen has always had an excellent sense of style and taste; even when she had little or no money, somehow she usually managed to create a warm, pleasant atmosphere wherever she lived.

"What is it?" El asked, knowing immediately that something was up.

I told her about my dilemma, admitting, "I don't know if I can pass this up."

"But why go back to him when you're not happy?"

I talked about what not going back was going to entail—an unpleasant, probably ugly divorce; putting off finishing college one more time; being stuck with a secretarial job again. Or, I told her, I could go back to a secure life and continue to ignore the problems in a flawed marriage until I completed the education that would allow me to be on my own.

Ellen looked at me, concern in her eyes, saying only, "Do what's best for you."

And so I took the practical route—the path of least resistance—and went back to B. and my scholarship. To independent individuals of a different generation, this must seem weak-willed. But for many women of my generation, especially those of us who put off school to marry and raise our kids, our options narrow as time goes on. We learn to survive and make do as best we can, sometimes, sadly, at the expense of marital happiness and our own self-esteem.

MY NEXT JAUNT down to New Orleans marked an important event—to meet Ellen's girlfriend Kim, with whom she was living at the time. This was the first time I had ever met any of Ellen's girlfriends, and I was excited about getting to know the person who had captured her heart.

When I arrived at their apartment, El greeted me with a hug and then gestured toward a warm, attractive young woman with dark, dark eyes and short curly auburn hair who stood by her side. "This is Kim," Ellen said. And to Kim, she gestured toward me and said, "This is Betty."

It was obvious that Kim cared for Ellen, and I liked her right away.

In those days they were renting a small half of a typical New Orleans shotgun double which, in spite of Ellen's terrific sense of style, they had painted and furnished in a dazzling pink and maroon color scheme. (Sorry, Ellen, I know you'll be horrified when you read this.) I happen to remember because I spent several weeks crocheting them a pink-and-maroon afghan.

We spent a lovely afternoon talking about how things were going. The good news was how well Ellen was doing with her stand-up. From the sound of things, she was about to become a big fish. It was also clear that Ellen's days as a gofer at the law firm were numbered. The humiliation of having to run errands and bump into the same people who saw her performing in the comedy clubs was becoming too much.

And at the office, whenever she made a mistake of some sort and explained that clerical work wasn't really her calling, that she was really a comedienne, no one seemed very amused. "OK, you're a comedienne," they'd tell her. "Could you copy this file?"

Ellen told me how she would protest, insisting, "Really,

I was big a little while ago. People knew who I was." That got her a laugh or two. But then—

"All right. We need some more coffee. Could you get that filter changed?"

On this visit Ellen and Kim shared their exciting plans with me. The two of them had decided to move together to San Francisco. "I'm going to do it right this time," El said. "I wasn't ready before. Now I am."

In fact, by the fall she was getting enough bookings in local and area clubs to quit the law firm. Since she and Kim were pooling their resources for the move, all systems were go. Saving the money still wasn't easy, though. I laughed again when Ellen wrote to me in January of 1984:

> I'm going insane here. Since I'm trying not to spend any money, that leaves me sitting at home and watching TV. Except this morning a man came and disconnected our cable, just because we were two months past due on paying our bill. Vance was about five months past due on his when they came and got his!

Ellen had had an impacted wisdom tooth extracted, and now she went on to describe the follow-up in detail. She was pretty well healed, she said, and noted that it cost twelve dollars to have the stitches taken out.

When I went to the mailbox a few days later I found a bumpy letter that appeared to have some kind of gift enclosed. When I opened it up, I discovered the wisdom tooth, a memento I still have. Oh, that Ellen.

Not many weeks later, I was thinking much the same thing: Oh, that Ellen, and Oh, that Vance.

To raise money for El's move, the two had come up with the idea of staging a farewell show at the Toulouse Theatre in New Orleans. On the drive down from Shreveport—where B. and I had relocated temporarily—I was already getting misty-eyed. Watching the show from my seat in the front row, I was proud of my son and my daughter. Vance was a masterful master of ceremonies and Ellen really delivered to these hometown fans, many of whom had been following her career since her humble beginning at the UNO Coffee House. There was a farewell party after the show, and it really felt like a family affair—all for an admission fee of only six dollars.

The reviews were raves. One of them, a local writer, mentioned that Ellen was in the running for Showtime's Funniest Person in America contest, a prestigious national comedy competition. He predicted that she would win it.

"El," I asked her on our last phone call before she left town, "did you read what he said?"

"Yeah," she said somewhat skeptically. "I also talked to a guy I worked with in Dallas who said that the guy who won 'Funniest Person in Dallas' heard through someone that they chose the national winner but haven't announced it yet. The rumor is that it was a woman who won. As far as I know, I'm the only woman in the finals."

"Ellen, that's wonderful!" I exclaimed. "I'm crossing my fingers and my toes."

Not wanting to get her hopes up, she said, "Oh, well,

we'll just wait and see. I mean, I doubt it was me. It couldn't be."

Then again, maybe it could. Before finding out the verdict, Ellen left with Kim for San Francisco. This time, armed with more experience and insight, she was ready for the big changes that were about to happen.

El had just turned twenty-six years old. On her birthday card I wrote:

> Ellen—You are a gift.
> You were a gift at birth—a beautiful, happy, peaceful gift.
> You've given to me all your life
> So, how natural that your life's work is giving joy and laughter—
> a continual unfolding of your God-given talent.
> You know you always have my deepest love,
> But also—I like you a lot!
>
> Mom

7

Big Breaks

"COMIC HAD TO LEAVE NO to Find Bucks for Yucks," read the headline in the New Orleans newspaper *Lagniappe* in February 1985. The story told of the dramatic strides a hometown girl had been making over the past year. The article described how Ellen had entered Showtime's Funniest Person in Louisiana contest—mainly for the $500 local prize, never dreaming that she would have a chance to claim the national title.

But not long after arriving in San Francisco, Ellen learned that, indeed, the Showtime judges had selected her to wear the crown as 1984's Funniest Person in America.

Was she surprised? Absolutely. Ellen did remark, however, "I think it surprised Steve Martin and Woody Allen even more than it surprised me."

Soon El had a manager and was being booked into prestigious comedy clubs all around the country. For the rest of 1984, my mailbox was always full of letters, cards, and clippings detailing her exciting adventures and showing that she was really coming into her own as a rare comedic talent:

5-20-84

I am in Los Angeles at this moment on an airplane that should have left for O.K. City approximately 20 min. ago. The pilot (or at least he claimed to be the pilot. It was a man's voice) announced that there is a small problem and it should take about 15-20 min. to "fix it." Immediately I heard a woman across from me tell her new acquaintance "Last time I was on a plane and they said it would be 20 min. it turned out to be 3 hours."

It's been 30 minutes now. If you ask me, the problem is a lot more serious than anyone is letting on. I just looked out of my window and there are 5 guys staring at the plane shaking their heads—one seems to be saying, "I don't know, it might make it." At this point, I'm remembering noticing a Christian Science Reading Room in the airport. Maybe I should've stopped in.

At this point, the woman across from me says, "What did I tell you, didn't I say that . . ." (her friend got up and left during the sentence, so she started to continue to me). I looked at her like Jack Nicholson would look at a woman like this. She shut up. . . .

The time now is 11:35. Since I last left you, we were told to get off the plane, that it was not able to take off. So I stood in yet another long line of angry strangers. The woman next to me was nice, she struck up a conversation with me and we exchanged our reasons for needing to be in Oklahoma City at a certain time. She said her daughter just had surgery and she wanted to be there when she got home. But I convinced her my reason was more important. So I won. Then, she started to hum some song, foreign to me, in an extremely high pitch. Dogs started circling us. I asked her to stop. She did.

Now I'm on the plane next to someone's grandmother, she must be 70 or so. Since I sat down, she hasn't stopped talking to me—telling me about her trip to Australia, showing me her menu from her last flight. I've had to open her packets of mayo, mustard, French dressing—salt-pepper—and finally peanuts. I wish she'd go to sleep. I have tried everything so she'd stop talking to me. I have on headphones listening to the sound for a news video which is being shown for *everyone* to see & listen. But she keeps tapping me and asking me what they're talking about. Shouldn't she just put her headphones on?? Then I tried to pretend I was going to sleep, I put on pajamas—just to stress this! But oh no, that didn't work either—She commented on the fabric. O.K., O.K. I'm going too far—She didn't comment on the fabric . . .

I'm exhausted—I just tried to put mascara on in the "bathroom"—but, uh, I started looking like Alice Cooper (he's the guy who wears black all around his eyes). And everybody thinks showbiz is all glitter and gold, HA!

If I get a part on a sitcom, I'll have to wake up for 5 a.m. every morning—but, I guess it's worth it for $9,000 a week! . . .

Although being named Funniest Person in America was a big break, it really put pressure on Ellen to prove that she was as funny as the judges at Showtime had said. It wasn't all smooth sailing.

I recall that El got her first taste of controversy in her

own hometown, when one writer for the *Times Picayune* took a bah-humbug attitude toward the next year's contest and wrote a negative article about the dearth of gifted comics in the area. Vance, the protective big brother, was angry and wrote a passionate letter to the paper, defending the importance of the contest and pointing out:

> As far as the career of ex-Orleanian Ellen DeGeneres goes, it's going just great, thanks. Winning the Showtime contest has done nothing but help. Ellen is spending much time on the road with Showtime—taping comedy segments and working long hours on her craft.

Because Vance was a local celebrity, his letter got a lot of attention. How gratifying it was—and is—to see how much brother and sister cared for and admired one another. I often hear stories about jealousy and rivalry between siblings who both pursue careers in show business, but that was never the case with Vance and El. Indeed, whenever Ellen is asked about influences and inspirations, the first person she always names is Vance.

The pressure to live up to her lofty title wasn't El's only challenge. She also learned quickly that life on the road can be exhausting—and expensive. Even when the accommodations were paid for and she was given a per diem for some expenses like food and transportation, it never quite covered the incidentals and other requirements for being ready to travel at a moment's notice. Also, once she began to have managers and agents, after taxes and commissions, the paychecks that seemed so much more ample than before weren't so large after all. Then there was the manager whose mismanagement put El in a financial jam. My mother, Noni, tried to help by giving her some down-to-earth advice:

> Ellen Honey, I am worried about you and your bills. You can't take the attitude, "Well, if I don't have it, I don't have it." Life doesn't work like that. If you have to sacrifice, deprive yourself, do it; but, hon, live on your salary. You'll find that you'll be much happier, and you'll enjoy your work even more.
>
> . . . Well, little sugar, all my love, hon, to you and Kim,
>
> Noni

Ellen's financial worries notwithstanding, within a year of having moved to San Francisco the second time, she was on her way to building a solid career. She regularly appeared at comedy clubs in Dallas, and I always managed to get there to see her and spend precious time with her. There were two shows each night—and for however many nights I was there, I watched two shows, always.

Between our letters and meeting up with her so often in Dallas, the distance between Shreveport and San Francisco didn't seem overwhelming. Whenever we saw each other, El wanted to hear everything that was going on with me—both good and bad. In early 1985, my good news was that the previous spring I'd proudly received my bachelor's degree and gotten started on my master's in speech pathology. That was going well, I told her as we sat down over lunch to get caught up. With a laugh, El brought up a recent letter she had received from me, in which I had written facetiously:

I had a really exciting weekend. I made two pairs of jogging pants and covered two cushions for our breakfast room benches. This living in the fast lane is going to wear me out!

I laughed too. The truth, we both knew, was that B. and I did work hard making our homes attractive. The house in Shreveport was really coming along. "It will mean so much," I said with a sigh, "when you and Vance can come see it." Then I became more serious, saying, "I was thinking the other day about the quality, as opposed to quantity, of the time we spend together. Goodness knows we have quality. Many mothers and daughters who live in the same town and see each other every day don't enjoy anything near the quality relationship we have, El."

Ellen nodded. On the other hand, she pointed out, she'd much prefer it if I lived closer to her. Nothing was said, but reading between the lines I knew that Ellen firmly believed I would leave B. sooner or later. She certainly would have preferred it to be sooner. "What was this about an unprovoked verbal attack?" she asked.

"Oh, it blew over," I said quickly, as usual doing my best to put a pleasant spin on things. B. had flown into a rage with me for no specific reason, only to back down the moment he realized how upset I was. "He's been super nice, trying to make up for it." Then I brought up my other bit of news—the diamond B. had given me for Christmas. It was over a carat and really gorgeous. "Did I tell you that we're having it set in my gold nugget ring, with six diamond chips set randomly around it?"

Ellen reminded me that I had written to her about it. "Remember?" she said. "You wrote me about all the strings attached." El was referring to the fact that B.'s sister didn't want to sell him the diamond because she wanted to "keep it in the family" and had sold it to him only on the condition that when I died it would go to his daughter. "That's a bunch of horse manure," El went on. "Like you said, you don't want to be in that stupid family anyway."

"It's put a damper on the whole thing," I admitted, repeating how I had told B. that when Ellen made it in show business she was going to buy her own diamonds—if she wanted any. "Just so you know," I told her, "if anything happens to me they can have the diamond back but the ring and little diamonds go to you and Vance. That's worth something, and you all can do what you want with it. Plus, you're going to get my silver, china, and crystal, and Grandmother Pfeffer's china—all the stuff that was mine before." Before I became too maudlin, I let her know that I had some genuinely exciting financial information. Brightening, I said, "I bought a $300 IRA. You and Vance are my beneficiaries—$150 each! The lady at the bank asked if you'd want it in payments or in one lump sum. I figured what the hell—live it up—so you each get the entire lump sum at once."

Ellen smiled with appreciation and thanked me for her future inheritance. Then she said, "And if anything happens to me, you and Kim can split my clothes. Since you have a car, Kim gets mine. But you get all of my notebooks and material, in case"—with a deadpan expression—"you want to continue on my career."

The subject somehow made her think of her father and how he had taken to sending her stand-up ideas on index cards. "They're funny. Well, some of them are funny," El said, "if he was to say them. They wouldn't be funny coming from me. " Ellen also mentioned that Elliott had asked after me. It made her feel good that we always spoke respectfully about one another to her.

I agreed. "It is nice that your Dad and I have friendly, warm feelings toward each other. When you talk to him again, tell him I heard the *Trout* the other day." Before Ellen could make too much fun of that comment, I explained that the *Trout* was a piece of music by Schubert that Elliott and I both liked.

The topic changed to Ellen's latest hope—that she would soon be moving to Los Angeles, the big time. Had she been content to continue traveling and working clubs around the country, she was doing well enough that such a move wouldn't have been necessary. But El had other things in mind: television and movies. For that, she knew L.A. was the only place to be.

"Oh, Ellen," I said, ever the practical one, "can you afford it?" She had just finished telling me about buying a brand-new TV she couldn't afford.

"OK," she shrugged. "The TV was impulsive. And I have to be impulsive while I'm miserable." This was a reference to her being single at this juncture and spending her free time watching TV. I smiled as she continued, "I'm just a very impulsive person. It was impulsive to move to San Francisco. It was impulsive to get into this business."

I understood, having my own impulsive streak along with my practical side. Still, the whole image of Los Angeles and Hollywood seemed so daunting.

Ellen's opinion was that it was necessary to take risks in life. "Look at Dad," she said, as I thought back to how painstakingly he deliberated over every decision. "Dad has never been impulsive, he always plays it safe."

"You know," I said, enjoying our long talk, "you're very insightful. You really understand people—all different kinds of people."

"That's why I can't wait to start acting," she said. "I can read people really well. And I see so many different fronts—all the different ways to handle situations or emotions. Somehow, whatever I'm made of is able to absorb that and let me feel it myself. I can feel an emotion and portray it in my eyes—in my own emotions."

This was a new development in her aspirations—a desire to have serious acting roles one day.

And so, in September of 1985, Ellen took her next step of consequence and moved to Los Angeles. Lest you think her days of struggle and stress were over, let me tell you that her first address was in East L.A. Upbeat and optimistic as Ellen can be, she told me it was advertised as having "New York charm." But once she moved she found that the neighborhood was being used in movies to show gang warfare and other horrors of urban decay. She was out of there after a few paychecks.

Soon El wasn't the only DeGeneres transplanted to Los Angeles. Just before Christmas, Vance also moved there. It was an important career step for him, given L.A.'s status as a music industry hub. Within no time, he formed a group called House of Schock with Gina Schock, the drummer from the Go-Go's, a very successful all-girl group of the 1980s. House of Schock quickly got an album deal that put Vance in the studio for many long months. He had never been the best correspondent before, and now I heard from him even less.

WHY WAS I feeling so low? That's what I was asking myself one Sunday morning as I drove myself to mass. It was a typically hot Shreveport day and my life was typically busy and activity-filled. B. and I were almost finished with the renovation of our house, and my course work in graduate school was interesting—albeit very demanding.

Though B. missed Atlanta, the move to Shreveport was a welcome change for me. With Centenary College and LSU, Shreveport offered a busy cultural life. It had a small museum, good shopping, and nice neighborhoods. It was a pleasant place to live. I even became active in a local community theater and made some new friends.

There really was no specific reason for feeling "not myself" that Sunday—nothing I could put my finger on. And yet, as I made my way to a seat in one of the pews close to the front, another wave of this inexplicable sadness hit me. Trying to fend off the tears, I sat down, hoping that the mass would start soon and help me feel better.

In Shreveport, I attended an Episcopal church regularly, although I frequently visited this Catholic church because of the priest, Father Clayton, who gave wonderful, thought-provoking sermons. This Sunday, Father Clayton spoke as passionately as always. But somehow his words failed to lift my spirits. Only once before—a few years earlier—had I felt like this.

That was on a cold night when B. and I were in the car, on our way out for dinner and a movie. I suddenly became overwhelmed. I started crying tears of I-don't-know-what—frustration, pent-up anger, sadness. The more I tried to stop, the more I cried. B. muttered something about my having really lost my mind this time. We had to turn around and go home.

My anguished feelings then and at mass this Sunday came from the same source. My life was a lie. My marriage was a pretense. As I sat in church and grasped this stark truth, I came face to face with my own shame. Why couldn't I find the strength to do what I knew I had to do?

With Vance and Ellen so far away, I missed them more than ever. Of course, I knew they loved me and missed me too, but they had their own lives to live. I couldn't change my life for them; I had to learn to do it for myself.

As painful as this experience was, it was a turning point that allowed me to make a vital decision—even though it would take me a few more years to act on it with finality. And as I look back at that dark, dark day over a dozen years ago, I realize that I went to that low point for a reason. I was being given a message that it was really time to reevaluate my life and do something, finally, to change it.

Slowly, with stumbling baby steps—learning to walk all over again—that's what I was getting ready to do.

Ironically, later on when I did leave and was really alone, I always remembered that day in church and that desolate feeling. I've never, ever, before or since, felt as lonely as I did then.

"MOTHER," ELLEN'S BREATHLESS voice whispered dramatically over the telephone, "are you sitting down?"

I sat down. "I'm sitting," I said, waiting to hear the big news.

These days, whether it was good or bad, Ellen's news was always big—even if she was just calling to tell me that she had the "most awful, terrible, horrible cramps." It was November of 1986 and over the past several months, the news had been mostly great, including being hired by Caesar's Palace in Las Vegas.

But after I made a quick trip to Los Angeles a few months earlier, Ellen had been so sad when I left to go back that she had seemed very down on her whole Hollywood experience. Around that time she wrote to me: "I wanna get out of the business. . . . It's tough, Mama! I need a break soon."

Well, I crossed my fingers. Maybe this was it. After a prolonged silence, I said in my own dramatic whisper, "The suspense is killing me. What is it?"

Then Ellen's voice changed as she sang out, "November eighteenth, I'm doing the *Tonight Show*! This is it! Johnny Carson!"

I jumped up, delighted, echoing her excitement with my own, telling her how thrilled I was.

"Now the hard part is going in front of Johnny and the cameras and millions of viewers and not fainting dead away on the spot!"

After assuring her that I knew she would be absolutely great, I let her know that the whole family would be glued to the television that night.

Ellen and I immediately got busy notifying everyone. El soon received the following from Noni:

> My Dear Ellen,
>
> Thank you so much for your nice letter, you are so busy, I didn't expect to hear from you. You can imagine how happy I was to come home from church yesterday evening and find a letter from you and one from your mother.
>
> Our church service was about to start, I realized a friend was sitting in back of me. I leaned over and whispered "Ellen, my grand-daughter, is going to be on Johnny Carson, Nov. 18th." It was too funny. I could hear whispering all down the pew—"Mil's grand-daughter is going to be on Johnny Carson Nov. 18th!"

I should note that I'd previously heard my mother's "whisper" in church. I was with her once when she spotted a friend, Joanne, sitting three rows ahead of us, vigorously fanning herself. Mother "whispered" to me, "Joanne's going through the change." I think that one got passed around as well.

Well, the big day arrived; but before we all sat down in front of our respective television sets, El called gloomily to say that she had been bumped at the last minute. The good news was that they had rescheduled her for Friday, November 28—Thanksgiving weekend.

B. and I drove down to Baytown, Texas, to Audrey and

Bob's house while Mother and Helen flew over from New Orleans. We all had a wonderful Thanksgiving together, and the next night we gathered, somewhat nervously, to watch El's significant first appearance.

From the moment I saw her walk out, poised, smiling, focused, I knew she could do no wrong. She got the audience laughing by talking about how mean her parents were to her when she was a kid: "Yeah, I remember one day when I was walking home from kindergarten. At least, they *told* me it was kindergarten. . . . I found out later I'd been working in a factory for two years."

The audience roared, and they roared harder as Ellen said what a healthy, fit family she came from: "When my grandmother was sixty years old she started walking five miles a day. She's ninety-seven now and we don't know where the hell she is."

By the time El got into her Phone Call with God, she was being applauded on every line. Amazing.

Then something even more amazing happened. After she finished, to thunderous applause, the camera cut over to Johnny. He too was applauding and on his face was the most delighted expression. He raised his hand as if to give her a thumbs-up but suddenly he beckoned her over. Unheard of! Rarely were any comics asked to sit on the panel with Johnny after their first appearance. And never before had any comedienne been "paneled" by Johnny after her debut. So when the camera cut back to Ellen, she stood there with an expression that almost said, "Who, me?" Realizing that he meant her, she floated over, smiling radiantly.

The second her part ended, I leaped to my feet and

screamed—overjoyed at how great she was. A few minutes later the phone rang, and it was Ellen to ask how we liked it and just share the special moment with us. Together, we relived the experience, talking about the whole thing from beginning to end.

This appearance proved to be one of the most important breaks of Ellen's career. Within the next six months she had four more appearances on the *Tonight Show*. She was a sensation—better and better each time, hilarious, infectiously likable, and smart. Everyone in TV-land started touting the newcomer Ellen DeGeneres as a blue-eyed blonde with brains.

At first, Mother acted very pleased about her granddaughter's success. But it soon became apparent that Noni's feelings were hurt because of Ellen's bit about her grandmother taking up walking. One day, on a visit, she blurted out to me, "I wish Ellen would leave me out of her act."

"Mother," I replied, as lovingly and carefully as I could, "she's not really talking about you. It's just a funny grandmother image. You know that when El talks about what mean parents she had, she's not talking about us. People know that."

I went on and on, trying to explain. Mother wouldn't buy it. In the meantime, Ellen's feelings were hurt too. She complained to me that instead of the simple congratulations she wanted from her grandmother, Noni was being harsh and critical.

I tried to give El advice about making her peace with Mother, and the incident blew over, fortunately. But a comment Ellen had made about family and unconditional love really got me thinking. After the blowup, I wrote the following to Ellen:

> Unconditional love is a very, very rare thing—and I feel like that's what I have for you and Vance. So why should I be half a continent away? Also, last night I talked to you on the kitchen phone—and [B.] was back in the sunroom. He heard me oh-ing and ah-ing and so on—but never ever asked me what we talked about. Needless to say, I didn't tell him, either. What I'm saying is—I'm tired of my life being so fragmented. I'm praying for a right answer to all of this. So—as another step along the way—would you please send me the mailing address for the L.A. County School District and the Orange County School District?

"I'm tired of my life being so fragmented," I had written to Ellen. These words came to mind in midflight between Shreveport and Dallas. I was off to meet Ellen, who was performing in Dallas at the Improv. She was now headlining there on a regular basis. It was May 14, 1988, the beginning of a much-needed week's vacation.

Although El had sent me information about job opportunities in Los Angeles, as I had asked her, I just wasn't ready to take that plunge. Instead, after proudly earning my master's degree in communication disorders at the end of 1986, I played it safe and stayed put. As I had no trouble finding work, I soon began my professional experience as a speech pathologist employed by the Shreveport and nearby Bossier City school systems. For the first time in my life, I experienced job satisfaction. I loved what I was doing and saw that I was having a positive impact on the lives of others.

But the fragmentation of my life became worse. To the outside world, I was a happy, working, thriving member of society, married, with two grown kids who were doing well for themselves in very tough fields. But none of this jibed with the struggle that was going on inside me—the fact that I was stuck in my marriage, wanting to move on yet unable to budge.

I stared out the window, watching the clouds go by, allowing my restless thoughts to float away for the time being, so that I could enjoy my vacation and have some fun. This was, after all, the week of my birthday and part of the trip was a gift from my favorite daughter.

It was a real joy—from beginning almost to the very end.

After two nights of watching Ellen dazzle packed houses in Dallas, I flew with her to Los Angeles. Ellen was now living in West Hollywood, a marked improvement from her first digs on Normandie, and single for the time being. Vance, who was living nearby, met us for lunch in the neighborhood.

More handsome than ever, Vance told me just enough about a new romance to let me know it could be serious. He also talked about his various new projects, including a contract as a music writer for a record label as well as some comedy and dramatic writing for television, which later would include a series called *Eerie, Indiana*, and then a steady succession of different shows.

In addition, Vance told me over lunch, he was starting to get more into visual arts too.

"You should see his paintings," Ellen raved. "They're incredible."

Then Vance remembered that Ellen was being featured in the new issue of *US Magazine*, and we made a dash to a newsstand to buy it. It included lots of praise and a great picture, and we were a happy trio as we stood there reading it together.

The rest of my stay was a whirlwind of delicious meals, sight-seeing, and people-watching. L.A. really did seem to be the place where the beautiful people lived. I had never seen so many good-looking, well-dressed individuals. Even the waiters and waitresses looked like stars.

For the culmination of my vacation, Ellen was taking me with her as she flew from Los Angeles to Valley Forge, Pennsylvania, where she was scheduled to open for the Pointer Sisters. The job paid several thousand dollars—a lot of money at that time—which was why Ellen was insistent on making a big deal of it and treating me to the flight. Feeling really flush from all this money she was getting ready to earn, she was spending very freely before we even left L.A. I wasn't sure that was such a good idea.

In fact, a few hours before leaving for the airport, Ellen needed to pack and asked me to go out and buy a set of flatware for her that she had seen earlier and absolutely loved. It was beautiful flatware but very expensive. "Buy it when you come back home," I admonished her.

El was quite put out with me at the time. Later she was relieved.

After a nice flight to Pennsylvania, we were driven to the

Valley Forge Radisson, where we settled into Ellen's lovely, large suite which had a huge Jacuzzi bathtub in which I spent a restful hour the next morning.

That evening, a limousine picked us up and whisked us over to the theater.

I accompanied El to her dressing room and then up to the stage, where she checked everything out before the audience began to arrive.

As performance time drew near, El introduced me to two of the three Pointer Sisters. Then, as performance time drew very, very near, Ellen was notified that the third sister had suddenly been taken ill and was going to the hospital.

"So what does that mean?" I asked Ellen, as she gave me the news.

"It means the show is canceled," she said, smiling, though not amused.

"Which means . . . ?" I didn't even have to ask.

Ellen just nodded glumly. "Right," she said, "which means I don't get paid."

The only positive thought I could muster was that at least she hadn't bought the flatware.

We got back in the limo and drove away in grim silence as hundreds of people were arriving, parking, and getting ready to go in—and hear the bad news.

With this turn of events, I decided to fly directly home, and to insist on paying my own way. Ellen didn't argue much.

Moral of the story: Show business is full of little bumps along the road, and some very large potholes.

• • •

ONE OF THE bright spots in my life in the late 1980s was Kerri Remmel, the owner and director of a private speech therapy clinic in Shreveport. Kerri was—and is—a remarkable speech pathologist, teacher, and, eventually, good friend.

I find it interesting which friends I've kept along the way in my many moves. Kerri Remmel is a definite keeper. She already had her Ph.D. in speech pathology when I went to work for her, and she would later get her M.D. and do a residency in neurology. Reading all this, one would expect a very serious woman, but Kerri is down-to-earth and lots of fun—very pretty, with a great personality. She is also very brainy.

As a recent graduate, I couldn't have gone to work for anyone better. Her clinic was well-appointed, with the latest equipment and an excellent library that I found most helpful. I worked with a variety of patient populations and speech disorders. The job was fulfilling, stimulating, and a definite step up in my career.

When Kerri first offered me the position, B. and I were already back in Atlanta, where he felt more at home. In fact, we were back in the same house we had lovingly rebuilt. The opportunity to work with Kerri was so good that I convinced B. it would be a good plan for me to get my own apartment in Shreveport. The idea, ostensibly, was that I would come home on weekends. I saw this as a practical way to ease into a permanent break. For the first time, I felt I had a viable plan of action.

At first, B. didn't like the idea. But when I showed him, on paper, how we'd be saving money, he went for it.

My own apartment. For so long, it seemed like a crazy

dream. In July of 1988 when I signed a six-month lease on a small, cozy apartment in Shreveport, it became a reality. But wait—before you start cheering for Betty Jane, let me warn you that I had a few more mistakes to make. Was I happy? Was the move toward independence everything I'd hoped it would be and more? No, not at all. I was scared and disoriented.

Nonetheless, that fall I finally broached the subject of divorce with B. He was battling any kind of permanent break. Understandably upset, he offered to pay for counseling for me—a very big gesture for a man with such a tight hold on the purse strings. I took him up on it, but after the second session the therapist dismissed me, saying, "Betty, you don't need to see me. You're healthy."

I made a note in my journal at that time, "What an eye-opener." It was a relief to have an outside person validate me and my feelings which I had allowed to become so squashed in this marriage.

This only reinforced my resolve to pursue the divorce, though it was soon clear that B. was going to be as ugly as he could about the division of assets. Now he wanted all of the house.

Again, those five stages of coping with loss—denial, anger, bargaining, depression, and acceptance—came into play. After years of being in denial about many of our problems, I was now getting in touch with my anger.

When Ellen and Vance heard that I was divorcing B., they both urged me to move to Los Angeles, and I would have done so had it not been for Mother's deteriorating condition. Earlier that year, she had had to get an oxygen tank in the house. As much as I loved the idea of moving to California, it was too far away.

And so, after much deliberation, by year's end I was making another drive—the seven-hour drive from Shreveport to New Orleans—my car packed full of my belongings. The good news was that the divorce was going through. The bad news was that I was moving in with my eighty-three-year-old mother.

Initially, this decision had seemed logical. I was living by myself in Shreveport, without much of a support system. Mother was ailing, living in her house alone, and my sisters and I were worried about her. We talked it over on the phone—with Audrey in Texas and Helen in Mississippi—and resolved that my moving in was the right thing to do.

I had barely unpacked my things when I realized it wasn't the right thing to do, for either of us. As helpful as I was trying to be, Mother just plain resented the fact that she needed help. She had always been active, a real do-it-herself person who loved working in her yard and walking. Not that she was a complainer, but she just simply wasn't used to being incapacitated. Bless her, Mother fought her debilitation all the way to the end. A few years later, when she could no longer leave the house, her priest came to visit her and said something about her being an invalid. Mother became quite indignant. She was hooked up to her oxygen tank twenty-four hours a day, but she most definitely did not consider herself an invalid.

Mildred Pfeffer was a darling lady, a true original. But she was not easy to live with. When I moved in with her, she had been living alone since Daddy died, for nineteen years, living her way all that time. A true creature of habit, she was naturally quite set in the way she wanted everything done.

During my years in east Texas and Shreveport, we had visited innumerable times. I knew, as well as I knew my name, that after each visit Mother washed the sheets on the guest bed. Yet every time, without fail, on the last morning Mother would say, "Bets, don't make the bed." It became our little joke. B. would say to me when we got up on that last day, "Bets, don't make the bed," only for us to hear it echoed a few minutes later.

For me to move into this highly structured situation was a disaster waiting to happen. I remember when Helen arrived for a visit and found Mother not talking to me. "What did you do this time?"

I shrugged my shoulders, bewildered. Helen understood that shrug so well. It meant that Mother's feelings were hurt. It could have been something I said or did, or something I didn't say or do. It could have been the distracted way I had said good morning. Whatever it was, I told Helen, "I've tried to apologize. It's no use."

Helen shook her head in dismay. She, Audrey, and I loved Mother, of course, and would never knowingly do or say anything to hurt her—and so we never understood why we were apologizing so often. Helen is, and has always been, the kindest person I know. Yet even she was not exempt.

In this particular case, I don't remember how or when the issue was resolved, but it was, as always—until the next time.

To complicate the picture, I wasn't especially happy in my new job. Though it was always possible to get work with a master's in speech pathology, my job was as an itinerant therapist—who travels to clients on an as-needed basis—and not in my particular area of interest.

All of this made it entirely too easy to reconcile with B. This would probably fall under the heading of the bargaining stage of loss. Bargaining is another form of denial or rationalization: you convince yourself that the death or thing that was lost was your fault, you promise yourself to do better, and you expect that everything will be fixed. I'll never know how I rationalized every aspect of B.'s behavior and our relationship that wasn't right, but I did.

Remember that he was a salesman, and he was charming and sexy. After four months of misery in New Orleans, when he said, "C'mon, Betty, honey, come on home," in his West Texas twang, I melted. The word "home" really got me.

And for a while, I was happy to be in my own home back in Atlanta once again. That stay proved not to be too long, as I soon procured an excellent job as speech pathologist on staff at the East Texas Medical Center Hospital in Tyler, Texas. So, doing the one thing that we did manage to do well together, B. and I packed up and moved to Tyler—a pleasant small town two hours east of Dallas—where we bought a house and began to put down stakes yet again.

On the one hand, my new work was fulfilling and I made a new circle of warm, supportive friends. On the other hand, an inner voice was telling me that going back to B. would never work. Somehow I told my inner voice to shut up and convinced myself that we deserved one more try. That was the bargain. And so it was back to the familiar pretense of normality—so much so that rather than just moving in together and seeing if we could make it work, we remarried. When someone suggested that we wait before tying the knot all over again, the first thing that came to mind was: Live in sin? What will people think? Or, more to the point, what will Mother think?

AS YOU READ my story, at this point you are probably wondering the same thing that Ellen, Vance, Noni, my sisters, and my closest friends were dying to know: When is Betty going to leave that guy once and for all? What is it going to take to get through that thick head of hers?

Well, fret no more. By late summer of 1990, just over a year since we had remarried, the house of cards was about to fall. After eighteen years with B., a span of time that included a handful of separations and a brief divorce and countless moves and relocating, I really and truly finally prepared myself to walk with determination and finality out the door.

No one incident was the final straw. It was really a series of realizations that jolted me into action. The first fact I had to face was that, no matter how hard I tried, denied, negotiated, or bargained, I couldn't get past the issue of his inappropriate behavior toward Ellen. My trust in him had died a long time ago. Somehow, the flame of love that had managed to burn in spite of that distrust had taken much longer to burn out, but now it was merely sputtering.

I had another revelation one day when B. and I were watching a news magazine show that featured a story about the Von Bülows. On the TV screen was a lavish mansion of the sort shown on *Lifestyles of the Rich and Famous*, and the narrator commented, "The Von Bülows lived in opulent decadence."

"Where's that?" B. asked.

I looked at him and then looked away in amazement. If this wasn't a clue that he and I had absolutely nothing in common, I don't know what was.

A week or so later, in late September, I arrived home from work and found B. waiting for me at the door. Without so much as a "How was your day?" he waved a bank statement in front of my nose and began to accuse me of stealing from him.

Because he was so miserly, I had opened up a small savings account in which I had been depositing a few dollars from each paycheck, so that I didn't have to fight with him every time I wanted to send a gift to my kids or another family member. It wasn't much, but it was mine and, as far as I was concerned, none of his business.

As calmly as I could I told him so, adding, "I contribute more than my share to our household; I've always pulled my own weight."

That was the truth, and he couldn't rationally argue with it. So he became irrational, threatening me by saying he would take me for everything I had—including my savings and my annuity, an investment I had made when I was single with money that wasn't his and that he had no claim to.

You stingy bastard, I thought, but I said nothing. After all those years of thinking that he was so charming and attractive, I looked at him for the first time and realized he wasn't at all appealing. In fact, as I stood there, just glaring, it dawned on me that he actually resembled Richard Nixon.

For the next several days, we waged a cold war—sleeping separately and hardly speaking. When that became unbearable for both of us, we finally broke our silence and behaved civilly. I think we both understood that we were at the end of our time together.

One last test took place in early October, when, as the marriage that wouldn't die was on its last breath, I flew to Los Angeles alone for Vance's wedding. Vance was marrying Mimi, a beautiful, bright young woman from a prominent Beverly Hills family. When I arrived, Vance went over all the festive plans for the days ahead—a cocktail party that Mimi's parents were hosting for us, along with the rehearsal dinner that I was arranging and hosting, plus the plans for a very beautiful garden wedding. Elliott and Virginia, having moved to San Diego a few years earlier, would be there. It was then that all my fears of being alone at these events ganged up on me. Somehow the thought of going through such an important life passage as a single was too much to bear.

Or, as I explained to Vance, "I'm just not ready to fly solo." So I went to the phone and called B., asking him to join me. For those few days, we put on a pretense of being a normal couple. We had the expertise.

The wedding was wonderful and elegant. As Mimi's family is Jewish, the ceremony had many traditional elements that I found moving and interesting. Elliott, Ellen, and I stood together in the beautiful *chupah* next to Vance, Mimi, her parents, and of course, the rabbi.

Someone asked if I minded that Vance was marrying a Jewish girl. The thought had never crossed my mind. I had grown so far by this point that I not only accepted it but was thrilled that our family would become even more diverse. In fact, if you'll forgive the cliché, it happens to be true that some of my best friends are Jewish.

At the rehearsal dinner which I had hosted the night before, I had a long, wonderful discussion with the rabbi and was highly impressed by his warmth and intelligence.

Clearly, Vance and Mimi loved each other, and that was what mattered to me. There were, unfortunately, some stresses on their marriage which had nothing to do with religious differences, but came from the fact that they were in different places in their individual and career journeys. As it turned out, they would not be married very long. Even so, they would part with love and mutual respect.

That was not unlike Elliott and myself. After eighteen years of having been divorced, we had gotten past our unhappy memories. Now, even though we weren't together, we could still feel the immeasurable joint pride of parenthood as we beheld the beautiful, fine human beings our two children had grown into.

To our mutual relief, B. flew home after the wedding while I remained for a few days afterward. At long, long last, something inside me finally let go. That was it. The sputtering flame had gone out. No more denial, no more anger, no more bargaining. Inside I felt empty and very sad; in those five stages of loss, this would be typical of moving into the fourth stage: depression. I would stay in that stage for a while to come. But I knew with assurance that we were through. That chapter of my life was over, and it was time to make my plans accordingly.

"Do you really mean that?" El asked as she drove me to LAX for my early-evening flight home. She had heard this from me before, so, understandably, she was wary.

"I do," I said emphatically. But then, watching the scenery fly by in a blur, I had to change the subject for a moment to ask, "Are we in a hurry?" Ellen always drives too fast for me, and since we were in no danger of missing the flight, I thought it wise to do what we could to avoid getting a ticket.

"Don't change the subject," Ellen said as she slowed to just above the speed limit, steering our conversation back to my need to make definite plans to break away once and for all and move to my ultimate destination—somewhere close to my kids.

"You're right," I agreed. "One hundred percent right. It's just that . . ."

"What?" El asked softly.

I said nothing. But knowing me as well as she does, she had only to glance over and understand my many fears and reservations. It wasn't just the ominous thought of being alone in a completely new city; it was also my desire not to live my life through her and Vance.

At the curb, Ellen helped me with my suitcases, then hugged me good-bye with tears in her eyes, saying thoughtfully, "Let me know as soon as you decide—whatever you decide."

On the plane I had a lot of time and a lot to think about. In my mind, I began going over logistics and formulating plans. Midway between Los Angeles and Dallas, I resolved that it was time for a complete change from the environment I had lived in for the last seventeen years. Thinking about all the advantages of living in a big city, I realized how much I had been missing out on.

I clearly remember that in those minutes I found myself looking out of the window, down into the blackness. Every now and then there would be tiny clusters of lights. At that moment I knew it was time to leave small-town life.

8

Come Out, Come Out . . .

I LEFT TYLER AT 6 A.M. on Thanksgiving Day, 1990, with my car completely loaded. I had done this departing act before. But this time it was different.

Having learned from past mistakes, this time I had laid my plans out very carefully and I was much better organized. And for the first time I was moving to a place where I really wanted to be, where I could see Vance and Ellen frequently instead of just during a few quick trips each year, as we had been doing for far too long.

After several telephone interviews, I'd been able to obtain a job with a private speech pathology company in the Los Angeles area. In the meantime, Ellen and Jan, her partner at that time—a tall, attractive young woman who is also a top-notch photographer—spent several weekends apartment hunting for me, looking for something in my price range in the Pasadena area, where I would be working, and ultimately finding a nice place in which I could begin my new life.

As I watched the rolling hills of East Texas fade behind me, the reality of leaving weighed heavily in my mind. I was sixty years old and starting all over again. Waves of fear, loneliness, and regret mixed in with my feeling of relief and excitement. The more I thought about what a huge leap I was taking, the smaller I felt. So, I resolved, I wouldn't think about the past or the future. Instead, I turned up my favorite Debussy on the tape player, hummed along, and made my way through central and West Texas. I tried to live in the moment, as the land around me flattened out for as far as the eye could see and the road ahead stretched to the horizon.

While I was used to driving alone from East Texas and from Shreveport, in the northwest corner of Louisiana, to New Orleans, in the southeast corner, I had never driven halfway across the country alone. Being practical, I reasoned that it might be a good idea to look as if I were not alone. So I put a lamp (without the shade) in the front passenger seat and put a hooded coat around it with the hood over the lightbulb part. The ruse seemed to work very well—that is, until I stopped for gas in New Mexico. A couple of the guys who were working at the station came up close to get a better look; when they realized what they were seeing, they laughed heartily at my "passenger."

"Not too attractive," I said with a shrug, "but she's a good listener."

Because it was Thanksgiving, there was very little traffic and the highways were nearly deserted. Watching the Texas flatlands give way to the rising cliffs and big sky of New Mexico was so fascinating that the time flew by. I got all the way to Santa Rosa, New Mexico, that first night.

On the second day, my spirits improving, I drove through

New Mexico and Arizona, stopping at Flagstaff for lunch. I loved the little I saw of it—the majestic rock formations, the Native American influences, and the western-style architecture—and put it on my list of places I'd like to go explore one day. That night I stopped at a motel in Needles, California.

"Hey, it's me, almost there," I told Ellen on the phone from my motel room. "I'm in Needles—you know, where Snoopy's brother Spike lives."

We laughed and then estimated the hours until my arrival.

Ellen was so happy, she said, it was going to be impossible to sleep. El had known for a long time that I would move out one day. She just didn't think it would take me as long as it did.

"Less than twenty-four hours," I sighed happily, knowing I would have no trouble sleeping. "I'll see you tomorrow."

The next morning I drove through the desolate Mojave Desert. That would have been a terrible place to have car trouble, but thankfully, my trip was uneventful, aside from seeing all that desert scenery I wasn't used to. Before I knew it I was on the Los Angeles freeways. What an experience! If you are unfamiliar with this phenomenon, imagine yourself on a horrific snarled web of six-lane freeways suspended in the air over and under each other, with overpasses and underpasses and exits and entrances appearing out of nowhere. The good news was that because it was the Saturday of Thanksgiving weekend, there wasn't much congestion. The bad news was that the traffic was flowing at a racer's pace. I stayed in the far right-hand lane, trying to stay out of trouble, but somehow exited the freeway without meaning to.

My car, the covered lamp, and I descended the ramp into what appeared to be a warehouse area of downtown L.A. Not a good place to be at any time, and on this holiday weekend, it was worse. The streets were completely deserted. Graffiti covered all the walls. Street signs were knocked down or missing. It looked like a war zone. For a moment, I panicked, but I must have had a guardian angel with me for the whole trip, and she didn't desert me now. After driving around several blocks, I managed to find another on-ramp and was on my way again.

The next thing I knew I was pulling into the driveway of Ellen's Spanish-style bungalow—the first house she had ever bought—behind her brand-new beige BMW convertible. (Remember the yellow Vega?)

As soon as I honked the horn, the door flew open. First came El, then Jan. Next came Vance and Mimi. I got out of the car and was swallowed up by hugs. "Welcome to L.A.," they all said, almost in unison.

We walked inside, all together, as I replied, "It feels so good to be here."

If home is where the heart is, I was home.

BIT BY BIT, step by step, I was starting to be the woman I had always dreamed of being—my own person. It didn't happen overnight. The idea that I had to be married to be secure took a long time to die. I felt an underlying depression, and at times I felt that I was lost in an abyss—a chasm between the known and the unknown, between my past life and what my life was going to be from then on. My bridge was my work, Ellen, Vance, and two kittens I'd taken on as roommates.

"Does it ever get easier?" I remember asking a therapist in Pasadena whom I went to see for some long overdue input. B. had been making attempts at another reconciliation and I knew it was time to arm myself.

My therapist assured me that it would get easier. Then she paused and asked quietly, "Betty, what do you want?"

The question threw me. I'd spent my life trying to do the right thing or the practical thing or the thing I had to do to solve whatever predicament I was in. But what did I want? I told her I'd get back to her on it. And that night I wrote the following notes in my journal:

> Whatever I want—it isn't my ex-husband—I can allow myself to explore what I do want. I'm going through grieving—a loss of home—place in community. I want to get out but angry that I have to at a time when my life should be settled. As you let go, you allow something else to come in.

During another visit, my therapist said, "Betty, do you realize that you've never mentioned your own sense of betrayal? You were violated by his behavior. But you haven't acknowledged that to yourself. Why?"

"It's my training," I reminded her. "I've been trained to deny my feelings. No, more than that—feelings don't count. You shouldn't feel that way. Don't make waves. Don't make a scene. Be nice."

She gently explained how I had turned my back on myself. Staying with B. was so important to me that I didn't even acknowledge his betrayal. Instead, I maintained a relationship with behavior that ignored me and my needs. My task, she said, was to recognize the part of myself that I had told to be quiet for so long.

This was a revelation for me: If we offer "nice" or any other guise that is not genuine, the relationship can't grow. Only when we offer our genuine selves can there be a solid relationship. Once I started acting on that premise—just being genuine old me—and thinking about what I wanted, it was amazing how much happier I became. And soon, at last, I moved into the fifth and final stage of my process, acceptance.

Meanwhile, as was my genuine way, I got busy fixing up my nest and getting to know neighbors and friends in charming South Pasadena.

Early on, I found my "church home," as they say in Atlanta, Texas—All Saints Episcopal Church, a vital, community-involved congregation. I joined their singles group and also joined a men's and women's golf group at a nearby par 3 golf course. Pasadena has a wonderful knit shop, Mariposa, where I took part in a Wednesday night group which included mostly women, and one or two men, who gathered there to knit and chat, and sometimes have a glass of wine and snacks—a thoroughly congenial group.

I loved my surroundings and my routine, but not the daily grind of freeway travel. So by the spring of 1992, I was living comfortably in Studio City—which was more convenient for my job and for seeing Vance and El. This was another area full of interesting shops and restaurants, close enough for me to walk everywhere. There were tennis courts nearby, and I signed up for refresher lessons and met a nice woman about my age, Angie Long. We've become good friends, and at some point we changed from tennis to golf. It's easier to chat along the way.

LIFE WAS GETTING better all the time. Then, in May 1992, on the afternoon when the verdict was announced in the trial of the policemen who had beaten Rodney King, all hell broke loose in Los Angeles. At first, the rage over the unjust acquittal seemed understandable. But as angry mobs started attacking innocent motorists, then destroying businesses and property in their own communities, I watched a terrible tragedy unfold on our streets.

When I awoke the next morning and all was quiet, I saw no reason to miss work that day, other than my two kids' warnings that it wasn't safe. Miss work? Not me.

The streets were eerily quiet, and when I arrived at work I found the facility closed. Annoyed, I turned around and headed home. Things started to get scary. Ahead, in the distance, I could see smoke rising from new fires. Businesses I passed were being closed up, some of them by owners carrying guns. On the car radio, I heard reports of rampant looting and burning through more and more neighborhoods. I arrived home to find panicky messages from Vance and Ellen. When I called to let them know I was all right, they did not fail to say, "We told you so."

We all spent the remainder of the day watching the news of the destruction, feeling sad and discouraged. Rodney

King's comment really hit home—"Can't we all just get along?"

The sad thing is that, although the burned buildings were rebuilt, we haven't made great strides in repairing relations between blacks and whites—not in Los Angeles or in any of our major cities. We need to do more. We need to tear down the walls that divide us, whether the divisions are based on race, religion, or sexual orientation. And we need to recognize that, as Ellen would later tearfully plead when she was subjected to bigoted attacks, "We're really all the same."

After the riots, I began having thoughts about ways that I could contribute to improving the quality of life for others. Any kind of political activism was still too foreign to me. Instead, I followed Ellen's example and found opportunities to volunteer at soup kitchens and at Project Angel Food, an organization which provides hot meals to patients suffering from AIDS.

In fact, that year I spent Christmas Day at Project Angel Food. El and Vance were both out of town, and it seemed like a good way to make use of time that I would otherwise have spent alone. That night I wrote in my journal: "Happy, contented day because I feel good about the way my life is unfolding."

One positive change had occurred in September of 1992, when I began work at Cedars-Sinai Hospital, where I would remain until my retirement—a great experience from beginning to end. I worked predominantly with patients who'd had a stroke, a head injury, or a laryngectomy. This was work I found extremely gratifying. To some, it may sound depressing, but for me it isn't at all. First of all, my graduate school training and my clinical experience had prepared me for this. And often, I could see wonderful progress.

Early on at Cedars I developed one of my closest friendships—with Ricki LeVine, a fellow speech pathologist who is warm, caring, and fun. Ricki and I became partners in crime, organizing staff activities that added some levity to our otherwise serious professional concerns.

"You know, Betty," Ricki confessed over lunch one day, not long after we became friendly, "I never expected you to be this much fun."

"What do you mean?" I asked.

"You seemed so reserved," she said.

Obviously, my more impulsive, light-spirited side had worked its way through. The truth was that I didn't think of myself as reserved; this was only a protective mechanism I had developed over the years. I resolved then and there to be less reserved, work on it, believing as I do that we're all capable of changing for the better and that it's never, ever too late.

So I continued to try to reach out, open up, and do what I could to let good people into my life.

By the year's end, I had settled happily into my work routine, had cultivated a support system of family and friends, and had, to my pride and joy, just bought a condo for myself in West Hollywood that I was busy furnishing and getting ready to move into. I received a check for new carpeting, and the following note, from Ellen:

MERRY CHRISTMAS BETTY
Happy New Year Too

Here's a little money
Because I Love You
Make your new home pretty—
You don't want it to look shitty,
That would be a pity.
I'm glad you live in this city.
I'm proud of all you've accomplished—
You're really one heck of a woman.
So feel good about yourself
And know that 1993 will be
your best year yet—
Now go out and buy cool stuff
for your brand new condo.

Love, Ellen

Finally, I felt I had really arrived. I had completed the process of letting go of all my disappointments from the past. Life was good and full of possibilities. There's an old saying that one should bloom where one is planted. In my case, I have adapted that saying to one should bloom where one is transplanted. It certainly worked for me.

A journal entry at the year's end:

12-31-92 Good New Year's Eve—worked—busy day—picked up vegetarian tostada—1/2 bottle of champagne—bed by 9:15. New Year's resolutions? Maybe—smile more—initiate friendships—do my very best to improve at work—enjoy everything and everybody. Enjoy and pay for my condo. Exercise. Swim. Go to museums. Get busy with hobbies. Be real. Be real. Be real.

Royce Hall on the campus of UCLA is a venerable 2,000-seat theater known for sold-out houses for shows by some of the world's greatest opera stars, dancers, and classical musicians. Famous poets and authors have graced its stage, reading from their works, as have a handful of popular musicians and groups. But rare indeed are comedy performers. On the night of October 2, 1993, though, one comedy great, thirty-five-year-old Ellen DeGeneres, appeared live and in person for a one-night concert performance of her own kind of music—laughter.

When the lights went down just before the show, I quickly looked around the packed theater and thought for a moment how far she had come. Just a few years before, it seemed, she was in that coffeehouse on the campus of UNO, performing to a crowd of ten or so. And here she was.

What made the evening even more exciting and special was that Vance was the master of ceremonies. He introduced the opening act, the talented Del Rubio Triplets—sisters of an undetermined age who had sung and played guitar all over Los Angeles for years and years and were always lots of fun. And then to have him introduce El, just as he had done for her farewell performance in New Orleans, made everything perfect.

During the past few years, like the years that had preceded them, Ellen had continued to move up the ladder. In 1989, she had made her long-hoped-for foray into the world of situation comedy, landing a role as a regular on the series *Open House* (originally titled *Duet*), in which she played Margo Van Meter, a ditsy secretary-receptionist.

El never failed to mention how fortunate she felt to be on

a weekly series. She loved the whole routine, she said, especially sailing through those famous Paramount gates. Though the show was canceled after the following spring, Margo Van Meter went on to become a kind of a cult figure. Years later people would come up to Ellen and quote lines of hers from that show.

After the show's cancellation, it was back to stand-up, but she graduated to concert performances like this one in Royce Hall. Instead of competing with food and drinks for attention, she was playing to audiences who had paid just to see her. The change was exhilarating for her.

Two different *One Night Stand*s on HBO, one in 1990 and the other in 1992, had gained her much new attention. And soon she went from being one of the best of a new breed of up-and-coming female comics to being simply one of the best, right along with the top male stand-ups.

As always there had been disappointments too—like the role in a new Sam Kinnison series that she thought was a shoo-in but didn't get. Then good news soon followed—she was cast in a regular (if small) role as a nurse on *Laurie Hill*, an ABC sitcom. But that series, unfortunately, wasn't on the air long before it was canceled.

When El called to tell me about this disappointment, I gave her my usual sympathy and pep talk, telling her what a shame it was but adding, "Something better will turn up. Sooner or later. It always does."

Ellen sighed in agreement. Such is the philosophy of the incurable optimists that we are.

Something better—a lot better—did turn up, and it was sooner than later. In just two weeks, on November fourth, I noted in my datebook: "El called with astonishing news about series deal with ABC, Disney, and Black-Marlens." Her own series, finally.

I should mention that as exciting as this was, I was also having some excitement of my own . I noted it the next day, exactly like this: "Defrosted *##&*# refrigerator. Turned it on and all the freon came out. No refrigerator at all now! Bummer."

My household problem was soon solved, of course. And in the meantime momentum was gathering for Ellen's new series, *These Friends of Mine.* Like her performance at Royce Hall, the shooting of the pilot earlier in the year had been a real milestone. Several of my friends from Cedars-Sinai came with their husbands, and I was, as always, a very proud mom.

Because of Ellen and Vance's experiences in show business, I was weathered enough now to know that there are far too many variables and unknown factors to ever predict how successful a series is going to be. Obviously, funny writing is important for a sitcom, and even more important is how the public relates to the characters and the actors who play them. In both respects, I knew this show was a winner. But other elements can make all the difference, such as programming—the night and time a show is aired—and how a network promotes the show.

Sometimes series are bought with an initial commitment for as few as six episodes. In the case of *These Friends of Mine*, ABC's initial order was for thirteen, and the network decided to bring it in as a midseason replacement in early 1994. For

Ellen, this was enough assurance that for the time being she could take a much hoped-for break from stand-up.

Since production would begin in the fall of 1993, Ellen spent the summer doing a "good-bye to stand-up" tour that took her all around the country. When an interviewer in Maine asked her about the rigors of touring and why she had decided to take a break from stand-up, El answered very seriously:

> I've learned that in life, it's way too important to be happy. If you do something that you're not happy doing—no matter how much you try to fake it—that will eat you up from the inside, that'll kill you.

A telling response, I would say—and another glimmer of things to come.

As Ellen became famous, the public and the media wanted to know more about her personal life. Whenever interviewers asked about her romantic status, her stock answer was, "My private life is private." That was a reasonable statement. After all, every celebrity should be entitled to have a private life—Meg Ryan, Tom Hanks, Ellen DeGeneres. But, then again, two of those three are in socially acceptable heterosexual relationships. To know that Tom is married to Rita Wilson and that Meg is married to Dennis Quaid shouldn't be any different from knowing that Ellen, or any other gay person, is in a loving, on-going homosexual relationship. These are just facts that we know about these people. Period. Otherwise, Ellen's relationships are really none of our business, just as Meg's and Tom's marriages are none of our business; unless, of course, they choose to talk publicly about their significant others.

Unfortunately, for Ellen and other gay people in the public eye, it's not always so clear-cut. It's OK to let your inner circle of friends and associates know, but the prevailing attitude in show business is that when it comes to acceptance by mainstream America, stay in the closet. Implicit in this attitude is the idea that audiences won't accept a gay actor or actress in the part of a heterosexual, and still less in a heterosexual love scene. Excuse me, but it is called "acting," isn't it?

The "velvet curtain" conceals one of Hollywood's big secrets—the fact that there have always been gay actors and actresses in movies and television, imprisoned by the pretense that they are straight. For some of our most famous leading men and women, being out is so taboo—even within an otherwise tolerant community—that some have gone to the extreme of getting married. It is commonly believed, for good reason, that coming out will ruin or seriously harm even the best career.

So, for as long as I can remember, all of El's career advisers—even those who were gay themselves—were adamant that she should not expose herself as a lesbian, especially now that she was making her way into television.

Sitting in Royce Hall that night, I recalled some of the untruths El was forced to tell—referring to women like her girlfriends Lisa and, later, Teresa as roommates; I thought of all the times she couldn't acknowledge her true partner but had to appear at special events with a male at her side—

sometimes a male friend, sometimes a manager or agent. It was even better for her to bring Vance, her brother, than to show up with a woman, even though the circumstances might be completely "innocent."

The residual effect of being herself in one area of her life but in the closet publicly worked like a slow poison. Unbeknownst to me, and maybe even to El at first, deep down she developed a feeling of shame for having to live a lie. In a perfect world Ellen should have been able to be out from the very start. But this being the very imperfect world that it is, I'm not sure she would have been met with the same wide-ranging acceptance. Nonetheless, as I knew well, having to keep any kind of secret or participate in any kind of pretense is ultimately destructive.

A day of reckoning would, of course, come. But for the moment, I celebrated with everyone at the end of the show at Royce Hall. This was, in fact, a farewell performance—the culmination of her farewell tour, the closing of the chapter that had begun her career, and the beginning of a new chapter.

As El stood onstage to deafening cheers and applause, I thought again of the other farewell performance that Vance had emceed a decade earlier. He too, had certainly come a long way since those days. People like Vance who are gifted in many areas often take a long time to find their niche—or to settle on the one thing that can give them financial success and creative happiness. For him, that one thing turned out to be writing for TV and film, and within a couple of years, he would be writing on the staff of his sister's show.

Needless to say, Ellen's Royce Hall show was a triumph—an hour filled with her best material and some new routines—all of which earned her a delighted standing ovation that seemed to go on forever.

When El came out for her final bow, on her face was a beautiful, unforgettable expression of pride, and something else—gratitude.

DURING THE FIRST few years that I lived in Los Angeles, I did my best to get back to New Orleans as often as I could to check up on Mother. As bad as her health had become, time and again she proved indestructible. She survived many crises, only to emerge all the stronger each time. Whenever my sisters called with news of concern, I'd think back to the time ten years before when I was living in Atlanta and Mother had come down with what sounded like a terrible cold. On the phone, she insisted that she was fine and didn't need to see a doctor. But after calling Cousin Maisie, Aunt Ethel's daughter, and asking her to check on Mother, I promptly made a plane reservation, packed, and jumped into the car for the hour's trip to the airport.

I sped like a demon down those country roads, actually hoping that a policeman would stop me and then escort me. How naive I was—I don't think it really works like that. In any case, it didn't that day.

When I arrived in New Orleans, Mother was in the hospital. I was told that she was deathly ill and might not have survived if Maisie hadn't gotten her to the hospital. And to think that Mother had said she was fine—leftover denial from Christian Science.

By the next morning, miraculously, the worst had passed and Mother began to rally. But for the next ten years, as Mother's lungs got weaker and weaker, there were more hospitalizations. Each was serious, and in one instance the doctor was sure that she wouldn't pull through. She did, though.

In late 1992, after her surviving her latest hospitalization, we were convinced she would do it again. This time, Helen insisted that Mother come home with her to Pass Christian. This was a first; in the past, Mother had refused to be anywhere but her own home. She spent a very happy few weeks at Helen's. Afterward, my sister lovingly described how many of her friends had stopped by to visit with cakes and cookies and delicious soups they had made just for Mother.

Because of my work, the earliest I was able to schedule a visit was for the middle of February 1993. Then, on February 1, two weeks before I was set to leave, Helen called.

"Bets . . ." she began, her usually steady, strong voice sounding strained. I knew at once that Mother had died. I broke down as I listened to the details.

Helen reminded me what a full, happy eighty-seven years of life Mildred Morrill Pfeffer had lived.

"I know," I said with difficulty, "even though she had such poor health, her spirit was so strong."

For the moment, my own spirit felt crushed. I was stunned at how difficult it was to accept that she was gone, even though we had been expecting it.

I called Ellen, who cried when she heard the news. El called Vance so that I could leave for work. All day at work, I kept my sunglasses on. I found that tears would start when

I least expected them. It was Vance who really helped steady me with his phone call.

He could hear how hard this was on me, and with kind, loving, thoughtful words he let me know that I had a right to my feelings. Vance has always been supportive when I really need him.

"I just feel so badly," I admitted to him, "about missing that last visit with Noni. There was so much to say, all those things you never say often enough—how much we all loved her . . ."

Vance said he was sure that Noni knew very well how much she was loved.

That night, I took the red-eye out of Los Angeles. When I arrived in New Orleans the following morning, I went directly to the funeral home. I approached the casket tentatively. Seeing Mother lying there was terribly, terribly difficult. I had to go into another room to compose myself.

Audrey, Helen, and I bonded more closely than ever at this time. We were deeply touched to see how many people came to pay their last respects to our mother. Some years earlier Mother's pastor and all the parishioners had voted her an outstanding senior citizen because of her "years of service and devotion to the church." She was honored at that time by the archbishop at a luncheon at the Marriot, along with senior citizens from the Catholic churches all over New Orleans. She was so well-loved. There was an endless flow of visitors for her last rites—friends from years back, friends from church, friends from her neighborhood, and friends of ours.

After the service, Helen, Audrey, and I went back to Mother's house and took care of everything we had to do, dividing her things among us and the grandchildren. Then I went to Helen's for a few quiet days before returning home.

While I was in Pass Christian, I took several walks on the beach by myself. I thought about how short life is, and how precious. Already, I missed Mother terribly—as I do to this day.

It's so important to appreciate each other while we're here.

ONCE AGAIN, I went through a natural process of grieving. Mother's death had given me closure on the many chapters of my life that took place in New Orleans and environs. The cord was cut. This was, all at once, liberating yet scary. Where my life was headed, I didn't know. There was something more I was yearning for, but I wasn't sure what.

Ever since I had moved to California, without giving it much conscious thought, I had assumed that eventually a man would appear in my life. That had always happened in the past. But now that I was finally ready, it wasn't happening. Initially, I attended a singles group for people over fifty, but that was so depressing—over seventy was more like it.

Here and there, I dated some nice gentlemen and even had a couple of serious relationships. Both were close calls; both decent men, but definitely not right for me. At moments, the temptation to fall back into a familiar routine was enticing, but I escaped unscathed. The lesson was long in coming but it finally registered with me that latching onto a man just to have a warm body nearby, and to not be alone, isn't worth it. I've learned that in these days, with so much going on in my life, it's much better to luxuriate in my aloneness.

It's amazing that the same person who less than ten years before was afraid not to have a man to take care of her could be writing this today. Never let it be said that human beings aren't capable of change.

But if that something that I was yearning for wasn't a man, what was it? Still unsure, I began to fill what spare time I did have, not simply with interesting hobbies as I had done in the past, but in areas that gave me a sense of meaning in my life. I did volunteer work at Project Angel Food; at the Jewish Family Service, where I helped immigrants fill out their citizenship applications; and at the Jeffrey Goodman AIDS Clinic, where I helped in the office.

My great, joyous pastime, of course, was sharing in all the excitement going on for Ellen. By the end of that first season, her series was a hit.

As Ellen's unapologetic number one fan, I was not surprised. In fact, it is rare for me to find myself truly surprised by her talent. But on the night of September 19, 1994, when she cohosted the Emmy Awards with Patricia Richardson from *Home Improvement*, I don't think anyone, including me, was prepared for the splash Ellen made. She was incredible. How much was written and rehearsed, I don't know; all of her bits were done with so much abandon and lovable mischief-making that they seemed totally spontaneous. At one point, after Bette Midler sang a medley onstage, Ellen grabbed a mike and had a cameraman follow her outside so she could sing Bette's medley to the people in the bleachers.

Stargazers covet these bleacher seats, but it was blistering hot that day and Ellen said she just felt so bad for those people that if they couldn't come in to the show, she would bring the show to them. Unheard-of!

Playing the role of roving reporter to the hilt, she headed backstage, catching celebrities off guard, and then she showed up in the director's trailer where the crew was in the midst of picking shots to send out live over the airwaves.

Elliott and I sat together, and as well as we knew our daughter's capacity for unpredictable shenanigans, even we were bowled over. The shocker, at least to those of us who know her well, was the sight of Ellen striding elegantly across the stage in a long, low-cut black gown. It was no secret that she hated dresses, and she probably hadn't worn one since her days working at the law firm in New Orleans.

This was no small matter. In fact, a year later, in her book of humorous musings, *My Point—And I Do Have One* (which debuted at number one on the *New York Times* bestseller list and sold over a half a million copies), Ellen devoted an entire chapter to the subject.

For days before the Emmys she practiced walking just the right way. The joke was that the person who showed her the right way to walk in a form-fitting dress was her hair stylist—a man. Whatever his secret was, it worked. Ellen floated majestically across that stage.

TV is such a powerful medium. In a review of the Emmys, the *Los Angeles Daily News* treated Ellen's performance as cohost as if it deserved an award: "Indeed, a star was born—or reborn, if you will." A wildly popular second season followed for her own TV show.

El's star was rising as never before, in spite of ongoing changes with her show. Originally it was filmed at Sony Studios in Culver City, but it later moved to Disney Studios in Burbank and its name was changed to *Ellen*—an eponymous title. I love that word!

Along the way, there were also cast changes, some that El didn't agree with—but hers was not the last word. There were almost constant changes in the night and time slot. Normally this would kill a show, but *Ellen*'s audience was undaunted and the ratings remained strong.

Although the producing and writing staff went through its own changing of the guard, I felt that the quality of the show stayed consistently high. For the entire four and a half years, I rarely missed a shoot. It was the highlight of my life. Ellen really liked having me there, and I think my feedback was important to her. Even before filming she would often have me read the script to tell her what I thought. She knows she can always count on me to be honest; just as I can count on her. In addition to wanting my input on her work, over the years Ellen has even managed to have me *put in* her work. My debut was doing promos with her for the cable network Comedy Central.

My next gig was doing promos with Ellen for *These Friends of Mine* before the series went on the air. After that, I became a virtual "Where's Waldo" in Ellen's multimedia world. I did at least three extra parts on *Ellen*, as well as a speaking part in one of her title sequences, and then appeared as an extra in *Mr. Wrong,* the first feature film in which El starred. Great fun! And, although I had no idea that I would later become a national spokesperson and appear frequently on television and radio, these earlier experiences gave me some good preparation.

While I enjoyed my onscreen appearances, I also relished my role as avid fan, audience member, and cheerleader to everyone in the cast and crew. One of the best perks of being a member of the *Ellen* family is my treasured friendship with Ellen's TV mom—the warm, outgoing Alice Hirson—and her charming husband, the actor Steve Elliott. Alice, a gourmet cook, and Steve, a marvelous host, entertain often and have had me over for wonderful evenings with their longtime friends from show business. At first, it was daunting to walk in and meet people I had seen for years on TV or in the movies. But fortunately, as time has gone on, I have outgrown being starstruck and am just happy to be in the company of interesting, down-to-earth, good people. There is nothing quite so energizing as an evening of stimulating conversation.

I recall one evening at home alone, when I got to thinking and had what must have been a prophetic thought about what I was still looking for in my life. I noted it in my journal:

> If I can tap the right reservoir, I have lots of importance to say.

I had no idea what reservoir would be right, but this realization was a breakthrough, the discovery that in spite of hard times, life had given me some commonsense wisdom I wanted to share. And out of that grew new dreams and hopes for the future. I still wasn't sure where, specifically, my path would take me, but at the young age of sixty-five I recognized that I was indeed on a path.

A short while later, during a bout of unusually wet L.A. weather, I made another entry in my journal:

> Rain—lots and lots of rain—gentle, steady, tiny drops; hard, pelting, wind-driven downpours—the kind that left me soaked from the hips down—only my upper half shielded by my oversized umbrella. This rain feels like home. Home. I've been away from New Orleans for over 20 years total—maybe almost 25—but that place is home. There's no denying our roots. Imagine people who never left. . . . I suppose I have ventured out into the world a bit. All in all, it has been beneficial for me—my life experiences—all the pluses and minuses—have so far left a total on the plus side. Thank God that in spite of everything, I remain an optimist—always hoping for the best—expecting things to work out. They don't always but I keep plodding on, hoping they will.

My life became a study in contrasts: Then versus Now. As a child, then five-year-old Betty Jane wept bitterly at having to leave home for kindergarten. As a coed, then twenty-year-old Betty wasn't too upset when her first marriage didn't work—because it meant going home. In my twenties, I dreamed and even wrote about traveling but never got around to it—why leave home? Home was everything to me. I won awards for writing about home improvements, and during my marriage to B., I put all my learning to good use. Home was such a priority that through my thirties, forties, and fifties, I put up with that unhealthy marriage—because I couldn't bear the thought of leaving home.

The Now Betty was a different creature altogether. Such were my thoughts in March of 1996 as I set off for a vacation—a group tour of Italy. This was a lifelong dream come true. In the past such trips had been impossible. Elliott and I couldn't afford it, and B. got airsick, seasick, and carsick.

Well, I was about to make up for lost time. The trip to Italy was a gift from Ellen The Generous—in honor of Mother's Day, my birthday, retirement, and I don't know what all. Sitting there on the plane on the first leg of the trip, for the first destination—Rome—I contemplated my retirement, wondering what I would do with my extra time.

I really wasn't ready to retire. But when Cedars began drastic cutbacks in its staff and offered incentives for early retirement, I took the bait. My working days were far from over, however, since I was able to continue as a per diem therapist at Cedars and two other hospitals, as well as doing at-home therapy through Cedars Home Health. Financially, I was better off than before. And, I reminded myself, I could use the extra time for golf.

My Italian vacation was a feast for the senses. I adored it

all—Rome, Assisi, Siena, San Gimignano, Florence, and Venice; the museums, the architecture, the age-old historical places, and, yes, the food.

I hadn't known anyone in my group before we left for the trip. But this was a congenial group, and after a week or so we all became quite friendly. I hadn't planned to travel incognito, but we all went by our first names only, so the fact that I had a famous daughter didn't come up until our next to last stop, in Florence.

It was one of those typical things. We were sitting over lunch one afternoon and people were talking about their successful kids—doctors, lawyers, accountants. I'm sure I wasn't the only parent with children in the arts but when someone asked me, "How about you, Betty; do you have any children?" the group became suddenly very quiet.

"Yes, I have two," I began with a proud smile. "A son, Vance, who writes for television and the movies . . ."

"Anything we might have seen?"

"Right now, he's working on *Ellen*, the TV show," I said.

A chorus of impressed comments followed: "Oh, I love that show." "I never miss it!" "She's terrific, that Ellen, as good as *I Love Lucy.*"

Then someone said, "You're lucky to have such a successful son. And what about your other kid?"

"Oh," I laughed, "she's Ellen."

You can imagine how big a revelation this was. Everyone in the group, it seemed, was a major fan of Ellen's.

When I returned to L.A., Ellen was tickled by this story. Seeing how thrilled I was by travel, she offered me another trip—courtesy of her abundant frequent-flyer miles. "Wherever you want to go, Mom," she said. "And fly first class."

I had flown first class only once before—a few years earlier, when I accompanied her to Chicago, where she appeared on the Oprah Winfrey show.

"Well," I said, thinking aloud, "if I'm going to fly first class, I want as long a flight as possible."

El grinned.

And so, since I had never been there, I chose Washington, D.C. I was very lucky—I arrived one week before the Republicans shut the government down. It was quite cold, but I'd brought along my trusty long silk underwear, and from my hotel near the White House I managed to walk everywhere—the Vietnam Memorial, the Lincoln Memorial, the National Gallery (where I could have spent weeks), and the Renwick Gallery, a wonderful museum of American arts and crafts. Thanks to ABC, a VIP tour of the White House was arranged for me. Talk about traveling in style.

The more I saw of Washington, the more I regretted that we hadn't taken Vance and Ellen there when they were in school. Our capital is so impressive, and it's a place that every girl and boy should see. Its sites and its history are a reminder of the spirit of freedom and democracy upon which this great nation was built.

I left wishing I had more time to see everything. Little did I know that I would be back; in fact, within a year, I would be back four more times.

"WHAT DO YOU think?" Ellen asked. It was late spring of 1996. She had just told me about a monumental decision. She, Ellen DeGeneres, was going to come out publicly as a lesbian. It was time, she said. But not only that: if she could get a green light from the network and the studio, her idea was to have Ellen Morgan come out in the series at the same time.

I was stunned. This wasn't an overnight decision—Ellen had been mulling it over for some time—but this was the first I had heard of it. As she explained to me, since she had begun therapy recently, she realized that all this hiding had given her a sense of shame, and she didn't want to live like that anymore.

We talked over all the risks.

I couldn't help pointing out that she might be jeopardizing everything she had struggled to attain in her career. Other concerns also came up, such as the invasion of her privacy. This is one of the great drawbacks of fame. Ellen had so little privacy as it was. Like other celebrities, she had to contend with the press and the public, who felt as if they owned her.

But, Ellen reminded me, there had been speculations in the tabloids anyway—like the hubbub over the facetious chapter in her book, about hating to wear dresses, which she called, "Ellen DeGeneres Is a Man!" Of course, the tabloids had also tried to make hay with the part in the book where Ellen talked humorously about her bad memory. Somewhere they got a picture of a pensive-looking Ellen and gave it the headline, "Woman Without a Past." Even I had been the subject of a tabloid story—a complete fabrication. The story said that Elizabeth Taylor and I had met while she was hospitalized and discussed our favorite comedian, Ellen.

As Ellen and I were having our discussion, the graduating class of 1976 of Atlanta High School in Atlanta, Texas, was planning to celebrate its twentieth reunion. Articles had appeared on the front page of the newspaper, asking, "Will Ellen Come to This Year's 20th Reunion?" Wonderful quotations were included from teachers and friends who remembered what a likable, funny person Ellen had been in high school.

Actually, Ellen was not planning to attend; but now, with the prospect of her coming out, I wondered if the town would still embrace her as an openly gay woman. I also wondered: What if she had come out as a lesbian but hadn't become famous? Would people have trouble accepting her? I wasn't sure of the answers, but I knew that none of this was going to be easy.

My old reflex, of course, was to wonder, "Why rock the boat?"

Ellen's reason was simple: "This is something I have to do."

My decision was just as simple—to support her all the way. I saw that her own struggles, her fears, and her weariness at having to hide part of herself had influenced her choice. And I saw that she was resolved and determined, prepared to accept the consequences. She knew well what they were.

As we talked it over further, I realized that not only did she have to do this; it was something she had the right to do, as any private or public person has the right to do.

Of course she had a right to be honest about who she is. I was reminded of some of the articles in the Universal Declaration of Human Rights adopted by the UN General Assembly in 1948:

- Article 1: All human beings are born free and equal in dignity and rights. They are endowed with reason and conscience and should act towards one another in a spirit of brotherhood.
- Article 3: Everyone has the right to life, liberty and security of person.
- Article 5: No one shall be subjected to torture or to cruel, inhuman or degrading treatment or punishment.
- Article 19: Everyone has the right to freedom of opinion and expression.

This declaration specifically says human rights. No one or no group is excluded.

These are rights we can all relate to. As a public person, Ellen had an absolute right to come out. And coming out made a lot of sense for Ellen Morgan as a character in a sitcom. In earlier shows, while she had dated and had some almost-successful relationships, her character arc and the show's story line seemed to have both become rudderless.

As for all her madcap, zany escapades—getting in and out of sticky predicaments—the writers were already feeling that they had exhausted those situations. Of course, many of these shows were classics. There is the hilarious episode in which Martha Stewart is coming to dinner and Ellen is cooking Cornish hens and twice-baked potatoes. Then there is an episode I loved, in which Ellen goes to a ballet class; and another very funny one in which she pretends to be a fitness trainer. Some of my other favorites were the episode of the bachelorette party with Kathy Najimy, the show about Paige's wedding, and the episode when Ellen tries volunteer work.

For Ellen Morgan to come out would open up a new avenue of writing possibilities, and it wasn't out of character.

While people often assume that the two Ellens are the same person, that is a mistake. Certainly, Ellen brought her own goofiness and offbeat humor to the character, but Ellen Morgan was not very successful on the job, was usually unlucky in love, and could sometimes be pitifully insecure, with a desperate need to please. In contrast, Ellen DeGeneres is very successful and has had very positive romantic relationships; and though it's important for her to be liked, she's not insecure about it. Ellen Morgan rambled and went off on tangents; Ellen DeGeneres has a point. Her book says so.

Most significant of all: the real Ellen went though her process of self-discovery and coming out in her late teens; Ellen Morgan was about to go through it as a woman in her thirties.

Ellen knew that even though other TV shows had supporting characters who happened to be gay, there had never been a homosexual lead in a sitcom; she also knew having a lead character go through the process of discovering her or his sexual orientation was something never before done on television. The odds that the network and studio would go for it weren't good. But Ellen had a powerful argument for trying. Grim statistics show that gay teenagers are more at risk of depression, suicide, and attempted suicide, and she felt that this was an opportunity to send a positive message to these kids—as well as to all gay people: "We're OK. We don't have to be ashamed of who we are and who we love."

The more we talked about the positives, the more excited I became. Over the last few years, as the public clamored to know more and more about her, I was constantly asked to divulge behind-the-scenes information: "Was she always funny?" "Where does she live?" "Is she married?" The first two questions weren't hard to answer, even though I was never specific about where she lived. With the last question, however, I had to be evasive—"No," was my stock answer, "she's married to her career."

For all those years, I couldn't even join P-FLAG—Parents, Family, and Friends of Lesbians and Gays, a supportive organization—because it would have meant "outing" Ellen. Now, it was a relief to know that I too would be able to come out of the closet.

After a top secret meeting Ellen had with the writers and producers, the next step was getting the go-ahead from Disney and ABC. That process began in August of 1996 with another top secret meeting at Disney. None of the executives there knew exactly what the agenda was. When Ellen told me about it, she described how she had started out by making a few jokes, loosening everyone up. And then, as she proceeded to present her idea, everything suddenly became deathly quiet and serious.

Ellen tried hard not to start crying, but the tears came. No one in that room could have had any doubt about how important this was to her. So no one was going to give her a flat no. Instead, she got a maybe—the possibility could be explored. But until there was a script in hand, there were no commitments.

It was then that the writers and producers came up with the code name "The Puppy Episode"—so hush-hush that when the other cast members and Tammy Billik, the casting director, saw it up on the storyboard for possible upcoming episodes, they had no idea what it was.

In September, with *Ellen* just starting back on the air for its fourth season, someone leaked the news to the *Hollywood Reporter*. This could have been a disaster. ABC and Disney were bombarded by calls and letters from all camps—pro, con, and simply curious. The official stance was a refusal to comment on the rumors.

For the next several months we were all on pins and needles. The secrecy surrounding the script was so intense that the drafts were printed on dark-maroon paper—making them impossible to copy.

Finally, in March of 1997, an inspired script for an hour-long special was given approval.

By now speculation had become so fierce that it would have been ridiculous to try to halt the momentum. The headlines had been blaring the news since the previous fall: GAY TV—WILL ELLEN DEGENERES' ALTER EGO COME OUT WITH HER HANDS UP? (*Entertainment Weekly*); AIRING OUT ELLEN'S CLOSET (*The Advocate*); MOST DRAWN-OUT UNOFFICIAL CLIFF-

HANGER (*Out*); IS SHE OR ISN'T SHE? (*People*); WILL THE REAL ELLEN PLEASE STAND UP! (*Curve* magazine); WILL ELLEN STILL WEAR PANTS? (*Newsweek*).

I was amazed at Ellen's focus and her relative calm throughout the hysteria, even when televangelists and religious extremists went on the warpath with their discriminatory, homophobic rhetoric. Of course it upset her, though, and it angered me. It was horrible. It was unchristian.

Funny, talented, smart, and a good, nice person, Ellen was used to having people like her. Now all of sudden, people like the right-wing extremist Jerry Falwell were saying hateful things, calling her "Ellen DeGenerate." Ellen could have become defensive and strident, but she did the true Christian thing and turned the other cheek. Later, when she was asked about Falwell's comment in *Time* Magazine's cover story, "Yep, I'm Gay"—which was published in conjunction with the coming out episode—Ellen said:

> Really, he called me that? . . . I've been getting that since the fourth grade. I guess I'm happy I could give him work.

I had wondered how the folks back in Atlanta, Texas, might feel about their hometown star coming out. *TV Guide* actually went and interviewed some locals. The wonderful principal of Ellen's high school, Barbara Qualls, was a hundred percent supportive—as were lots of people, including several old friends of Ellen's and younger students now attending her high school. Others, such as an old boyfriend of Ellen's, were not so broad-minded.

While all this was going on, a less vocal but no less energized coalition of gay rights activists were busy on the Internet, preparing for a major celebration.

Indeed, the two weeks in which "The Puppy Episode" was rehearsed and shot felt like one long party. And it seemed like a party nobody wanted to miss, as the list of stars making guest appearances grew longer and longer—Laura Dern, Oprah Winfrey, Demi Moore, Gina Gershon, Dwight Yoakum, Billy Bob Thornton, k.d. lang, Melissa Etheridge, and others.

With my usual soft-focus memory, I find it hard to pinpoint specific moments from this experience. Instead, I'm left with fragments of memories—a blur in which my clearest recollection is the palpable exhilaration felt by all, for taking part in something important and meaningful. There was also a sense of fun. I have memories of the rehearsals in which, under the direction of Gil Junger, a hilarious and touching piece of writing came to life; memories of the breaks between scenes and seeing El and all those guest stars relaxing on a sofa and chairs and quietly talking together; memories of exchanging proud smiles with Vance; memories of the filming itself and the roar of the live audience whose cheer of jubilation was literally deafening as I, an extra in the scene, looked on in "surprise" when Ellen turned to Laura Dern's character and unwittingly leaned into an airport loudspeaker and spoke her truth: "I'm gay."

Most of all, I am left with the memory of the look of utter relief on El's face at the end of the shoot. She cried and I cried, mirroring her emotions.

• • •

ELLEN LIKES TO joke that I need to live within one mile of her. It happens to be true, if for no reason other than convenience. It does save gas. And then there are Trevor and Murphy, otherwise known as my granddogs. I am their official dog-sitter. Often when El is going out for a long night, I'll sleep at her house and take care of the "boys."

One such night was March 25, 1997, Oscar night. The last *Ellen* of the season had been shot and the wrap party for the year was to be held in a few days. When Ellen left to attend the exclusive *Vanity Fair* Oscar party at Morton's, along with her then manager, Arthur Imparato, it struck me that my daughter was especially beautiful that night. She had her hair and makeup done, as she does for most public events, but that wasn't the reason. There was a glow and a lightness about her, as if some heaviness she had carried for years had been lifted off.

I watched some of the post-Oscar coverage on TV before drifting contentedly off to sleep, only to be awakened in the wee hours by the barking of Trevor and Murphy, who heard the limo pulling in. As usual, when this happens, I threw on an old robe and stumbled outside with them, hoping we'd all be able to sleep in a little later in the morning. The air was cool and from where I was standing in that part of the yard, I could look through large windows into the entrance hall and dining room. In my half-asleep state, I noticed that with Ellen and Arthur was an elegant young woman I had never seen before.

And that's how I met Anne Heche—a memorable meeting for all of us that night. They later described to me how, the moment El walked into Morton's, she looked across the room at Anne, who was looking at her, and the attraction was instantaneous. Anne later described it as a "chemical change." She took the initiative, letting El know right away what she was feeling. El felt it too but was cautious. After all, up until that night, Anne was known as heterosexual. But Anne's position was, and is, that love and attraction aren't about those distinctions. As she has said, "It's not about what's between your legs. It's about what's between your ears and in your heart."

El and Anne have been together since that night.

I liked Anne right away. That night I made a note in my journal of things to be grateful for: "El's new happiness and meeting Anne." March 27, two days later, I noted: "A wonderful talk with Anne." Then on March 29 I was grateful for: "Anne for El—so far." And on April 5: "El and Anne's happiness."

The more I got to know her and the more I saw the purity of her love for Ellen, the more impressed I was with Anne as a person, and with her intelligence, even her brilliance. And I quickly learned about her marvelous acting, watching videos of *Donnie Brasco* and HBO's *If These Walls Could Talk*, and, later, attending the Los Angeles premieres of her films, *Volcano* and *Wag the Dog*.

God works in wondrous, powerful ways. How interesting that Ellen did what was no doubt the most important show of her life and less than one week after that began what is undoubtedly the most important relationship of her life.

Anne really seems to have been delivered to her by no accident—"an angel," as Ellen calls her.

I feel that God has sent me someone special too—my other daughter, Anne.

THREE YEARS EARLIER *PrimeTime Live* had done a wonderful feature on Ellen in which Judd Rose had accompanied her back to New Orleans to retrace her humble origins. In conjunction with "The Puppy Episode," *PrimeTime* decided to do another interview, this one conducted by Diane Sawyer.

This was the first time that Ellen had talked about her own coming out at age twenty. Diane arranged to interview the whole family. Before the day of my actual interview at the Peninsula Hotel, I was going to get a chance to meet Diane when she came to El's house (where I was living briefly during repairs to my place) to get a few shots of her and Ellen walking through the house and talking.

This had been planned for some time and the house and gardens were shiny and pristine in preparation. I was reading the morning paper at the breakfast table when Anne and El came into the kitchen. Ellen said something about "when Diane Sawyer gets here," and what happened next I have no memory of. I can only relate what Ellen and Anne told me afterward. Apparently I asked, "Oh, is Diane Sawyer coming here?"

Anne looked at me as though she thought I was kidding, but Ellen knew right away that I wasn't.

The next thing I remember is Anne sitting next to me

with her arms around me and El standing in front of me, with tears in her eyes, asking me questions.

"What happened?" I said, upset and scared.

When they described it to me, it was obvious I had "checked out" for a few seconds. This was serious. Having worked in a hospital with stroke patients, I'm familiar with TIAs (transient ischemic attacks) and I realized that's what it could have been.

When I felt reasonably calm, I called my doctor's office to try to get an appointment right away. As I talked about the incident, I became very emotional. In spite of my grave concern, when I was informed that I couldn't be seen until the afternoon, I opted for another day. Why? Because I didn't want to miss the last class of the commercial workshop I was taking—if I missed this class, I couldn't take part in "agent" night, a chance to show what we had learned in front of agents who came to look us over. I already had an agent, but I just couldn't bear not getting my money's worth. Never let it be said I don't have my priorities straight. I went to the class.

In the meantime, however, I did talk to my doctor and made an appointment to see her so she could arrange for a CAT scan and other tests. It occurred to me then that my checking out that morning may have had a lot to do with being more caught up in all the excitement than I let on—even to myself.

A few days later, I had the tests and, thankfully, I'm all clear. Since then I have tried to pace myself and take good care of myself.

In the midst of all this, I had my interview with Diane—who is as beautiful and thoughtful in person as the image she projects on TV, and very down-to-earth. She had on a lovely blouse her mother had made for her, and as she was pinning it at the neckline to make it less low-cut, I said, "Don't you have people to do that?"

Diane smiled and said, "I am my people."

We talked about that day on the beach in Pass Christian. Later, when they ran the interview, they used a shot of the rocky Pacific coast for the beach. It worked, except for the people on the Mississippi Gulf Coast who know that there are no boulders on their beaches. I had no idea how pivotal my taking part in this interview was going to be in my own life's journey. I only knew how liberating it felt to be rid of a twenty-year-old secret.

SO THAT'S MOST of the story that led to my sitting in the auditorium at CAA watching history unfold. Everything had built up to this moment as it erupted with *the* show. There were so many special people there that night that my memory is again sketchy. Vance, of course, was there. Reserved though he usually is, that night he was practically euphoric. Oh, and I remember meeting Sir Ian McKellan. How could I not remember that mellifluous voice?

And I know that Shirley MacLaine was there because, before the show she was sitting in an aisle seat and I saw her as I hurried past. I wanted to stop and tell her how much I've always admired her work, but I was too awestruck to say anything at all. Ellen's good friends Kathy Najimy and Dan Finnerty were there—which I know because I captured the two of them in that picture I took of Anne and El.

I know that at the end we all clapped and cheered and stood up and applauded for Ellen. That's all I remember, like facets of a prism—just wonderful little glimmers of light.

PART III

APRIL 30, 1997, TO THE PRESENT

I know the truth—give up all other truths!
No need for people anywhere on earth to struggle.
Look—it's evening, look, it is nearly night
what do you speak of, poets, lovers, generals?

The wind is level now, the earth is wet with dew,
the storm of stars in the sky will turn to quiet.
And soon all of us will sleep under the earth, we
who never let each other sleep above it.

MARINA TSVETAYEVA

Blessed are the peacemakers: for they shall be called
the children of God.

MATTHEW 5:9

9

Journeys

ON THE MORNING AFTER —May 1, 1997—I awoke to discover that I had gone through a virtual overnight transformation, from being the mom of a famous person to being something of a famous mom. Incredible. And it was all because of the *PrimeTime Live* interview with Diane Sawyer, which had aired the previous night just after the coming out episode.

The response was amazingly positive, immediate—and surprising. Everyone asked how I could be so calm and articulate, wondering if I had known ahead of time what Diane was going to ask me. No, I kept saying, I didn't know what she would ask; but because I was talking about my kid, I didn't see any reason to be nervous. Then again, at that point I still had no concept of the magnitude of all that was going on. We knew the show would be groundbreaking, a first. But I don't think any of us realized how truly historic it would be and how much it would mean to a great many people.

It hadn't occurred to me during my interview with Diane

that my simple statements of love, support, and acceptance would send a message the public hadn't heard before—or at least had never heard in such a large public forum.

Suddenly, the very next day, and then in the days and weeks that followed, strangers recognized me on the street and in stores and showered me with thanks, wanting to tell me their stories. If their parents were supportive, they were happy to tell me that. If they weren't, they would say, "I wish my Mom were like you," and we'd talk about it for a while. And some, even if they weren't gay and had no gay family members, just wanted to say how much they admired Ellen—and my vocal support for her.

I even received my first piece of fan mail:

> In light of all the things your daughter has been brave enough to stand up for and all the media hype—this is a note just for you, from a group of girls that watched the *PrimeTime* interview and wanted to say we would ALL be very proud to call you mom.
>
> Sincerely,
>
> The girls in the band CAT B'LUES

At Bloomingdale's one Saturday, I passed two older women at the jewelry counter and overheard one say to the other, "It's her. It's her mother." Then she grabbed my arm and said, "You're her mother."

Of course, I agreed—and we never even said "her" name.

At a party, a young man approached me and introduced himself, telling me that although his mother knew he was gay, she had never acknowledged it. But then, he told me, after watching me on *PrimeTime Live*, his mother called him the next day from Ohio and said, "Well, if that woman can say that on national television, I guess you and I can talk."

An estimated 40 million viewers had watched Ellen Morgan come out, and many of those had stayed tuned to *PrimeTime Live* to hear Ellen DeGeneres and her family talk about her own coming out nineteen years earlier. When the heads of the network and Disney called the episode's director, Gil Junger, to report the astonishing ratings, they said it was the equivalent of a movie having an opening-weekend box office of $280 million. A record-setting blockbuster!

And then there were the *Ellen* parties. This was how I first heard about the great work of the Human Rights Campaign, the nation's largest political organization for equal rights for gays. I found out that they had put together party kits, including everything from an *Ellen* trivia quiz to sample invitations to a party poster to a video from HRC. Initially, they anticipated getting requests for a few hundred kits; instead they got, and filled, requests for over 2,500. In Birmingham, Alabama, where the local ABC affiliate refused to broadcast the show, an entrepreneurial young man named Kevin Snow arranged an *Ellen* party in a hotel ballroom for a private showing—via satellite. Nearly 3,000 local celebrators attended. (Since then, Kevin told me, the gay community in Birmingham has become more organized and cohesive.)

On that very morning after, an exuberant Alice Hirson, my dear friend and El's TV mom, called to tell me about a party she had attended at a nightclub in West Hollywood. It was festive, packed, and noisy. Alice said, "When I got there, I thought, oh, no, we'll never be able to hear the show. But the minute it started, you could've heard a pin drop." Of course, she went on, there was lots of laughter for the punch lines, but then there would be quiet again for the dialogue.

From what I continued to hear in the days that followed, that scenario was repeated all over the country. I heard from a lot of gay men and women that even as they laughed, they were crying tears of happiness throughout the show. Many said they watched in absolute wonder, not believing that this was finally happening on network TV. Others described a huge feeling of relief—somehow this show was taking away their collective pretense of normality by saying to the world that gay people are normal and that pretending otherwise isn't healthy for anybody.

This was beyond everyone's wildest expectations. It seemed almost like a dream, almost too good to be true. I kept wanting to pinch myself, wondering when the bubble would burst. But it wasn't a dream; it was real. Without bloodshed, Ellen DeGeneres had returned from the battlefield victorious, to find that her personal victory was shared by everyone who had a stake in fairness and equality for our gay and lesbian citizens.

A new day had dawned. That week the actress and gay rights activist Amanda Bearse said in *People* magazine:

> The ice has been broken. We are in every job, we're every color. We're not out to take over the world. We just want to live in it.

I've heard it said that the best way to get someone to change or open their minds is first to make them laugh. Maybe, because of her gift for comedy, that's why Ellen had stepped—pretty much unwittingly—into the role of a pioneer. Thanks to her talents and those of her director, writers, producers, guests, and fellow cast and crew members, the coming out episode probably packed its punch because it was so well done and so funny.

It was thrilling to see praise for the show in all the major media. Just as meaningful to me were the letters I received from several of my family members. "Dear Bets," Helen began, as she always does, in the note she sent enclosed with a positive local review from Mississippi:

> Tell Ellen I have continued to have very positive comments on her shows. One friend told me today that even her pastor from the pulpit spoke favorably about it. Even my friends from Vermont, now 90 and 93, wrote to say "hooray." So Ellen must be feeling very good about it all.

This came from Audrey:

> Whew! I'm exhausted—so I can only imagine how you and Ellen and Anne must feel. I've never seen anything like the media coverage this last week. Well, you three came through with flying colors. I don't know that I could have begun to face the cameras and questions with the poise and ease that you exhibited. I hope for everyone's sake that it calms down.

P.S. I went to church after writing to you. So many people had good things to say about you—and Ellen's program. And I enjoyed seeing Vance, too.

Like Audrey, we were also expecting that, as the weeks passed, life would soon quiet down and return to its regular routine. We were wrong. The excitement and the tide of good feeling continued. And as the days took on a sort of enchanted, inspired quality, they were just as eventful. Every day we heard reports that because of Ellen, lives were being changed for the better; indeed, lives were being saved.

"I keep waiting for the other shoe to drop," I said to Vance, as we sat down together over a Mother's Day lunch to which he was treating me.

"I know," he agreed, and with his typical dry humor he made some funny remark about the first shoe that dropped. As a result of Diane Sawyer's interview, Vance was being recognized too—as El's proud, protective big brother who loved his sister unconditionally.

Becoming serious, however, he admitted that he still felt angry about the bomb threat on the set the last day of shooting. "I blame the right-wing rhetoric," Vance said. "Those extremists—how they can call themselves Christians and preach hate, I just don't know."

I felt the same way, recalling how one televangelist had made the absurd comment that he didn't believe Ellen was really gay because, "She's so popular. She's such an attractive actress"—as if only unattractive people could be gay. Ridiculous, derogatory, and unacceptable. Another one, purporting so-called "family values," said that Ellen was a blond, blue-eyed girl next door who could be Miss America, so why on earth would she *want* to be a lesbian?

And, yet, in spite of the ignorance of some people and in spite of the controversy that was brewing about Ellen and Anne, nothing could stop the momentum. Throughout it all, the bad and the good, El and Anne were the epitome of grace under fire. New media darlings, the two were soon being sought by everyone for television talk shows, magazines, and newspapers, while their professional and social schedule became busier and busier.

Before we knew it, Ellen was being given such honors as the ACLU Bill of Rights Award and UCLA's Jack Benny Award, and topping all the "Most Fascinating" and "Most Influential" lists for the year. Without planning or intending it, by the summer of 1997 El found herself in the role of—to borrow a phrase from the great Candace Gingrich—an "accidental activist."

At the ACLU banquet in her honor she spoke about how unexpected this new role was for her:

> I feel like I'm being honored for helping myself. I had no idea how many other lives would be affected by what I've done.
>
> . . . I got to a place where I needed to live my life freely. I didn't want to feel ashamed of who I was anymore. Thank God, literally, thank God for allowing me to get there. Some people never do. Some people hide a little bit of who they are because it's safer in this world to hide than to be yourself.

Rather than celebrate individuality, society would rather have others feel uncomfortable and stay quiet, or better yet, be invisible.

. . . How sad. I feel overwhelmed sometimes. And I feel a responsibility to continue to simply be myself. I want to continue acting, entertaining, making people laugh, making people feel good. And I will also dedicate my life to making it safe for all people to live their lives freely—whatever that means.

In living up to that pledge, Ellen soon learned about many issues of gay rights that were new to her. In another speech, she told about getting a thank-you letter from a seventy-six-year-old lesbian, a retired teacher, who said she never thought she'd see an openly gay lead on a TV show done with such "poignancy, taste, and humor." Ellen joked, "And me being new to this, I didn't know there were seventy-six-year-old lesbians."

In my happy role of number one fan and cheerleader, I could not have been more proud. Then one day in late July while I was catching a few minutes with Ellen and Anne to go over their busy itineraries and to tell them of my latest encounters with people saying they wished I could be their mom, a light came into Ellen's eyes. She said, "You know, maybe there's something else you can do to help. Why don't you call Tammy?"

She was referring to Tammy Billik, the terrific casting director on the *Ellen* show—a friend of ours and an active member of the Human Rights Campaign. So I called Tammy. And the rest, as they say, is history.

Through Tammy, I was put in touch with Elizabeth Birch, HRC's executive director. As we spoke on the phone, her kindness, gratitude, and excitement were humbling.

Elizabeth said that my desire to help felt as if it was coming to their cause by divine intervention; as if, she said, I had come down as some kind of angel. "Betty," she told me, "your involvement could be so important. There is so much you can do, so many lives you, personally, will be able to touch. There is a real hunger in so many gay people for a parent figure like you."

In effect, what she was asking me to do was something I knew a lot about—being Mom.

The more we talked, the more excited I became. Then she hit upon the idea of my becoming their National Coming Out Day spokesperson. We were both aware that my taking on this role without any background as an activist would be like jumping in at the deep end. But I was ready to give it a try.

And thus began my new journey as spokesperson and activist. Aside from being a mother, and my early training with Aunt Tillie, little had prepared me for this highly public role in which I would be speaking out. But I wasn't very nervous. To become HRC's first non-gay national spokesperson meant that I had a chance to make a difference—to say "enough," enough of hatred and bigotry and ignorance and fear; to be, simply, a voice of calm and reason amid all the hysteria and hateful rhetoric masquerading as religion.

This was also a chance, I was about to discover, to go out and meet America—in states and cities, large and small, in every corner of the country—and to see for myself that fair-mindedness, tolerance, love, and goodness are alive and well, growing stronger all the time.

Two days after my phone conversation with Elizabeth Birch, I was in Washington, D.C., walking into the offices of the Human Rights Campaign headquarters, where I met the entire staff of sixty—some of the most wonderful, brightest men and women I have ever met. From Cheryl Henson, the warm, friendly African-American woman who answers the phone and greets visitors, to Elizabeth herself, a good-looking, extremely articulate dynamo, I loved them all.

Over the next days and weeks, I would hear more about the personal journeys that had made activists out of all these extraordinary individuals at HRC. Elizabeth had left a high-powered job in corporate law to come to HRC, because, she said, "I decided to spend the next years of my life doing something truly meaningful."

Along with the several individuals at HRC with whom I would be interacting in the months to come, I quickly became good buddies with David Smith, the handsome, intelligent, friendly communications director and senior strategist. That first morning David put me at ease right away as he brought me up to speed on many of HRC's current activities—lobbying Congress, providing campaign support, and educating the public—all with the goal of ensuring that lesbian and gay Americans can be open, honest, and safe at home, at work, and in the community.

Then there was Donna Red Wing, HRC's national field director, whose compelling story I would later hear in more detail. To meet Donna, a striking part Native American woman, is to be immediately impressed by her vigor and her great gifts as a speaker. Few would suspect what I later learned—that Donna has an inoperable brain tumor. Instead of debilitating her, it has empowered her to work even harder, doing what she believes will make her life—however long it is—really count for something.

After the introductions that first morning, I got started right away with briefings on the National Coming Out Project. I loved the emphasis that was being placed on coming out as a way to create a dialogue and to open channels of communication. I knew well from my own experience how important it is to simply talk. Many families, I was finding out, have a conspiracy of silence—not because of a lack of love but because of a lack of skill at talking. And not talking about being gay means staying in the closet. What's wrong with the closet? I knew that from Ellen DeGeneres–Ellen Morgan: It's suffocating. Gay men and women have the same right to be out in the open, breathing the same air, as any of us.

During these briefings, I was also given some background on HRC's past spokespeople. The list included Chastity Bono, as well as the actress Amanda Bearse, the actor Dan Butler, and Sean Sasser of MTV's *Real World*.

One of the most vocal and most widely recognized past spokespersons for HRC is Candace Gingrich, who pronounces the name "Gingrick." In the months ahead, I would have the pleasure of getting to know Candace. Outgoing and friendly, she is a tiny little bundle of energy.

Candace used the title *Accidental Activist* for her book about her unlikely journey from a conservative background to the path she eventually took. A gifted speaker, she was so effective as a spokesperson that after her stint was over, she was asked to stay on as part of HRC's permanent staff.

Just after these morning briefings were over, I was given a copy of my schedule for the rest of the day. My first question was, "When do I get to go to the rest room?"

Every minute was planned. Even lunch was a meeting so that I could meet the summer interns who were there to learn about campaigning and helping out at the grassroots level. What an exemplary group of smart, clean-cut young men and women they were. Looking at them and thinking of the ignorance and discrimination they face—just because being gay or lesbian is a part of who they are—when it was my turn to talk, I had to choke back tears.

The following day I was taken to Capitol Hill, my first visit there, by Suzanne Salkind, who manages HRC's political action committee, and Winnie Stachelberg, HRC's political director. They're both attractive, warm, and brilliant. They introduced me to Senators John Breaux and Mary Landrieu from Louisiana and Senator Barbara Boxer from California, and took me to the House of Representatives, which was in session.

HRC's legislative agenda, about which I was getting an education, included lobbying Congress to support the Hate Crimes Prevention Act, headed for a vote in 1998 and the desperately needed Employment Non-Discrimination Act (ENDA), a bipartisan bill which polls showed an overwhelming majority of Americans support. It was a shock to learn that only eleven states in this country have laws to protect gay and lesbian workers from unfair discrimination on the job. (Tragically, a few months later the number of states would diminish to ten.)

ENDA had come within a hair of passing in September of 1996 when the vote in the Senate was 49 to 50—one vote short. Now our goal was to make sure it passed when it came up again, we hoped in 1998. The fact that a handful of Republicans had crossed party lines to stand up for fairness was encouraging. And, as Elizabeth Birch would later say:

> The real miracle was not in the Senate chamber but in the large, ornate room outside. There gathered were leaders from the NAACP to great religious denominations and from corporate leaders to the AFL-CIO. In that room, we were already one America. When we got down to the final hours of the vote, Coretta Scott King, Dorothy Height, and Rosa Parks herself were urging us on.

After two days, I headed back to Los Angeles, fired up and ready to go, taking home as much reading material as I could fit into my suitcase and my carry-on bag. As spokesperson, I wanted to be as knowledgeable as possible. Although National Coming Out Day wasn't until October 11, my interviews would start in September.

On the airplane, I remembered how Winnie Stachelberg had told me that, for her, coming to work for HRC was "love at first sight."

I knew just what she meant. I took out my journal and began making notes about the crash course I had taken on this trip. At the end of my entry, I noted with great joy, "This truly feels like my mission in life."

ON OCTOBER 4, 1997, I stood up to give my first official speech at an HRC dinner for 1,200 in Minneapolis. Over the past two months, I'd been warming up with media interviews. That was easy, but this was a challenge. This was the first time since 1963—thirty-four years before, when I addressed the insurance convention in San Francisco—that I actually had to stand up, walk to the podium, and speak. Before I said a word, I was given a standing ovation—wow! I got another one after I spoke as well. Good thing.

Also speaking that night were Donna Red Wing and Dr. Joycelyn Elders—two fantastic speakers. Luckily, I didn't have to follow them.

The love and gratitude everyone expressed to me was overwhelming. As I looked around at all those faces, few of whom I knew, I felt that none of them were strangers to me. We were family—part of something that was larger than the sum of its parts.

A week later—when I was back in Los Angeles to acknowledge National Coming Out Day and officially kick off my work as spokesperson—there was a reception at the Universal Hilton. P-FLAG ran a blurb in its local newsletter with the headline, BETTY DEGENERES COMES OUT AS EVERYONE'S FAVORITE STRAIGHT MOM.

Watching me go to the podium, Ellen and Anne were very moved. Ellen was so unabashedly teary that a reporter asked why she was crying. As she dabbed at her eyes, she said, "To have a mom like this, not only to accept me and love me but to come out and be a spokesperson and travel—I'm so proud of her." Ellen added, "I'm just a mush—I cry at commercials!"

Now that I was official, I got started on a speaking itinerary that took me to all corners of the map, primarily for events hosted by local HRC groups. Every city and every event amazed me as I hopscotched around the country, back and forth from Los Angeles: Detroit; back to Washington, D.C.; Boston; back to Washington, D.C.; Boston again; San Antonio; New York; Chicago; back to Washington D.C.; to Portland, Maine, and to Portland, Oregon; to Raleigh; Denver; Philadelphia; back to Washington, D.C.; Dallas; Myrtle Beach; New York; to London (that's London, England); Atlanta; and then to my hometown, New Orleans.

There is not enough space for me to describe every magnificent reception I was given and every remarkable individual I met along the way. Instead, I'd like to offer a sampling to give you a general sense of this unfolding adventure. Many of my trips include three days of events—a cocktail party on Friday, a black-tie dinner on Saturday, and a brunch on Sunday. Often, interviews, lunches, and other meetings are also scheduled.

Though I sometimes speak at smaller events, most of the time I give my main address at the dinners, speaking to audiences of anywhere from 600 to 1,500 and more. From the start, though I felt slightly jittery, I had no real stage fright—thanks again to Aunt Tillie! Besides, I always remind myself, I'm speaking from my heart. And my message is so simple: We love our sons and daughters unconditionally; our gay family members have the right to be who they are, to live their lives in a healthy, open manner—just as we do.

Of course, the more I spoke, the more confident I grew in my new role. One of my few instances of genuine nervousness was on the night of November 8, 1997. Everything about this evening at the Grand Hyatt Hotel in Washington, D.C., was historic. It was the Human Rights Campaign's first ever annual national dinner—a sellout with 1,500 attending. President Clinton spoke—the first time that a sitting president had addressed a gay civil rights organization. And HRC also presented its first National Civil Rights Awards, three of them: to Dorothy Height and Wade Henderson, two officials from the Leadership Conference on Civil Rights; and to the actress and comedian Ellen DeGeneres.

Knowing that I would be speaking on the same bill as the president of the United States did make me nervous. But since Ellen was the one receiving the award, her speech was an even more daunting assignment. Before going down to the dinner, I joined her and Anne in their suite, along with David Smith and a few others from HRC, while she worked on her speech. She agonized over it, but of course, it turned out to be warm, honest, funny, and wonderful.

When it was time to go downstairs, guards arrived to escort us the back way—through the kitchen and boiler room, not exactly the scenic route.

From the instant that the guards led us inside, to a VIP cocktail party, the energy we all felt was electrifying. There were banks of photographers and reporters and a huge crush of people at the cocktail party. We went into the ballroom for dinner, through metal detectors because of the imminent arrival of President Clinton.

In introducing the president, Elizabeth Birch noted how isolated and ignored the gay community had been by previous administrations. Given the movement's needs and the expectations, she pointed out, it was inevitable that no one leader could live up to those needs. "But, Mr. President," Elizabeth said, in spite of some shared disappointments, "you have played a brave and powerful and indispensable role in the march toward justice for us, and all Americans."

President Clinton took the podium and gave a rousing speech that was positive and encouraging. It was marvelous to hear him recognize many different individuals who were part of the administration and were attending that night as members of HRC. His whole speech would be worth quoting, but one point I especially recall was in reference to the need for ENDA:

> All America loses if we let prejudice and discrimination stifle the hopes or deny the potential of a single American. All America loses when any person is denied or forced out of a job because of sexual orientation. Being gay, the last time I thought about it, seemed to have nothing to do with the ability to read a balance book, fix a broken bone, or change a spark plug.

I was on later in the bill, thankfully, and my speech was brief. Though I was not so nervous anymore, I did rush a bit, and I felt somewhat unnecessary compared with all the luminaries—even if I did get a standing ovation. On the other hand, I wouldn't have missed the opportunity to be part of an event of such importance.

The evening built up gloriously to El's award and speech. She was introduced by members of HRC's Youth College, one of whom said, "There are two known cures for what ails America—an end to homophobia and Ellen DeGeneres."

The standing ovation when Ellen went to the podium and stood there was absolutely incredible. As many times as I had watched her being thunderously applauded, this was on a level and in a context I had never witnessed before. Before she spoke, Ellen looked around the room at what must have been a blur of faces and through what must have been a blur of tears, slowly allowing the love that was being showered on her to help her gain her composure. Then she spoke, and she was great from start to finish. Wild applause followed her explanation for her decision to come out on TV and in person:

> I finally got to the point where living honestly and being proud of who I am was more important than fame. Ironically, my being honest made me more famous. So much for those who said it would hurt my career. I was willing to risk all and I was rewarded for it. My life is better than it's ever been—I found love, and there's nothing more important than that. . . . I never wanted to be an activist—I just wanted to entertain people to make them feel good. But if by standing up for what I think is right makes me an activist—I'm an activist.

The minute the program was over, the guards took us back upstairs to have a glass of Dom Pérignon, which Tammy Billik had generously brought. Cheers!

AS I RECOUNT these steps along the way in my own growth as a mother and human being, I realize that it may be hard for some of you to relate to the path of activism I had chosen. Some of you may have only recently gone through a coming out of a gay family member or friend. If you have only begun your process of acceptance, my work as a spokesperson may seem like something you could never do. I just want you to know that twenty years ago, I would have said the same thing. Others among you may have already reached acceptance for your gay loved one but may wish to keep that information a private, family matter—just as I did all those years after Ellen came out the first time. Still others may be looking for ways to speak out or take a stand but haven't found the right avenue yet.

To all of you, I want to emphasize that in order to be supportive and loving, it's not necessary to pursue a course of activism. On the other hand, by sharing my experiences with you, I also want to stress the amazing rewards that can come from reaching out—sometimes beyond what you think you are capable of. I can tell you that everywhere I went I heard stories from people about how Ellen and I were making a difference in their lives.

In Los Angeles, I met a man who told me that he has been with his partner thirty-five years and that his partner's mother has always accepted them but has refused to talk about it. Then, he said, "She saw you on Larry King and was so impressed that she's been talking about it ever since." He smiled and added, "She even said the G word!"

At an HRC luncheon in Washington, D.C., a young woman who came out a year ago to her parents told me that I have advanced them "months" in accepting her. "You've relaxed them about the whole thing," she said.

Another woman I met there is a psychologist who said that Ellen and I are literally saving lives. "It's true," a handsome young man interjected. "I tried to commit suicide when I was a teenager. If you two had been around back then, I don't think I would have felt the same despair."

In Detroit I met a teacher who reported having asked his ninth-grade class to name some current heroes—and several kids named Ellen.

In Chicago, an attractive young woman in her thirties told me, "I lived up to every expectation my parents had for me; whatever they wanted I did—including becoming a doctor. But the one thing they wanted that I couldn't do was change my sexual orientation." She said that for the last five years they were unaccepting—until El's coming out episode, when finally, they understood that this wasn't something she was doing to rebel or to upset them. "They are so accepting now," she went on, "it's a miracle."

Amidst these affirmations about positive changes were reminders of the many obstacles still to be overcome. While waiting to board a plane as I was heading off for a weekend, I did a telephone interview one morning from Los Angeles International Airport. The interviewer said, "My brother is gay. Mom insists he just hasn't met the right girl yet."

"Oh," I said, remembering that notion. "She thinks the right girl is going to fix him." I told her the lesson I had to learn about that form of denial, and apparently a difficult lesson for many parents: our gay family members don't need fixing. This is who they are. They are giving us their gift of their true, honest selves, living their lives as they were meant to.

This brought us to a subject of grave concern—recent attempts by extremists to "convert" gays and lesbians.

As El would point out, the gay people of this world aren't asking for anything or asking anybody to change; they simply want to be allowed to live their lives as who they are. By what right do others presume to change this whole segment of society? And yet there are organizations that push families to "rehabilitate" or "deprogram" their gay family members. Most people with common sense know that being gay is not the same thing as joining a cult. I am especially concerned about the full-page ads in major newspapers that show throngs of so-called "ex-gay people" who have supposedly "fixed" themselves with religion.

The rhetoric is scary, and it's being aimed at vulnerable family members who may think something can be done to change the fact that their son or daughter or sibling or parent is gay. My heart goes out to all the victims of this rhetoric.

Please, wherever you are in your level of understanding, don't let anyone else impose ideas on you or your loved one about who they are.

Another area of serious concern is the lack of freedom so many gay citizens have in their place of work. At an event in Boston, I spoke to a teacher who has been teaching for twenty-six years and can't risk letting anyone know she is a lesbian. Obviously this woman is well thought of and has a wealth of experience to share. The knowledge that she happens to be gay shouldn't change one single thing in her life, or in the lives of her students, her students' parents, or her coworkers. But sadly, she feels certain that if word gets out, she will lose her job.

You might ask, "Why tell?" This is why—because she shouldn't have to spend twenty-six years of service and hard work being afraid of the possibility of losing her livelihood simply because one person or several may be homophobic.

At first, when I started hearing stories like hers, I searched within for something to say to soften the hurt. But after a while, I understood that this wasn't what mattered. What mattered was that I was listening, that I cared. And the more I listened to stories, both heartening and discouraging, the more I grew in the role of witness—an unexpected dimension of what I was doing—and the more motivated I became to continue working for change.

As this phenomenon grew—with more and more people coming up to me at events, wanting to tell me about themselves—my HRC colleagues got the idea of sponsoring a contest over the Internet for people to write in and "Tell Betty Your Coming Out Story," offering an extravagant prize, a free T-shirt. The number of responses was staggering. Everyone's story was unique. Some stories had happy endings—like the gay woman in her fifties from Texas who finally came out to her seventy-six-year-old mother, only for her mother to say, "I knew that. It's OK." All those years of living in fear and hiding—unnecessary.

Then there were heartbreaking letters like the one I received from a seventeen-year-old girl who lives in a very small northwestern town. She asked if I could please talk to her parents and tell them it's OK that she's gay—because, she said, "they don't like me anymore." Her letter continued:

> I told my parents and they didn't accept it. They took me to a shrink. Now I've lied to them and told them it wasn't true so my life could be normal. But they still question me and we fight all the time. I hate living here. I guess I just wish that my one and only parents could accept me. I need someone to help me help them.

Here is my reply to her parents, and to any other parents like hers:

> Dear Mom and Dad:
>
> Your daughter has taken a brave, courageous step. She has shared with you the deepest truth about herself.
>
> It sounds like you are having a terrible struggle accepting this news. Or maybe you aren't even struggling—just outright rejecting that this could possibly be true. Maybe no one else in your family or circle of friends is gay. Or maybe they are, but you just never imagined it could happen to you.
>
> Well, it has. All your daughter needs from you right now is your continuing love and support. Please stand by her as she explores and grapples with this newly discovered information about herself.

A tremendously supportive and healing step would be for you both to attend a P-FLAG meeting. If there isn't a chapter near you, write or call the national office and ask for helpful literature and information.

No doubt your fears are similar to mine when my daughter told me she was gay—who will take care of her, will she be the target of hatred and bigotry, can she be happy?

Granted, being gay or lesbian is not the easiest path in life given society's difficulty accepting anything different from the perceived "norm." But it's a thousand times easier than asking your daughter to live her life as a lie.

Please allow her to be who she is—and help her to be proud of who she is.

Note to readers: You'll find the phone number and address of P-FLAG's national headquarters at the back of this book. This organization is a godsend—the most wonderfully supportive group of people imaginable. At our L.A. chapter, we often have excellent guest speakers. During another part of our meeting we divide up into rap groups of about ten people. Each group has a facilitator who makes sure the group stays on track and no one person dominates. People pour out their hearts—sons and daughters whose parents have rejected them; mothers and fathers who are beautifully loving and accepting; parents who have just learned that their child is gay and are in shock, struggling to understand and going through their own process.

For many family members it is a struggle, a gradual process; they may attend several meetings before they finally reach acceptance. But, at least, they are reminded, they've come to the meeting. It's the first and most important step and because they've taken it, you know that their family will be fine.

I will never forget what a glorious and humbling feeling it was to finally attend my first P-FLAG meeting, a few days after the coming out show had aired. It was thrilling not to have to hide anymore and a relief to know that I was never alone in that experience. I discovered that most families—gay and non-gay members—do have to "come out" every day, and have to continually make decisions about the people with whom they share this information. Of course, my situation is different from most people's. Because of Ellen's fame, and the way she did it, I no longer have to worry about that. Usually, everybody already knows. That makes it much easier for me. I wish it could be so simple for everyone.

No matter how tough it is for families, the importance of talking and keeping the lines of communication open cannot be overemphasized, as the next letter shows:

> The biggest indicator of how hard my coming out was on my mother was the fact that she stopped calling me by my name for over a year. It was as if I had died, and knowing my mother, had I let her alone, she probably would have never spoken to me again. I'm the one who kept calling, kept writing, and kept exemplifying to her that though I was gay, I was the same boy she raised and loved. It worked. Mom and I are now as close as we ever were; heck, she's even gotten to the point where she can ask me how my lover is doing. I always knew my mom was cool.

James Bryson from Philadelphia, who is active in HRC there and on the national level, including the board of governors, wrote to me about coming out to his mother eleven years earlier, a few weeks before her eightieth birthday. He said that although she was accepting, he felt that she really didn't get it. A week later, his mom sent him this letter:

Dear Jim,

Needless to say, your news did throw me. I was prepared for almost anything but that. How could I have been so blind? I'm sorry my reaction was so lacking in warmth and understanding.

I'm sitting here now, in the middle of the night reviewing all the wonderful memories of the past years and realizing that nothing has really changed the joys I've had in watching your growing up, and loving the man you have become.

And there have been dividends, your two lovely daughters (my granddaughters) of whom I'm very proud.

So we just go on from here the same as always with a hope of deeper dimensions of understanding.

Much love,
Mother

James told me that his mother welcomed his new friends; set an example for other family members, his daughters among them; and began listening more closely to news about gay issues. Their relationship grew stronger, deeper, and more trusting. He expressed his belief that all people can grow in understanding, if only they'll give themselves a chance.

Many of the letters I've received about coming out are, at heart, love stories. In fact, at one HRC dinner, I was introduced to two girls—both pretty in a quiet way, friendly yet shy—who met through an Ellen DeGeneres website on the Internet. They had lived in two different states, but now they had been together in the same city for almost a year. Who couldn't be happy for them?

The more gay couples I met, the more examples of love, devotion, and true commitment I saw. These are partners who have been together not because of society, but in spite of it. They don't have society's blessing or society's permission to celebrate anniversaries—they don't even have legal sanctions available—but they are life partners in loving, monogamous relationships.

Knowing this makes more odious the Defense of Marriage Act—a mean, hateful, needless piece of legislation passed a couple of years ago. Heterosexual marriage undeniably needs some help, given the 50 percent divorce rate, but that abominable act isn't it.

I stand beside the group working with the Hawaii Freedom to Marry agenda, who say, "Same-gender marriage confronts the American people with a core reality: that gay and lesbian people exist and that their relationships deserve equal treatment under the law. Equal treatment under the law. No more. No less."

FROM THE MOMENT I had come on board with HRC, any kind of regular social schedule in my personal life became a thing of the past. Though it didn't last long, at first I kept my part-time on-call status at Cedars. Some of my colleagues were surprised by my new work, telling me they had no idea about that side of me.

"If we had known this before," said one, "we could have put you to work a long time ago doing speaking engagements for us."

"But nobody asked," I said with a laugh.

They were really impressed, they all said, with the way I had been handling the tough questions being put to me on radio and on television, not to mention my endurance in doing interviews every day—sometimes, as many as five interviews a day.

This was an area of my work that was somewhat daunting. In the beginning, it made me quite nervous knowing that I was being watched and heard by millions of viewers and listeners. But after a couple of weeks' practice, it was fun. Rarely did I feel tired or "talked out," because callers and interviewers were so appreciative. After only a month on the interview circuit, I was thrilled to see how much speaking out seemed to be helping. Frank Butler of the HRC excitedly informed me that they'd never gotten so many calls for their excellent "Resource Guide to Coming Out." There were 500 calls after Elizabeth Birch and I did *The Ricki Lake Show* and, after that, they started averaging 100 calls a week.

The interview questions that were the hardest for me had to do with the extremists' negative rhetoric. When one interviewer asked me what I thought of Jerry Falwell's name-calling of Ellen, I nearly started to cry. "She's my daughter," I said. "And she's a good person."

Friends with more experience being interviewed gave me

sound advice about not letting myself become rattled. They suggested phrases such as, "Next question, please."

That became an effective way for me to respond to gossipy questions about Ellen and Anne. For instance, one radio host was determined to know precisely where, when, and by what means they would have a baby.

Next question?

One of my most gratifying interviews was with Liann Hansen of *Weekend Edition* at National Public Radio. After years of listening to NPR's evenhanded, in-depth reporting, I felt as if I were going to a holy place. Liann was warm and delightful, as one would expect her to be, and her questions were thoughtful and fair.

The day after that interview, Elizabeth Birch and I appeared on ABC's *This Week* with Sam Donaldson, Cokie Roberts, William Bennett, and George Will. Their green room was the best, with two attendants in tuxedos and all kinds of food, from breakfast dishes to boiled shrimp. Bill Bennett was in the green room with us and was very pleasant—off-camera. On-camera was another story. George Will was very stern and seemed intent on not smiling. When I was talking about working for equal rights for our gay and lesbian family members, he said, "Ellen certainly doesn't seem to be oppressed."

I said, "Well, in thirty-nine states she could be fired from her job or evicted from her home simply because she's gay."

Will didn't answer. And there was still no sign of a smile.

After my segment I watched Elizabeth from the green room. Bill Bennett went off on a tangent, talking about polygamous marriage and pedophiles. He made no sense at all. Elizabeth kept her cool. She was reasonable, even brilliant.

Incidentally, I had an interesting interaction with Cokie Roberts. I had long been a fan of hers from her NPR days, so I had been dismayed by a piece Cokie and her husband had written a month earlier in their syndicated column. They had sharply criticized statements by Vice President Gore, who applauded *Ellen* as a good show for family values because it opened minds and furthered acceptance of diversity. They said that the show Gore should have praised was *Touched by an Angel*, for its message about spirituality. I wrote immediately to say how disappointed I was that they found it necessary to put *Ellen* down in order to praise another show. My point was this:

> Certainly, *Touched by an Angel* has an inspiring, positive message and is good for families to watch together. *Ellen* also has a positive message—about accepting diversity, about having friends, setbacks, joys—and sexual identity being only a part of who we are as a healthy person. That wouldn't be a bad message to get as a family. And you will get it from watching *Ellen*.

When I first arrived on the set of *This Week* and was introduced to Cokie, I brought up my letter, saying again how much their piece had troubled me. She had no comment at that time. A few months later, I received a warm reply from her in the mail.

As you can see, my growing political awareness was another transformation. After coming from my staunchly conservative background, I had changed over time because of personal issues, and now I was actually meeting political leaders and becoming part of the political process.

During one of my many trips to Washington, I went again to Capitol Hill and met more allies in the cause for equal gay rights: Representative Zoe Lofgren from San Jose, California; Representative Barney Frank, who is openly gay; Joe Kennedy, Jr., and his wife; Kennedy's sister Kathleen Kennedy Townsend; the lieutenant governor of Maryland; and Representative Richard Gephardt, the Democratic minority leader of the House.

It was on this trip that I went into the gallery and saw the House in session while Candace Gingrich's brother was speaking. She would later tell me, sadly, that her brother won't give her the time of day. His attitude is that gay people should be tolerated as alcoholics are. And, she would say, his definition of family is a mother, a father, and children—nothing else. That excludes a lot of adults and children who thought they were families.

Four months later, I was back in Washington. David Smith had called to say that I was urgently needed for a press conference on Capitol Hill. This was HRC's response to a luncheon being held that day in the Senate Dining Room by a right-wing religious extremist group. Use of the dining room was obtained for them by Congressman Dick Armey, who is infamous for referring to Congressman Barney Frank as "Barney Fag." When Armey received more bad press than he had probably anticipated, he said it was a "slip of the tongue." Congressman Frank's response was, "That's funny. In fifty years my mother has never once been called Mrs. Fag."

In our press conference, I gave my usual message, urging parents and siblings to love and accept their gay family members. I thought that day of the words spoken by Dr. Dorothy Height at the HRC dinner in Washington when she reminded us of the links between the struggle for gay rights and the fight for equal rights for our African-American brothers and sisters:

> The climate that was there in the 60's is not there now. It is not there for so many of the issues; and so many of the gains that we've thought we've made seem more tentative than they ought to be. . . . It only means for us that we have to recognize that we have a long way to go, but we have to go that way together.

Those words gave me inspiration, as did the courageous examples of the many people I had been meeting. I thought of the longtime activists all around the country—the mothers and fathers who have been working tirelessly, usually with little fanfare, for equal rights for their gay sons and daughters. I thought of those on the frontline, like Richard Zaldivar, who spoke at one of our P-FLAG meetings about the program he heads in East L.A. The vital work Richard is doing includes three support groups he has established for HIV-positive gay Latinos; he has also founded *Las Memorias*, a wall memorial to victims of AIDS from the Latino community. Zaldivar is a true hero.

I thought about a true heroine I had met—the amazing Mary Fisher, who delivered the keynote address when I attended an HRC event in San Antonio. I was fortunate to spend time talking to her about her work and experiences. Mary contracted the HIV virus from her husband, who has since died of AIDS. She became famous when she addressed the Republican convention in 1992 about the AIDS crisis. After she spoke so poignantly, it was impossible for those who heard her to continue to ignore the epidemic. She has created a foundation and lectures tirelessly around the country for funding and greater tolerance for all people—straight and gay, old and young—who are struggling with AIDS.

Mary told me how frustrated she feels when people say, "But you look so well." Her regimen of medications generally keeps her able to meet her demanding schedule: mothering her two little boys, working as an artist, and speaking publicly. But sometimes the virus gets the upper hand and she has to cancel her engagements. What an inspiration she is! And her books, which she kindly autographed and gave me, are equally inspiring.

I also thought that day of Coretta Scott King, a great humanitarian whom I was honored to meet. I had not realized how accomplished she was in her own right, before she ever married Dr. King. Among other things, she was a graduate of Antioch University, where she had majored in peace studies, a perfect preparation for the important role she would play in the great movements of the 1960s and later. I recalled her keynote address at the Los Angeles HRC event and how she had quoted her husband's simple reminder: "Injustice anywhere is a threat to justice everywhere."

• • •

AMID ALL THIS activity, it wasn't easy to find time to spend with my kids. I did get to spend a cherished Thanksgiving with Vance, for which I prepared a New Orleans–style vegetarian gumbo and candied yams.

When Vance arrived and we sat down to dinner together, we had a heart-to-heart talk that was very much overdue. In his understated way, he let me know he was glad that I was happy in my life.

Pretty amazing, I said, feeling full of Thanksgiving spirit. How interesting, I told him, that even though I was single, I was more fulfilled than ever before in my life; and that opening myself up had brought me new friends, new experiences, new vistas. "And how are you doing, Vance?" I asked seriously.

He paused. Looking at him—with his handsome, young face, his dark hair and those green eyes, his still lean physique—I had to remind myself that he was already in his early forties. He still could pass for early thirties. "Everything's great," he said. "I've got lots of stuff cooking."

I brought up his love life, but Vance shrugged uncomfortably. "You know, Mom," he said, "I'm private about that stuff. Like you."

"Private?" I asked.

Yes, he asserted, he and I both are private and even standoffish, because, he said, of the German in us from the Pfeffer lineage.

Standoffish? That somehow didn't fit the way I was starting to see myself. Obviously, I was changing, I told him.

Saying nothing, he raised his eyebrows as if to say that

maybe he too could work at getting past his cool reserve. Then, in classic DeGeneres fashion, he added some levity, saying, "Mom, the yams were delicious. And everything else too—the, uh, succotash, really healthy. Really, *really* healthy."

I laughed as I corrected him, letting him know that it was actually gumbo. He said he knew that but just liked to say the word "succotash."

Catching up with Ellen and Anne had to wait until Christmas, when I met the two of them in New York. We celebrated Christmas Eve together at Park Avenue Café, a five-star restaurant. It was one of the most memorable dinners I've ever had—wonderful food, beautiful presentation, appetizers that were compliments of the chef, scrumptious architectural desserts, and a truly extravagant French red wine Ellen ordered, which was sublime.

The most delicious part of the meal was our conversation. We found it hard to believe that it was only eight months since our lives had taken such a dramatic turn. Most years aren't as life-changing as the past one had been. We usually go from one year to the next hardly noticing any difference in the pattern of our lives. But because of what Ellen had had the courage to do, our lives—hers and mine—were changed forever. And Anne's life had changed too—because they are so honest about their relationship, they've made the way easier for countless other same-sex couples. This is the most gratifying part of our changes—that so many people feel so good about themselves.

Before this trip to New York, one of the few times I had seen El was when I went to the set with some of my HRC colleagues to watch *Ellen* being filmed. In the fall of 1997, Ellen and her producers and writers were exploring a story line that followed her character's experiences as a single gay woman dating different women and then developing a relationship. Not every episode dealt with a gay issue. Nonetheless, I consistently heard, from gay and straight people alike, how relevant and courageous the show was. Many people felt that the episodes were better written and funnier than ever. My personal favorite featured Emma Thompson and Sean Penn as guest stars. But in spite of critical praise, the ratings were flagging, and support from the network and the studio was not forthcoming—they did nothing to offer alternative time slots or more promotion to help boost the show.

At the same time, El and Anne told me about the positive responses they'd been getting everywhere they went: families telling Ellen they love her show, people giving them the thumbs-up sign. The day before, they were walking hand in hand, as they always do, and an elderly woman who was walking toward them with her husband said, "Good for you two!"

As they were telling me this, we noticed a family of seven at the table next to us. A short while later, one of the group, a girl about six years old, walked up to Ellen with a card on which one of the grown-ups had written: "Ellen, Merry Christmas and thanks for your show. Sarah and Family." Those are good family values!

My heart was full as I looked across at Ellen and Anne. They were sitting with their hands intertwined, two women in love. Only eight months before, Ellen could not have openly shown affection for a girlfriend. In fact, it occurred to me then that, before Anne, I had never seen El hold hands with, or kiss, or show affection for any of her partners. Twenty years earlier, a show of affection may have made me uncomfortable. But now, I saw their sincere expression of love as the most natural thing in the world.

I told them how heartbreaking it is when I meet couples who must hide their relationship. Hearing such stories is always hard for Ellen. It is also a sensitive matter for Anne, whose family has not been at all accepting. One story concerned a man in a twenty-one-year relationship who had told me that his parents were completely supportive until suddenly, last Christmas, they cut off contact. It seemed that a niece had become a fundamentalist and turned the whole family against him and his partner. "You have to wonder how they could be so easily swayed," I said.

This raised a related issue: the increasing number of incidents of discrimination and gay-bashing we were hearing about. Anne articulated it—"Why does it bother other people so much who I love?"

It was getting late and we knew that the battle against intolerance wasn't going to be solved by the three of us in one sitting. Still, it felt good to know that we were part of the battle, sharing a dream for the future—a dream that a day will soon come when people will look back in disbelief at today's discrimination.

It was not so much what was said that made this Christmas Eve so special for me. It was simply that the three of us are grateful for each other and enjoy each other's companionship so much. This is a gift not to be taken lightly. I'm truly sorry that, by her own choice, Anne's mother is missing out on all of this joy.

THE NEW YEAR brought more unforgettable encounters and adventures. Everywhere I went, there was an outpouring of love—from people whose parents are supportive, from people who wish their parents were supportive. I was immediately embraced as part of their lives and their stories.

While traveling to Portland, Oregon, I was approached at the airport by a small group of fellow passengers who thought they recognized me. One of them said, "Aren't you David Letterman's mother?"

I said, "No—Ellen's." They were just as excited.

In Portland, I stayed at the Benson, a truly beautiful, charming old hotel, in one of the loveliest suites I've seen—complete with a fireplace and a double-size Jacuzzi in the marble bathroom. On my first day, I had lunch in the lobby with Julie, another darling, helpful new friend from HRC in Washington; and Craig, the terrific chairman of that night's event.

Craig said, "I'm one of the lucky ones. My mother's always been very accepting of my sexual orientation. But after she saw you on Larry King, she called me and said, 'You know, Craig, I should do more.' "

I loved that. Julie nodded, saying that her mother was also accepting and that they'd always been close. Then she added, "My mother and I were both at the national dinner.

After your speech, Mom said it made her realize how very special our relationship is. She had sort of taken our relationship for granted, not realizing how many gay men and women long for what we have."

Craig and his partner adopted two children at birth. In fact, they were present for both births. Craig proudly showed pictures of a darling brother and sister who look alike, although they aren't biologically related. This couple have been together over twelve years, and both knew that they wanted children. Before they went into it, however, Craig said they talked over every aspect for years, including their families and an adoption counselor in their discussions. They both have lots of flexible time, and one of them is almost always with the children, even though they have a day nanny. There's a large extended family, and there are lots of family trips with the grandmothers. So much love—what lucky children.

Craig said that there's complete acceptance in their neighborhood, with all the children going back and forth to each other's homes to play.

Once again, the night of the big dinner was another wonderful evening of meeting many fine men and women who were so appreciative that I was almost embarrassed. My message is so basic—that a family should be the safest place on earth, a place where our sons and daughters receive unconditional love.

The next morning, I awoke to find an envelope under my hotel room door, from Philip, a tall young man who had been at the party the night before. He had gone home, written a two-page letter, and returned with it at midnight. Of the many congratulatory and thoughtful words he'd written, these in particular touched me deeply:

> You are witnessing to hundreds of thousands of parents that it is OK to affirm our gay and lesbian children. For children who hear you, you are setting an expectation that their parents can and should accept and affirm them. . . . Your role is offering joy to parents who can empathize with the authenticity of what you are saying and doing: Accept our children gay and straight. They are as God made them and they are ours. . . .
>
> I hope and pray that you have the life and energy and commitment to continue carrying that gospel (well, heck it means Good News!) to more and more people.

I loved the comparison to the gospel. Indeed, the spreading of love and acceptance is good news. And I am proud to accept Philip's words of thanks on behalf of all the mothers, fathers, family members, and friends all over the world who also carry that gospel by standing up for fairness.

One such parent activist, whom I met in Denver, is David Dinwoodie, a past president of the Fort Collins P-FLAG chapter and the father of Rebecca, who worked at HRC in Washington and is now with the ACLU.

David is a walking encyclopedia of knowledge about the fight for equality for gays and lesbians, and he has worked tirelessly for change on the local and national levels. His wife too, he said, has been very active with him in P-FLAG.

Rebecca, an attractive, vivacious, red-haired young woman, is their only child and, he said, "our pride and joy."

He described his daughter's coming out as a gift, letting me know how much he loves the work he does and the other admirable parents he meets in the course of that work. David made a familiar comment, "My life has just opened up in so many wonderful ways I couldn't have imagined."

I told him I could certainly say the same thing. And this feeling was shared by many at the HRC dinner in Raleigh, North Carolina, for example, where the theme was "Bring Your Mom."

I will never forget two mothers, Patsy and Eloise. Both had sons who died of AIDS, and they are now activists because they loved their sons. Patsy said her son went quickly, but Eloise cared for her blind, incontinent son for eighteen months.

Eloise told me, "I was so grateful I could do that for him."

With tears in my eyes, I said softly, "I can't imagine losing a child. I think I'd collapse and not be able to function."

Patsy said, "No, you wouldn't. You'd continue to speak out and be active, just as we're doing."

Eloise said, "That's what keeps us going."

I met a very handsome young man, Crae Pridgen, and his mother, Marie, who live in a small town in North Carolina. They told me that five years ago Crae was beaten up by three Marines. He and his mother went to court and finally won a judgment.

In Raleigh, as in many other cities, several people I met

were there simply because they had good friends in the gay and lesbian community. One young woman was a straight writer who was being persecuted simply for being friendly and supportive to the gay community. In the neighborhood where she lives with her husband and children, people put signs with hateful messages on her lawn. Still, she perseveres in living up to her highest sense of what's right. God bless her.

The next morning at brunch, I was sitting at a table with another mother. With her were her two sons, Patrick and Rick. Her son Rick's partner was there; his name is also Rick. After I spoke, this mother said she'd like to say something. She stood up and said, "I'm sixty-five years old, and I lived on a farm. When my youngest son told me he was gay, I didn't know what that meant or anything about it, so I had to get books to read."

Then she looked at her youngest son and said, "Patrick, I want to apologize to you in public for the way I treated you." She continued, "He left home—not right away, but he left. Several years later Rick told me he, too, was gay, but it was easier for me to hear by then. Patrick says he paved the way for Rick. And I just wanted to apologize in public to you, Patrick, because I have never done that."

She went over and hugged Patrick, and then Rick, and by then there wasn't a dry eye in the room. It was a precious, special moment that none of us will ever forget. I'm grateful I was there to witness that love.

Everymoms of the world unite. We're everywhere!

As you can see, again and again on these journeys to new and different places, I heard testimony about the transforming power of love. Love can transform ignorance to understanding and rejection to acceptance. As it has been said, with love all things are possible.

My personal transformation is a case in point. In fact, another unexpected offshoot of my work for HRC is that I am now represented by a speakers' agency and have the great pleasure to speak to a variety of groups.

As much as I enjoy speaking, sometimes the best part of my journey is listening to others speak. One of the most moving speeches was from Carol White, who spoke at an HRC event in Denver.

Carol was the minister of music at a large church in Houston, Texas, but had been fired when the church discovered that she is a lesbian. "And there I was," she said, literally on the street, "with two worthless master's degrees"—both from Southern Methodist University, one in sacred music and the other in choral conducting. At this turning point, she could have seen herself simply as a victim of bigotry. Instead, to quote from her bio in the dinner program, "She set out to heal the world of homophobia through music, activism, and leadership." This she has done in music and in the Methodist church throughout Colorado.

"Whatever the music is inside of you," Carol said that night, "play it, dance it, sing it. . . . Don't let it die inside of you."

As she said those words, I thought of Ellen and Anne and all the openly gay and lesbian people everywhere. That's what they're doing—playing and dancing and singing the music inside them.

• • •

AMERICA IS A great country. As my travels have shown me, Americans are a great people. I feel blessed to be meeting many unsung heroes—gay and straight—who are standing up for diversity and who recognize that we are all family. I know that we still have many miles yet to travel toward equal rights for all our gay, lesbian, bisexual, and transgender family members. But I have also seen firsthand how closely we are all bound together on this journey.

That sense was strong for me when I attended the Ninth Annual South Carolina Gay Pride Festival and March in May 1998—my first participation in this kind of event. This was also the first time the event had been scheduled in Myrtle Beach. It was a rousing success in spite of opposition.

Flying in, I heard that local zealots had forced a cancellation of the Indigo Girls, who were scheduled to perform in a town near Myrtle Beach. The Indigo Girls are lesbian, and the cancellation was all the more upsetting to me because they're friends of El's.

The mayor of Myrtle Beach had done everything he could to have the entire festival canceled. When he failed, a local landowner put pressure on all his business tenants, forbidding them to advertise the event and demanding that all rainbows (a symbol of diversity, used to show support for gay rights) be removed from the buildings he owned. Another local business had a rainbow in its company logo but changed it just for the weekend.

In spite of the controversy, it did not rain on our parade. *Au contraire.*

Saturday dawned bright and clear. Several blocks in downtown Myrtle Beach had been roped off, and the police were plentiful—in cars and on motorcycles. I made it a point to say hello to several officers that I passed. "I hope you have a quiet day," I said, and they did.

It was estimated that 8,000 men and women attended, most of them from South Carolina, North Carolina, and Georgia. I wasn't the only non-gay person participating. I met a number of supportive family members sharing in the celebration, lending moral support to the concept that gay men and women have every right to come together, feel comfortable, and celebrate who they are.

One of the first people I met was Harriet Hancock, the matriarch of what has to be one of the first families of the South Carolina gay community. When Harriet's son Greg told her that he was gay, she not only stood by him but stood up next to him. She jumped into the fray for equal rights, immediately organizing P-FLAG in South Carolina and going on to work tirelessly in all nine South Carolina Gay Pride Festivals. No question of her love for her son.

When we discussed Harriet's background, I felt a close kinship with her. She too had gone back to college in her forties, getting a law degree when she was fifty-two. She now specializes in family law and does pro bono work in cases involving AIDS patients versus insurance companies.

Of course, I also met her son Greg; his sister, who was there helping out; the sister's five-year-old son, Tommy (Harriet's grandson), who wore a T-shirt saying "I Love My Gay Uncle." Talk about family values! Greg and Tommy led the Pledge of Allegiance to start the program.

I also met two young men who were there with their two adopted children, both of whom had been born drug-addicted. The men said that because of this, they keep the children's routines and schedules highly structured so the children know just what to expect every day. These young men couldn't have been more caring and proud. One wore a T-shirt that said "Daddy," and the other's said "Father." Grandmother was there, too, with her much appreciated love and help. Her T-shirt said "Nana." Each daddy was a speaker, as was I. At the end of their speeches their little boy was supposed to tell the audience good-bye. Instead, to everyone's delight, he sang the alphabet song.

Mandy Turner spoke, too. She's a bright, articulate African-American who is a devoted gay rights activist, in addition to being national field director for the National Black Lesbian and Gay Leadership Forum. She is a credit to South Carolina. Candace Gingrich was there, as well. No matter how many times I hear Candace, this tiny, dynamic speaker never loses her impact. I love her.

My own speech was heartily received, and I was soon deluged with more thanks and words of admiration for Ellen and what she has done, as well as for me. I feel like I met all 8,000 people there—or at least signed their programs, their T-shirts, and their hats, and smiled while having my picture taken with them.

This weekend brought a pleasant surprise—I reconnected with some people I had met in other places along the road. Steve Gunderson and his partner of sixteen years, Rob Morris, whom I'd met in Washington, were there. Steve is a former Republican congressman from Wisconsin and Rob is an architect; they are smart, warm, great guys. And the two Ricks were there—one an artist and one a doctor—familiar faces from my weekend in Raleigh, North Carolina. From Birmingham, Alabama, there was Kevin Snow, the young entrepreneur who had organized the private *Ellen* party for 3,000 when the ABC affiliate refused to run it.

At one of the booths, I bought a necklace of rainbow-colored wooden beads on a black string. I often wear black, and I love these colors against it. Rainbows celebrate all of us, gay and non-gay.

The parade itself was a joyful one-of-a-kind experience.

Six of us marched in front holding a banner that read, "Pride 98—United for Gay and Lesbian Rights." We were followed by marchers, a small brass band from North Carolina, a few motorcycles, and a truck filled with girls and a glamorous drag queen lounging on the hood. We were a modest-sized but vocal group doing our call-and-answer chants:

"What do we want?" "Equal rights!"
"When do we want them?" "Now!"
And, with spirit, "Hey, hey, ho, ho, homophobia's got to go!"

The leader of these chants was a young man, small in stature but with the loudest voice I've ever heard. As an activist, I was happy; as a speech pathologist, I worried about his vocal cords.

Along our one-mile route our audience ranged from enthusiastic supporters to older couples and people watching with a baffled expression—"What in the world is this?" We smiled and waved at all of them.

And as I marched along, chanting, smiling, and waving, I thought of Carol White's words, realizing how well they applied to everyone, including me. What an incredible feeling to be in touch with the music inside of me and to allow myself to play it, dance it, sing it, and live it!

10

Speaking Out, Speaking Up

"MOM, WHERE ARE YOU? We have to leave in twenty minutes," Ellen said as I answered the phone one morning in the spring of 1998.

"We?" I asked. "Leave for where?"

"I'm speaking at that high school, remember? Anne and I want you there with us."

Now I remembered. A few weeks earlier there had been a powerful story in *Buzz Magazine* about how hard it is to be a gay teenager. It described two high schools here in Los Angeles which have clubs that are gay-straight alliances, and it featured the two boys who were presidents of those clubs—Garrett at one school is gay and Noah, at the other, is straight. Both are heroes.

When Ellen read the article, she was so impressed by Noah's activism that she called him to say how proud she was of his efforts to make things easier for his gay friends and fellow students. During the course of their conversation, Noah asked if she would speak to his club.

Somehow Ellen had forgotten to mention the date and

time for the event until now. For a moment, I deliberated. My desk was piled high. I had a new speech to write, not to mention a book. And I had to do laundry and pack for a trip the next day. Then I thought again. This was an event I didn't want to miss. Grabbing my keys and my purse, I told her, "I'm on my way."

Ellen, Anne, and I piled into El's car and went to Harvard-Westlake for questions and answers from the whole school. Along with us was a baby bird that we rescued on the way.

It was understandable that Ellen had forgotten to tell me about this event: things had been crazy lately. Rumors of *Ellen*'s cancellation had been flying around for weeks. The network wasn't going to make an official announcement for another month, but Ellen wasn't at all hopeful. ABC-Disney had tried to put a parental warning label on the show—evidence that they were unable to stand up to the antigay invective from right-wing organizations who had targeted the show from the moment the closet door had opened. Much was made of a prank kiss between Ellen Morgan and her straight friend Paige (Joely Fisher). El thought this was unfair, especially because scenes with similar prank kisses between two men had been shown on two other ABC sitcoms without critical comment or warning labels.

A week earlier I was asked by an interviewer from Florida about the rumored cancellation and how Ellen was handling it. I answered matter-of-factly, "It's a stressful time for her. I feel like any parent. When any of your children are hurting, you hurt too."

Another question I had been getting was how I felt about

comments that perhaps the story line had become "too gay." I would say that disliking the show for being too gay is the same thing as disliking it for being gay at all. To be fair, I realize that this criticism came not necessarily from extremists but from middle-of-the-road people. Still, the implication was that it was OK for Ellen Morgan to come out of the closet, but now that she was out and the show was still talking about it and raising so many issues—both humorous and serious—which openly gay people must face every day, those critics wanted her to go back into the closet and stop talking.

But now that an amazing national dialogue had begun, stopping wasn't possible. Obviously, *Ellen* was spurring change that seemed to be scaring some people—whether they might be gay themselves, middle-of-the-road, or homophobic. The status quo had been challenged.

What was changing? Most dramatically, from my point of view, a growing number of gay people were deciding to come out, and a growing number of straight family members and friends were taking an active, supportive role.

El and I received hundreds of letters about how gay sons and daughters had used the show to help facilitate family understanding. "Mom, I'm like Ellen," became a new way for many young women to come out to their mothers.

At one HRC event, a young woman said, "When I told my mother I'm gay, she called a priest and a doctor. After Mom watched the show, she decided maybe I'm OK after all."

A young Hispanic man's story echoed hers. "My parents

weren't accepting at all, either," he said. "After the show, they called and asked me to come home so we could have a long talk."

Another woman, also young, said that right after the show aired she was in a grocery store and overheard a cashier and another employee talking about gay people in a derogatory way. Had it not been for the show, she said, she wouldn't have the courage to say something. But she spoke up immediately, saying, "I beg your pardon, but I'm gay and I resent the way you're talking."

More and more, I was hearing that people around the country were allowing themselves to speak out and speak up—like a woman student at a small college in the Midwest who wrote:

> Your daughter gave me the courage to come out on my college campus and to organize the only gay and lesbian student organization here. We watched the show at our first meeting, and that was a wonderful way to begin our dialogue and for me to start my coming-out process. Our membership has grown to almost fifty people, students and faculty, on [this] small, conservative Christian campus. If not for Ellen, I and so many others across the world may still be hiding. She's my hero, as are you for supporting her.

Then there was this note:

> The steps Ellen has taken for many of us who have struggled with explaining to our parents the true person that we are has meant a monumental step forward. Her show's tell-

> ing of our story has given strength to those of us who didn't even realize we needed strength. It has given us a feeling of normalcy that many of us didn't even realize we were missing as we've lived our lives from day to day, thinking things were OK.

Ellen was also creating change and stirring conversation in other communities. Whenever I was on television or radio shows there were always several calls from non-gay people thanking me and thanking Ellen for opening up their awareness. On one show in Philadelphia, I got a call from a heterosexual married woman, a mother, who said she loved watching *Ellen* with her twelve-year-old son because it was such a great opportunity for children to see that gays and lesbians grapple with the same issues as everyone else.

Her call was followed by one from a heterosexual married man who watched regularly with his wife and kids. He was genuinely upset about the rumors of cancellation, saying, "I can't believe it. There's nothing else like it on TV. How can they do that? It's terrible and awful and makes no sense." He vowed to start a local letter-writing campaign to protest to the network.

I remembered that man's passion as Ellen drove us through the streets of Los Angeles on our way to Harvard-Westlake. El really didn't have time to take a morning off to speak at this high school. But given our growing awareness about issues concerning gay teens, this was just too important to miss.

Indeed, if people need a reason to become active in the fight for equal gay rights, they need only look at the alarming statistics that show gay teenagers at risk of severe depression and suicide. Of all teenage suicides, 30 percent are gay. Gay teenagers have the same sensitivity as any adolescent, and in addition they are subjected to bashing—verbal abuse and physical violence. These kids desperately need our support. Organizations with suicide hot lines report that low self-esteem related to sexuality is one of the leading reasons why their adolescent callers are contemplating suicide.

TEEN-LINE is one such hot line in Los Angeles: an extraordinary service for teen callers whose calls are answered by other teens trained to listen and help. A few days before our trip to Harvard-Westlake, Ellen and I were honored at TEEN-LINE's annual lunch and fund-raiser at the Beverly Hills Hotel; the teenagers and their board had voted to present us with humanitarian awards. It was my first award for the work I'm doing now—a cherished honor.

That day, many of the teenagers who work the phones told us that they feel Ellen and I have directly reduced the panic and fear in the gay teens they have counseled. The young man who introduced Ellen to the audience said that for millions of gay teens, El has been a "life raft" in a sea of discrimination and rejection.

As Ellen took the podium, she made a funny remark or two to loosen up the crowd; but then, because of all the controversy, she broke down. This was tough for her. El had gone from being a person whose main motivation in life was to make people happy and have them like her to being an outspoken activist. Now she was being criticized, even by some she had considered friends, and in extremist camps she was being demonized. Now it seemed likely that the TV show in which she starred, the show which she had dreamed of and worked so hard for, was going to be ended. There was silence in the ballroom. I was a few steps away from Ellen on the dais, and I instinctively moved next to her, putting my arm around her shoulder as she regained her composure.

El said, finally, "If I have been your life raft, then you have been mine." She went on to reiterate that in spite of the controversy and the attacks, knowing that she has touched people and made a difference—"even if it has been just one person"—is all that really matters to her.

And so, feeling empowered by that conviction, Ellen, Anne, and I went to meet the diverse group of students at Harvard-Westlake.

THE QUESTIONS RANGED from students wanting to know how Ellen had gotten started in show business to how these teens can help work for equal rights. We talked about gay-bashing, about homophobia, and about all the risks of coming out. We talked about the impact on straight family members—parents, kids, and spouses—when a loved one comes out. We talked about gay marriages and gays as parents.

These weren't only important issues to me, they were personal concerns of real people I had met over the last year. In my mind, I could see these people's faces and recall their names. I could vividly remember the anguish in their voices as they told their heartbreaking stories.

For example, there were painful recollections about partnerships which are not fully acknowledged. When I traveled to the HRC event in Denver, I was met by Tom, a handsome man in his fifties with whom I shared a quiet dinner that night. Tom told me of his experience when his partner of eighteen years was dying of AIDS. He put a hospital bed in a large bedroom and a mattress on the floor for himself so he could be there all night for Paul. While carrying this heavy burden, Tom continued working every day. Yet he couldn't share with anyone on the job what he was going through at home. He said if that had been his wife dying, he would have had all kinds of support.

At the other end of the spectrum were the many accounts I heard from men and women who tried to stay in heterosexual marriages, hoping to hide or deny their sexuality. They all attested to the fact that being forced into traditional roles is destructive. How could living any kind of a lie be otherwise? What a waste of life and time. Unless you believe in reincarnation, this is the only shot we get. How tragic to live it as someone you're not.

In San Antonio, I recalled meeting a woman in her fifties who came out to her adult daughter after her husband of thirty years passed away. Thirty years of hiding.

Difficult though many of these accounts sound, I have been inspired over and over by hearing how resilient loving families can be. One woman I met, Ruth, said that when their children were grown her husband admitted, to himself and to her, that he is gay. They remain friends, and she is entirely supportive. "My anger isn't with him," she said, "it's with society and our rigid rules that force people to pretend to be someone other than who they are."

I thought of my dear friend Phyllis, who is a writer. She shared with me a very powerful piece she wrote about what she went through when her husband told her he was gay and left their marriage and family. She described her feelings of devastation in emotional detail. Then, she wrote:

> Coming out of my solitude, I sought solace from my friends and family and was met with confusion and lack of understanding. I'm so grateful to those who had the wisdom to say that they didn't know what to say. . . .
>
> Now it's becoming increasingly clear to me that my issue is not that my husband is gay, but the person I have become and the person I want to be. . . .
>
> I want to be a source of strength and encouragement for other spouses. They need to know that all their tortured feelings are appropriate and that they are not alone in their suffering. I want society to not diminish or take lightly our struggle. But mostly, I want to believe heart and soul that I am enough.

Indeed, she is "enough." She is now an active member of Straight Spouses, a national organization and support group for men and women whose spouses have come out—and she is also a devoted mother. Her life has purpose and meaning.

Then there were the memorable stories I heard in Dallas, where I did several interviews along with Nancy McDonald, the national head of P-FLAG. One morning we were interviewed at KERA, the National Public Radio station in Dallas. The subject was gay parents coming out to their straight children, so joining us were Pat Stone, the Dallas head of

P-FLAG, and John Selig—who both had personal experiences to share.

Ten years ago Pat's daughter came out to Pat and her husband. A year or so ago, Pat realized that she, too, is a lesbian and divorced her husband of thirty-five years, knowing that she could no longer be the wife he expected her to be. She said during the interview that her ex-husband has met someone and that she hopes he is having a happy, fulfilled relationship.

John took up where she left off, saying, "In my case, the marriage was already falling apart and my wife was the one who asked for the divorce." He was then able to admit to himself that he is gay. Extremely intelligent and articulate, John expressed his hope that people stop picturing gay men and women as stereotypes—"flamboyantly effeminate men or masculine-looking women in black leather." Instead, he hoped people could be given more diverse images of gay men and women. For example, one image he knew well, as a father who happens to be gay, was putting a Band-Aid on his son's scraped knee.

John's son was small when his parents divorced and chose to live with his father. Saying that his son's well-being has always been of the utmost importance to him, John added that the boy is now a young man—twenty-one years old and "110 percent masculine," complete with girlfriend. John, his son, the girlfriend, and her parents all get along well.

John recalled that once his son had a friend over for the night, when he was younger. The friend knew that John was gay and asked, "Your father isn't going to come in here in the middle of the night, is he?"

John's son replied, "My mother's a sexy, attractive lady. If we were at her house, would you ask if she was coming in here in the middle of the night?" What a kid.

In Philadelphia, I saw another example of true, positive family values when I met Chuck and Jay. They treated me to a visit to the Philadelphia Art Museum—which is a joy, especially with a wonderful Impressionist collection. Then we met Jay's daughter, Jen, for lunch in the museum restaurant. She was home from college for spring break—a lovely young woman, very bright, friendly, and focused and planning to go into civil rights law.

Jay and his wife divorced when Jen was four. Their relationship was amicable almost from the start, and they wanted their daughter to know that she had the love of both parents. Jen had her own room in each parent's home, and Jay remains friendly and in close touch with his ex-wife and his former in-laws. I could see that Jen loved both her Dad and Chuck. It was evident how much she appreciates and respects their caring, committed relationship.

Our discussion at Harvard-Westlake about gay parenting reminded me of a few encouraging news items I have read about gay and lesbian couples adopting children; something that is happening more and more. New Jersey, obviously an enlightened state, has just passed a law giving gay and lesbian couples the right to adopt. On one of the news reports, there was an interview with a woman from an organization that calls itself "profamily" and opposes gay adoption. She said how selfish it was to deprive children of what they need most—a mother and a father.

To me, the true profamily stance would be to recognize

that what children need is a parent or two parents, who love them unconditionally, who give them a safe, loving home filled with joy and laughter and mental stimulation. Furthermore, unlike heterosexual couples, who often have unplanned pregnancies, gay couples must go to a great deal of trouble to become parents. Their children are truly wanted, and they are part of a true family.

Since many dysfunctional, abusive households have a mother and a father present, it's clear that being heterosexual is not necessarily a qualification for being a good parent.

I recently met a woman writer for a gay newspaper who said she and her partner have four children. The daughter had to explain this fact to her two best friends at school. The daughter told her friends that she has two mommies, and their response was, "Oh, that's neat."

I was introduced to a man in New Orleans not long ago who identified himself as a gay foster parent. He told me his amazing story: "Three years ago, I took on a twelve-year-old boy who could spell his first name and that was as far as he could go. The state said he was nothing but a 'special ed.' child—but the real causes were abuse and the prescribed drugs that he was strung out on. Now, three years later, he's in ninth grade, he's getting more A's than B's, and he has just blossomed. He plays five instruments and he tap-dances, and all the people at P-FLAG just love him. As a child he was abused by his parents and thrown around the system for four years in several two-parent foster homes and four institutions before I got him, and he was just shell-shocked, like a Bosnian child. Now he may end up being a medical doctor—that's his goal. So in three years he's gone from kindergarten to ninth grade."

Then this wonderful father laughed and added, "And as far as I know, he's going to be a straight boy."

To which I replied, "He's just going to be what he's going to be."

My new hero of the moment (I meet so many) agreed and said, in a down-home accent that was music to my ears, "My kid hugs on everybody and everybody loves him."

Then there were the two men I met in the South who told me they have two adopted children—a boy, six; and a girl, two—the joy of their lives. I asked to see pictures, and they proudly showed me the happy, smiling pair—both black. I told them they were very brave—a gay white couple living in the South and adopting black children. They said it hasn't been a problem at all. One of the men is a "room mother" and helps out at school events. He was there the previous day for a party and some boys were asking his six-year-old son, "How come you're black and your Dad's white?"

His son said, "Look, I have a birth mother but I don't know her, so I have two dads. OK?"

Remembering them, I could not be more proud of their family and their community for teaching and practicing love and acceptance. I really believe that these tolerant communities represent the majority of Americans. I am convinced that it is the intolerant people who are in the minority and on the fringes of society.

In fact, that point was raised by one of the gay students

when he stood up and said that the majority of his straight peers treated him with respect and dignity. But there was one student who was overtly intolerant and belligerent.

Someone suggested that perhaps the intolerance grew from that person's insecurity about his own sexuality; in order to compensate, the other student was just trying to show how macho and mean he could be. This brought to mind Shakespeare's lines: "The lady doth protest too much, methinks."

Another student, who is straight, asked a follow-up question. He said he had tried to talk to a fellow student about tolerance, only to be given a lecture on the immorality of homosexuality. He wondered if there was a way to talk reasonably to a peer who is intolerant.

Ellen thought about this question and then said, "It's hard to be rational with irrational people, especially when they're convinced that they're right and you're wrong. I don't know what it taps into, and . . ." she sighed, "sometimes people hide behind religion and the Bible, and don't get me started on that." El did get started, though, enough to say, "A lot of these people who are so hateful are using God and the Bible to justify their hateful actions, and that's just the opposite of what I believe God is—which is Love."

There was quiet as many young people nodded in agreement. Ellen said that people who justify intolerance by citing specific passages in the Bible ignore other passages—passages which don't support their argument. She also questioned the idea of following a narrow, literal interpretation of rules laid down thousands of years ago. "I know this from doing interviews that when somebody sits there with a tape recorder and has every single word that I've said on tape, and the article comes out and I'm misquoted. . . . Here's a guy with a chisel and a stone, and he's writing the words out. Something's gonna get lost in the translation."

Everyone laughed.

As we laughed, I had some of my own thoughts on this complex subject.

MANY OF YOU reading this may know from your own experience that when you or your family member comes out, it can call into question some of the religious values you have been taught. This is a highly personal issue, and it is not my intention to tell you what and how you should believe. By the same token, I am alarmed by the increasingly strident rhetoric of extremist groups who are making all possible efforts to dictate what and how you believe. Because of my own religious values, I feel a need to speak out against their hypocritical message.

In *Angels in Our Midst,* given to me by Mary Fisher, AIDS activist and author, I saw this letter:

> Dear Mary,
>
> I am a mother and a grandmother, and my daughter and grandson are HIV-positive. It's been seven months since we learned of their infection. I love them to pieces. . . .
>
> I felt that I needed to seek support, and what better place to seek it than the house of the Lord, the church I have attended for more years than I can recall, where I taught children and youth in Sunday School. I felt that these people would love me through the toughest trial to be visited upon me. But reality struck hard in this community of brothers

> and sisters, and they have more or less closed their hearts, minds and doors to me and my family. It is so lonely here that sometimes I feel as though the world has closed me out and there is no one to help me back. Does it ever get easier?

And they call themselves Christians? How could they be so heartless? How could so many have gone so far afield from the teachings of the One they profess to follow?

The activist Paul Monette wrote of "a world that wallows in holy wars and ethnic bloodbaths." Regarding the movement toward greater visibility for gays and lesbians, he told of a friend who was "worried about the backlash, having an instinct for the savageries of which religion is capable." Monette used the terms "Stepford Christians" and "Christian Supremacists."

There are enlightened Christians everywhere who embrace the teaching of love and don't fall for inflammatory rhetoric like the rhetoric of televangelists whose main message seems to be "send money." I recalled a night when I was channel surfing and saw some "Christian" network on TV with a ranting minister saying, "Now, child of God, send in a thousand dollars right now." He kept saying "child of God." What a subtle message to those who aren't mentally alert. We're each and every one of us a child of God and we don't have to send a thousand dollars to anyone to prove it.

The bottom line is that no one person or group has a monopoly on God or faith. I appreciated that sentiment, and the live-and-let-live philosophy, expressed in this letter, which followed the coming out episode:

Hello, first of all I am a blk/f/36 and thought the show was very funny. Ellen has a lot of talent and I loved the show. The topic did not upset me at all. That was my first time watching her show. I've seen her do stand up before . . . and the lady has it. Gay, Straight, Black, or White has nothing to do with the entire person. From my church teaching it is wrong to be gay, but she has to deal with that. Who am I or anyone else to judge a person for who they are, that is not for us to do. JOB WELL DONE. Ellen is one funny person, and I wish her the best.

Contrasting with that truly Christian attitude was a disturbing letter shown to me by my good friend Dr. Jim Gordon, a psychologist and fellow activist. It was from a Baptist minister writing to a gay magazine, and it included rhetoric such as "this sickening perversion"; "those who are enslaved in this type of lifestyle and feel they cannot be free or know they can in fact be normal"; and "sinful, learned behavior." Almost laughable, if it were not so malevolent, was his comment, "We love you people but hate your lifestyle and wickedness."

That's not love by anyone's definition. Behind the double-talk, what he's really saying is, "We despise you and we are spreading a doctrine of hatred, fear, ignorance, and religious extremist supremacy."

It's very hard for me to read the hypocrisy of so-called men of God, knowing as I do all the wonderful, brilliant gay men and women I have met all over this country of ours—men and women, sons and daughters, mothers and fathers, sisters and brothers—who are doing good in all walks of life and are contributing to our society in magnificent ways.

However, our country, where "all men are created equal," also has free speech as its cornerstone. Hence, we must let the extremists rant. But because we too have that right of speech, there are times when we must reply.

Wouldn't it be better if the inordinate energy and money spent by right-wing religious extremists to rant about what others do in the privacy of their own homes could be spent in causes that are actually family-friendly? Not long ago there was an article in the *Los Angeles Times* about the casualties of the Orange County welfare system—a real-life horror story. It mentioned one mother who has five drug-addicted babies, each by a different man, and each man now in various state lockups.

In four out of five cases of child abuse, the mother or father is a drug user. Now, there's a project for the fundamentalists. Go after abusive parents; educate women having multiple babies by multiple fathers; go after drug dealers and users. More than 4,600 children are under the court's protection in Orange County. Here's a startling figure: Since 1990 the number of children whose cases end up in these courts has risen 54 percent.

And then there's the terrifying phenomenon of kids and guns. Children bring weapons to school and murder their classmates. It's happening all across the country, even in "all-American" towns where people tell themselves, "It can't happen here." Where is the outcry on behalf of those innocent children whose lives are being taken from them? Think of the good these preachers could do. While they're at it, the inner cities could also use some help—there are more than 58,000 gang members in Los Angeles County alone.

If we need an example of how we can make a difference in these children's lives, just think of the gay foster parent who transformed a drug-addicted boy—a kid that the system almost gave up as a lost cause—into a well-rounded good student.

I am heartened by stories of those who question hateful rhetoric. When I was in the South, I heard of a Baptist couple who stopped going to their church because their pastor said such demeaning things about their gay son.

At an HRC dinner in Atlanta I met an African-American mom, Heloyse. She and her gay son sat next to me at my table. He was a fine man, successful in business, and his mother loved him just as she did her other two children. When we talked about mothers who, on the grounds of religion, reject their gay sons and daughters, Heloyse said, "Well, we'll just have to pray for them."

Religion should never be an excuse not to love. That's what I said to the young gay woman I met in the Midwest who told me, "My mother won't have anything to do with me—she's Catholic."

As it happens, I know plenty of Catholic parents who are entirely accepting of their gay children. At a P-FLAG event in New Orleans, there was a staunch Catholic woman who goes to mass every morning and is the mother of ten. Three children are gay, so she's very active in P-FLAG, but she has no conflict with her religion. Another Catholic mother initially had problems when she found out that four of her five children are gay (three sons and one daughter). She went to her priest and he told her, "Support your children."

In my own family, of course, in her later years Mother returned to the Catholic church and remained totally accepting of her granddaughter. My sister Helen is also very active in the Catholic church, and she too is completely supportive of her niece. Helen recently sent me the latest opinion on homosexuality, from a report in *America*, a Jesuit magazine. The article, "National Dialogue on Gay and Lesbian Issues and Catholicism," reported on a symposium of over 650 men and women—all ages, from forty states—who gathered to hear theologians, bishops, psychologists, and others. A nun spoke of these issues as a concern for Catholics and for the public as a whole—especially because there are those who still practice discrimination, even violence, against homosexuals. She asserted that gay people have the same right to equal protection under the law as heterosexuals.

The article quoted statistics just released by the National Coalition of Anti-Violence Projects, indicating an increase in violence against gays and lesbians since 1995. A priest who spoke about discrimination against homosexuals in employment and housing went on to recommend justice for an "already undervalued minority."

His is good argument for activism. To that end, in January of 1998, I made one of my most memorable HRC trips to Portland, Maine, in order to help out with the "Maine Won't Discriminate" campaign.

After Maine passed an antidiscrimination law, making it the eleventh state to have such a law based on sexual orientation, an extremist group from the religious right took advantage of a loophole that had never been used before and got enough signatures to have another election, trying to overturn this law. Talk about poor losers.

I traveled to Portland, Maine, with Susanne Salkind from HRC; Martha Fish, my ebullient, delightful new friend from earlier HRC events; and Martha's dear friend Adrian. In Portland, we were fortunate enough to stay in one of the loveliest bed and breakfast inns that I've ever seen, the Pomegranate Inn, owned by Isabel Smiles. (What a name to be blessed with!) Isabel once owned an antique shop and she and her late husband collected art, so the inn is full of wonderful furniture and artworks.

While we were there, the area was being hammered with its second big snow and ice storm of the season. We found ourselves snowbound at the Pomegranate Inn.

The warmth of the people more than made up for the weather. Saturday morning all the houses across the street from the inn were without electricity, so neighbors wandered into Isabel's kitchen. We all seemed to gravitate there—guests, friends, and strangers alike. Isabel told the neighbors to fix their own breakfast, and they did. One man cooked scrambled eggs for several others. Before long, we were all old friends, talking among ourselves in little groups. It was the loveliest spontaneous gathering imaginable.

When one of the guests—a woman from Boston who said she generally does not talk to strangers—heard that we were there to help with "Maine Won't Discriminate," she wrote a check for the campaign!

Then, two weeks later, upon my return to Los Angeles, I heard devastating news: Maine had voted to repeal its antidiscrimination law aimed at protecting gays and lesbians. A combination of inclement weather and deceptive advertising by religious extremists contributed to the defeat. I sat down and wrote the following letter to the *Portland Press Herald:*

I just saw a small news item in today's *Los Angeles Times*, "Maine Becomes the First State to Repeal Its Gay Rights Statute." My heart goes out to all the good, fair-minded Mainers who worked so hard to see that this travesty of justice would not happen. The article quoted a leader of the Christian Coalition as saying, "We feel great." That's painful to read. The word "Christian" should not be in the same sentence with elation over making discrimination and hatred against any group OK. The fight for fairness is a long-term struggle, and we should all take heart that in the end the American people will come down on the side of fairness.

A month later, I received this next letter from one of my new friends in Maine, a widow with grown children:

I waited to write to you until after the vote, thinking it would be a celebratory epistle. Alas those hateful, Bible-thumping Christian coalition got the better of us—for now. Still I want to express my gratitude to you for all the energies you expended for Maine Won't Discriminate. It was greatly appreciated.

We had our first obvious gay-bashing since the vote—a psychiatrist, who with his partner, has adopted 3 children—

trying to lead a quiet life. He was jumped and badly beaten when out for his daily run. What next?

My reaction was sadness and anger—not only at the perpetrators but also at those who incited them. The leaders and ministers who use religion as an excuse to preach hate and judgment should be held accountable. To anyone who hears such rhetoric, I have a simple plea: As a mother and average citizen, I beg each of you, allow yourself to question ideologies of blame and punishment. Remember Jesus's simple instruction, "Love one another."

THE QUESTIONS CONTINUED from the group at Harvard-Westlake. It was an amazing experience. Ellen was definitely in her element—funny, poignant, brilliant. Anne also spoke, in her no-holds-barred way. She was as honest, direct, and articulate as only she can be.

Anne had a different take on the question of how to talk to a peer who is intolerant. "You know," she said, "remember that there's safety in numbers—so the more support we can garner and gather from our friends, the more we spread that support among people who are open to listening. You're not going to convince the one guy. . . . but think of it this way—" Anne nodded to El, explaining, "Ellen used to say, 'I'd be performing for two thousand people, and one guy in the front wouldn't be laughing—and I'd care about him.' Remember, there are 1,999 other people who may be open to listening, to supporting tolerance and love. So that one person is going to feel pretty outnumbered pretty darn soon if we keep building gay-straight alliances where everybody comes together. One day he's going feel like the people he's been making fun of."

Everyone cheered. And once again we cheered for Noah and his fellow activists.

Activism is not without risks. I was very impressed by a journalist, an African-American, when he told me that some members of his community have criticized him for being sympathetic to homosexuals. He believes that there is a close parallel between the black civil rights movement and the fight for equal gay rights. "Whenever I hear African-Americans making discriminatory remarks about homosexuals," he said, "I make a point of telling them to watch what they're saying because in ten years they're going to look back and realize they sounded like George Wallace did to us back then."

STRAIGHT BUT NOT NARROW read the sign held by an African-American man who was interviewed during a gay pride march in Washington a few years ago. When asked why he felt it was important to show his solidarity with the gay marchers, he said, "The same people who hate them hate me. If I don't stand up for others who are being persecuted, who'll stand up for me when it's my turn?"

Activism can take many forms—including, for someone who is gay, coming out. What is being risked goes beyond rejection from family, as is illustrated in this letter I received:

> I came out in 1973 my last year of college. My mother took it very hard. . . . It's a long and painful story but we finally over the years worked it out.

In 1985 I lost a very good job as a supervisor of a non-invasive cardiac lab . . . because I'm gay. So . . . I know how hard coming out can be. But we have to keep on trying to make it easier for those who follow.

From a letter printed in a gay newspaper in Dallas:

> Two years ago I was fired because of my sexual orientation. Since losing my job, we had many troubles financially. . . . Before I lost my job, I just wanted to live quietly and let the "radicals" and "politicals" fight for our rights. Now I am one of them. It has helped me heal and given me such insight, and I have met so many wonderful people I would never have known had I not become active: Ehrhardt (Harryette, State Rep.), my P-FLAG family, and Betty DeGeneres, to name just a few.
>
> We must all fight the fight, even if it's just to write a letter, vote, make a phone call, or march in a parade. No one in this community should sit idly, expecting others to correct the wrongs aimed at us.

For all of us, gay and straight, activism can be as basic as sitting down with a family member or friend and talking to one another openly and honestly. As one handsome young African-American man put it, "I'm not asking my parents to join a cause or march in a parade or throw me a party. I just want them to know who I am so that instead of asking me when I'm going to meet a nice woman and get married, it would be great if they'd ask if I've met any nice eligible young men lately."

For other parents, like myself, it is important to take a stand by joining the cause and marching in the parade. As the slogan goes, "Equality through visibility." This is reflected in polls which show, overwhelmingly, that when you know people who are gay or lesbian, you are much more likely to vote for antidiscrimination laws and much, much less likely to be homophobic. That's why the more visible our gay sons and daughters are, and the more visible we are as supportive family members, the better we will be able to help them achieve equality.

I hope that some day before too long these admirable gay-straight alliances won't be found only in progressive schools but will reflect our society as a whole. Who knows? As El has said, a day will come when we'll all look back and see her coming out as "one big so-what." Eventually, in a still better world, coming out won't be necessary because the closet itself will have ceased to exist.

I pray for that day—a time when, instead of hate, love is carefully taught and children will grow up without hearing derogatory remarks about their gay and lesbian family members and neighbors; and the more enlightened among us who already accept each other without regard to race, color, or creed will include sexual orientation in that list.

11

Questions

WELCOME TO BETTY'S Town Hall Meeting, where you can ask me any questions you want, about anything. Or at least, you can ask about anything that someone else has asked and that I've included here.

I call this a Town Hall because I've been asked these various questions by many different types of people and in many different settings, friendly and hostile. Let's start with some of the more common questions.

Why is it important for people to come out? It's not only important but vital for gays and lesbians to come out—to be able to live openly, truthfully, and unafraid. Until more and more gay men and women feel comfortable and safe taking this healthy step, we in the heterosexual world won't know how many of the friends, neighbors, and coworkers we like and admire are in fact homosexual.

On that wonderful day in the future—when homosexual-heterosexual no longer matters, when your gay coworkers can proudly bring their partners to company functions, can display pictures of their loved ones on their desks—then this will finally become a nonissue and won't have to be discussed ever again. What a blessing that will be! Then our religious leaders can spend their time and money exhorting their flocks to keep the Ten Commandments. They can invite all of us, all of God's children, to join with them in striving to be the very best we can be—honest, loving, and compassionate.

Then teenagers can be accepted for who they are, as they are, and not be the target of jokes or harassment. How beautiful and simple! Let's strive for it. Give all people the sense of self-worth they deserve. Let them know they're OK just the way they are.

This quotation from Anthony Trollope applies to all of us: "Never think you're not good enough. A person should never think that. People will take you very much at your own reckoning."

What's the best way to come out? There is no right or wrong way to take a stand for honesty. My simple prescription follows three important points. First, remember what really matters. For all families, that is the unconditional acceptance, love, and support for each other. This has recently been confirmed by the National Conference of Catholic Bishops: it is important to realize that when children or parents or siblings come out, they are not changed at all. They are just giving you their own gift of honesty and love, and asking that you begin to understand.

Second, be patient. Whether gay or straight, we all need

time to think, to reflect, and to care. Before we blurt out words we'll regret later, we should stop and really listen to each other. For straight family members, this is a time that we begin to be more honest ourselves.

Third, celebrate your honesty. The first step of coming out demands courage, but almost every step that will follow is exhilarating and rewarding. You'll find out personally how much better your life can be, how close your family and friends will eventually become, and how strong you feel once you have embraced the truth.

And, finally, every step of the way, don't hesitate to reach out and use the resources available in your library, in your community, and from organizations like P-FLAG.

What is P-FLAG? Parents, Family, and friends of Lesbians and Gays is a wonderful support organization primarily for parents and straight family members of gays and lesbians. It was founded by a courageous woman named Jeanne Manford. After her son, Morty, was beaten up while distributing leaflets at a New York City political dinner in 1972, she became increasingly active, urging parents of gays to unite. About this same time, in Los Angeles, Adele and Larry Starr, parents of one gay son (of four children), began a parents' organization which grew to the national level. There are now over 400 chapters across the United States. Generally, monthly meetings are held, consisting of informal rap groups and then a guest speaker for the whole group. Support is also offered to gay men and women whose families aren't accepting; many attend meetings to learn ways of reaching out to resistant family members.

Through P-FLAG, I meet many parents who are every bit as proud as I am. Peggy Olson, in her president's message in the L.A. newsletter, writes: "What an incredible journey the past eleven years has been! Learning our son is gay has opened up a new world for me, and I am so grateful, grateful to so many of you in P-FLAG who have enriched my life." A mother I met in Chicago always wears a large button that says, "I'm a P-FLAG mom." When people ask her what that means, she is only too happy to tell them.

What advice do you have for children of gay and lesbian parents who come out? The same advice I have for parents of gays—realize that they are the same parents you know and love; they are just being more honest with you. Be patient and allow yourself to go through a process of acceptance. You may not accept this overnight, but your parent didn't accept this news overnight either; he or she probably struggled with it for a long time.

A loving family atmosphere at home and, ideally, a large, loving extended family will help younger children cope with whatever prejudice and ignorance they may face outside the home. For children who are older, or grown, it's vital to go through the process of acceptance, keeping in mind that your parent is no longer able to maintain the facade of living a lie and is giving you the gift of his or her honest self.

Why should I have to know about other people's sexual practices? You shouldn't. And this is where people get confused. When you learn that someone you know is homosexual, you don't know anything about his or her sexual practices. That is strictly none of our business—just as your own sexual practices are no one else's business. I've heard it said that with the word "heterosexual" the accent is on "hetero" and with the word "homosexual" the accent is on "sexual." What a shame that we, as a society, are so hung up on this. After so many generations, we are still, deep down, puritanical. Puritanical and hung up on sex—what a combination! I'm positive that for a committed, loving homosexual couple, sex is no more or less important than it is for a committed, loving heterosexual couple.

Not long ago, I heard the great writer Toni Morrison being interviewed on *60 Minutes*. As an African-American, she said, "When you know somebody's race, what do you really know about them? Nothing." How true and this can be applied to sexuality. When you know somebody's sexuality, what do you really know about them? Nothing. It should be just a fact and should not enter into the equation of the sum of that person.

What about "outing"? As far as I'm concerned, a definite no-no. I know that coming out is a healthy, positive step. Coming out, however, is something that must be done in one's own time, at one's own pace. I think outing someone before he or she is ready to take this step is unbelievably cruel.

My friend John Selig takes the other side, at least in one regard. He says that if an elected official is closeted and votes against antidiscrimination legislation, he or she should be outed. Actually, that's an exception that I too would go along with.

What is bisexuality? One explanation I've been given is that bisexuals don't have the same boundaries as those who seek partners of one sex over the other. Whereas a heterosexual is attracted romantically and sexually only to the opposite sex and a homosexual is attracted romantically and sexually only to the same sex, a bisexual may honestly be attracted to either sex. This may be hard for those of us with rigid boundaries to understand. Ideally, as with anyone else, if bisexuals are lucky enough to find the one true love of their life, that's where they'll stay.

What does transgender mean? *Mom, I Need to Be a Girl* is the title of one book on this subject, which I received recently along with a note from the author, who calls herself Just Evelyn:

> I really appreciate your efforts to promote family support for gay and lesbian children. Transgendered children and their families experience the same types of discrimination and also need support and understanding. I want to give you this book about my transexual child and our journey from anguish to joy. As a fellow mom, I am sure you will see the similarities and need of love and acceptance for all our children.

P-FLAG has a helpful, informative pamphlet on this subject, "Our Trans Children." In it, a transgendered person is defined as "someone whose gender identity . . . differs from conventional expectations of masculinity or femininity. Gender identity is one's internal sense of being masculine or feminine, a man or a woman, a boy or a girl." Sexual orientation is defined as "someone's sexual attraction for others who may be of the opposite sex, the same sex, or either sex."

Why do we have all these distinctions and labels? Good question. In a perfect world, we would not need any special names. We could all just be people. Nonetheless, until we have awareness and tolerance for homosexuals, we need respectful labels to help get beyond ignorant street slang and old stereotypes. There is a tendency to overdo "political correctness." But then again, why not err on the side of courtesy? "Gay" is fine to use in designating men and women, though "lesbian" is a more precise designation for women. In order not to mislabel anyone, however, you should know that many people who consider themselves bisexual don't call themselves gay. This also applies to transgender individuals and to transexuals and transvestites, who may or may not be homosexual.

Note also that some gay women dislike the term "lesbian." To some, it sounds foreign or alien, as it should, being derived from a foreign place, the Greek island of Lesbos, which in ancient times was inhabited by a group of strong women. "Queer" was once a derogatory term for a homosexual. Now many gay people—especially young gays and lesbians—use the term proudly to describe themselves.

We get into another murky area when we search for a polite label for a gay person's significant other. "Partner" is usually appropriate for men and women. Anne and Ellen, who are not married, call each other "wife" and "Mrs." The two Ricks I mentioned earlier are not married either, but they call each other "husband." When there is no long-term commitment, "girlfriend" or "boyfriend" or "lover" can be used.

The best advice I can offer about what to call gay people and their partners is this: When in doubt, just ask them what they prefer.

Is homosexuality a lifestyle choice? Hardly. A person's sexual orientation is not a lifestyle; it's a life. As to the precise factors that determine homosexuality, there are no definitive answers yet. Are gay people born that way, is their DNA "hard-wired," as many suggest? Is homosexuality passed on from other family members, genetically or culturally or both? Do experience and environment play a part? Is there a choice?

My own observation is that while both genetic and environmental factors shape who we are, very few people choose to be gay. For most gays and lesbians I have met, this is a fact about who they are, much as the color of their eyes is. As Ellen has said, it is as much a part of who she is as the color of her skin.

HRC's excellent "Resource Guide To Coming Out" (available for just a phone call to HRC in Washington—phone and address at the back of this book), says:

> Homosexuality Is Not a Choice;
> Homosexuality Chooses You—
>
> Some people say that homosexuality is a choice to discourage you from being in a gay or lesbian relationship. But think about it for a minute: Did you choose to have feelings

of same-sex attraction? Why would you? The fact is: Homosexuality is not a choice any more than being left-handed or having blue eyes or being heterosexual is a choice. It's an orientation, a part of who you are. The choice is in deciding how to live your life.

Can people be recruited? Definitely not. If so, I'd sign up! After all, I have more and more good friends who are gay and lesbian. I love them, but I am hopelessly heterosexual. Society needlessly worries that young people can be influenced, but this isn't true. We have the orientation we have and we love whom we love.

What about gay and lesbian stereotypes? What about heterosexual stereotypes? One heterosexual stereotype might be a muscular, macho man, maybe on a motorcycle. Another might be a tanned, handsome young lifeguard. Yet another, a Sharon Stone–type beauty. That doesn't quite describe all of us who are heterosexual, does it? Well, the same goes for gay and lesbian men and women. The stereotype of the effeminate gay man or the "butch" lesbian is just that—a stereotype.

This is yet another important reason for our gay family members to come out—so the world can see that gay people are all around them, in every walk of life. Gay people include our police officers, teachers, doctors, professional athletes, artists, models, oyster shuckers, and vacuum cleaner salespeople.

A psychologist recently told me that Ellen has made her life so much easier, personally and professionally. Before coming out, she never had anyone to point to and say, "Look, she's gay and she's successful."

Why is a gay person's process of self-discovery and acceptance so difficult in so many cases? Again, look at the messages gay people get from society. At a time when teenagers are aware of romantic feelings for the opposite sex, our gay children are becoming aware that this isn't happening to them, that their romantic feelings are for friends of the same sex. And they may be hearing an ugly array of derogatory nicknames for gays and lesbians. At their houses of worship, they may hear hellfire and damnation preached against what they are.

Imagine how they must feel—confused, ashamed, concerned. They are simply living the lives God gave them, and suddenly they're a target of discrimination and prejudice at best and hatred and physical violence at worst. Which brings us to . . .

Why is it so hard to accept diversity? Or, more accurately, why is it so hard for some people to accept diversity? God bless those among us with a live-and-let-live attitude. Bless those enlightened souls who realize that we don't all come out of one mold or one cookie cutter, who acknowledge that their fellow human beings come in all shapes, sizes, and varieties and accept this as a matter of fact without trying to change others to fit their own particular shape, size, or variety. Why can't we all be accepting? I think the reason is all too obvious. We aren't born with prejudice, hate, or discrimination. "You have to be carefully taught."

How can you ask your child tough questions? For many of these questions, there's no one way or one answer. So much depends on the age of your son or daughter when this discussion comes up. With an adult child, straightforward questions seem appropriate. One mother had met her son's partner as a "friend" and had grown to know and like him. When her son and his "friend" got a one-bedroom apartment, she began to wonder about the friendship. She said her son had always insisted on having his own bedroom. She asked, "Son, is this more than a friendship?" and he honestly replied, "Yes, mother." His secret and his hiding were over, and now he and his partner are embraced by the family.

One of the wonderful students who welcomed me at Colorado State University when I spoke there recalled that she came out to her mother on July 19, 1994, at 4 P.M. (I wish my memory were that precise.) "In fact," she said, "my mother told me I was gay. We were sitting at the dining room table and talking about a friend of mine, and mom said, 'She's gay, isn't she?' I said, 'I don't know—I guess so.' And mom said, 'You are too, aren't you?' I didn't know what to say and she said, 'It's OK.' I started crying and she said, 'I said it's OK.' I said, 'I know, but it's such a big deal—I've been worrying about telling you for a year.' "

If you begin to have questions in your own mind when your child is a young teen you may want to help the child explore his or her feelings. Many times, parents see all the signs but don't say anything. Years later, when the son or daughter finally works up the courage to be honest, the parents say, "Oh, we knew that." How much better and how much more helpful it would be for parents to broach the subject when children are younger and are going through the difficult process of discovering who they are and learning to accept themselves. That's a lonely, difficult journey for our gay sons and daughters. Which brings up another good question . . .

Why do we need gay clubs, or gay-straight alliances, in high schools? These clubs are wonderful starting points for ending this pitiful form of bigotry. The gay clubs give our gay adolescents a safe place to meet and—in a friendly setting—talk out their worries and concerns with friends going through the same trials. It's important for them to know they're not alone.

Gay-straight alliances are an even better bridge to acceptance. My hat is off to the straight kids like the group at Harvard-Westlake who are mature and intelligent enough to reach out a hand in support of their gay classmates. It's sad to report that often they stand head and shoulders above their local school boards, which try to stop the establishment of these positive groups in their schools. More fear and ignorance to be overcome!

A young woman who leads a gay and lesbian teen group in Washington, D.C., told me that when some members have mothers who aren't supportive, they say, "I need a Betty." How flattering—I'm a commodity!

These terrific clubs sprouting up around the country are literally saving lives. Some experts in denial have challenged the statistics about suicide and depression among gay teenagers, claiming that gays are no more at risk of violence than other teenagers. They're wrong, and the reason is painfully obvious. Look at the message gay teenagers have gotten: "What you're feeling is wrong, unnatural, abnormal, sinful, abominable, an aberration."

Is it possible to have a healthy dialogue between people who disagree? As an incurable optimist, I'd say yes. And the old saying "You can disagree without being disagreeable" might be a good starting place. Also, respect helps tremendously—self-respect and respect for others and their beliefs.

The qualities needed to accept diversity are the same qualities needed for a healthy dialogue about differences of any kind—race, religion, orientation, ideology, or whatever we can imagine that divides us. On this issue, Carl Jung makes a point worth repeating, "Everything that irritates us about others can lead us to an understanding of ourselves."

How can all of us build a bridge to reach more heterosexuals who don't have gay or lesbian family members? The key to building a bridge to acceptance by heterosexuals is coming out. As people begin to realize that acquaintances, coworkers, service people, and professionals they already know and like happen to be gay or lesbian, their ignorance and fear will vanish, as it should.

The best cure for homophobia is getting to know a gay person. If you suffer from this "curable" disease, make the effort to go out and expand your horizons.

• • •

SOME OF THE questions I'm asked are rather personal. After a speech at a university, one student asked how many marriage proposals I'd received over the Internet. None, I answered, at least to my knowledge! At another speaking engagement I was asked if I would consider remarrying and, if so, what kind of a mate I would consider ideal.

My answer was, "I'll have to think about that and get back to you." After thinking about it and acknowledging that "ideal" is by definition elusive, I came up with a few characteristics for a suitable candidate. First, he would have to be well-educated—self-educated or through traditional avenues. Broad-minded, well-read, interested in many things—art, theater, history, astronomy, travel. A nice appearance, good taste in clothes, healthy, active, a good sense of humor. It wouldn't hurt if he was a wonderful cook. Of course he should be an oenophile, or at least know what that means! A sailboat would be nice, as would a house on the ocean. Other than all that, he can just be an average guy.

Having said all that, I agree with Katharine Hepburn. A few years ago, when Barbara Walters asked her if she had any interest in a new relationship with a man, Ms. Hepburn replied, "Well, at my age I'm not going to attract the strongest lion in the jungle, so why bother?" My sentiments exactly.

Some of the personal questions I've been asked, like those that follow, are a bit more serious.

Do you consider yourself religious? Yes, but not in the sense of following a structured religion—and certainly not a denomination that proscribes your every thought and idea. I appreciate the Bible, and I pray the prayers in Psalms, The Lord's Prayer and the Beatitudes and so many of the beautiful teachings of Jesus. I talk about this often with Ellen and Anne, and like them, I try, more and more, to live up to my highest sense of right. And we thank God for each day and for all His blessings.

Has your new role given you a new perspective about your own life? A big, definite *yes*. It has been and continues to be life-changing, challenging, and rewarding in the best possible way. It has given my life, my days, a clear direction and purpose such as I have never known before. I have learned and grown from this powerful, intense experience as a parent, as a woman, and as an individual concerned with all human rights. My "antennae" have been fine-tuned as I become more aware of injustice wherever and however it may manifest itself.

I've discovered that I have a strong point of view and can engage in debate and not be thrown by the few negative comments I've gotten here and there. This, along with the love that I've felt everywhere I go, has created a sense of empowerment new to me. I am experiencing a truism about life. When we are given greater challenges, we rise to the occasion.

As Everymom, do you think your voice of common sense and reason is being heard more readily by those who wouldn't otherwise listen? It seems to be—and there are moms and dads like me all across this country, active in their local P-FLAG chapters, speaking at schools and civic clubs, successfully getting out the same message, that our gay sons and daughters need to be treated fairly and equally.

I also think that because Ellen and I show how much we have gained in our mother-daughter relationship, other kids and parents may be noticing what they could be missing. I heard a story about a man who attended the HRC national dinner and sat right behind Ellen, Anne, and me. After hearing my speech and then Ellen's, he walked right out and called his mother and came out to her. She was fine with it.

What have you learned that you would most like to share with other parents of gays and lesbians? Above all, I've learned that there's nothing so important and so wanted as a parent's love. I can't even begin to describe the sadness I see in the eyes of men and women who tell me that their parents have rejected them. I would like these parents to know that their sons and daughters are some of the finest people I've met. It's never too late to examine your heart and welcome your child back into the family. An old Turkish proverb puts it well: "No matter how far you have gone on the wrong road, turn back."

Shed the burden of the past, and let your vision of a realized future guide you.

—Deepak Chopra

EPILOGUE

It's All About Love

LOS ANGELES, 1998

MAY 20TH, 1998. WELL, it's my birthday, and I've been celebrating all week long. The high point is here at the Ivy with my three favorite people in the whole world—Vance, Ellen, and Anne, who are treating me to dinner before we dash off to a screening of Anne's new movie, *Return to Paradise*.

With its Louisiana-style cuisine and its pleasant "nouveau southern" decor, the Ivy has a homey feeling for us New Orleanians. It's always a good spot for special occasions.

Over dinner, Anne makes an announcement. "Mom," she begins, "you know the *Six Days Seven Nights* premiere is in two weeks?"

"In New York," Ellen jumps in a bit glumly, "I can't go."

"Why not?" I ask with concern.

El and Anne explain. Ellen has just started filming *Ed TV*, directed by Ron Howard. There's no way, she says, that she can get time off from her shooting schedule.

Before I become too sad for the two of them, Anne continues, "So I wanted to know, would you and Vance come with me as my escorts? I mean, you're my family and it would mean a lot to have you there with me."

Vance and I exchange surprised, excited looks and then tell Anne: "We'd be honored."

We talk about plans, including the possibility of flying there with her in a private jet. Of course, I realize that more and more celebrities enjoy this perk when they're working. That is, I say, if they don't already have their own private jet.

(Listen to me—once starstruck, now an authority.)

Well, this will be a first. I'm having more and more firsts at this late date. These are not bad years at all.

We chat about other projects in the works. El is in talks to star opposite Kate Capshaw in *Love Letter*, a Steven Spielberg production. Then there's Anne's next movie, a remake of *Psycho* in which she's slated to play the Janet Leigh role.

Vance says, "Is it true they're rewriting that part a little? Instead of getting stabbed, I heard that you just get punched in the stomach."

Ellen and I crack up. Anne looks somewhat puzzled—she is not quite used to Vance's sense of humor. Later, she's quicker on the uptake when a reference to the movie *Dead Man Walking* prompts Vance to say, "I heard they're making a sequel. They're going to call it *Sick Man Jogging*."

This time, we all laugh and groan in unison.

Becoming more serious, Vance asks El and Anne about the volunteer work they've been doing, helping gay and lesbian young people, many of whom have gone through rejection, abuse, and homelessness. Ellen and Anne meet with a group once a week to direct a workshop in creativity and building self-esteem, and to send a simple message of love, to reinforce in these young men and women the idea that they are worthy and have a lot to give.

I beam at my three kids, so thankful to be here, celebrating not just this birthday but the rich feast of experiences with which we are being blessed. I flash back to my last birthday, another high point following Ellen's history-making show. Many other events from this incredible event-filled year come to mind—so many emotional highs, and some lows too.

PROBABLY THE TOUGHEST time for me came at the end of last summer. On August 19, 1997, a few weeks after being named Spokesperson for the Human Rights Campaign's National Coming Out Project, I flew to Texas, as did my sister Helen, for an impromptu visit with Audrey, who had just a few weeks before been diagnosed with a rare, inoperable form of cancer. This was devastating news. Up until her diagnosis, she had led an extremely active, healthy life—in her church, in her community, traveling with her husband Bob, and often bringing along one or more of their eight grandsons.

Her illness rapidly took its toll. I had to hide my shock at seeing her. Helen said I did a good job. As debilitated as Audrey was, her ever-present smile and laugh were still there. We spent as many hours together as she felt strong enough to manage, the three of us sitting in the sunroom overlooking the bay, reminiscing about everything from the inconsequential to the momentous.

Eight months earlier, Audrey had given Helen and me

each a copy of the book, *Sisters*, full of photographs and essays about sisterhood. She signed mine, "To a wonderful little sister—from the one 'forever in the middle.' Love, Audrey."

As we sat together I thought how connected we were, yet how different our lives had been.

My oldest sister Helen was just as she always was—kind, thoughtful, serious, and studious from the start. Helen finished LSU with a double major in speech and Spanish. When her three sons were young she commuted from Pass Christian to the University of Southern Mississippi at Hattiesburg and got her master's degree in Spanish and French. She taught both languages for years at St. Stanislaus, a Catholic boarding school for boys on the Gulf Coast.

In the course of her teaching, she discovered the art of weaving and soon had her own studio with quite a business going—making jackets, shawls, and placemats; taking custom orders; and teaching weaving. When she retired from St. Stanislaus, she became even busier full-time, easing up only recently so that she could devote more time to tutoring at the local elementary school. Helen is also an accomplished writer. I love her poetry.

A truly good, giving person, Helen struggled for years with her first husband's addiction to alcohol. He was a brilliant engineer and a good person but hopelessly enslaved to drink. It destroyed him and their marriage. Helen was alone for a number of years and then married René, a longtime friend who was more than twenty years her senior. They had three very happy years together until they were parted by his death. Their age difference was not at all significant. Why should it have been? After all, it's all about love.

Audrey—the outgoing, effervescent one, throughout the years always with a smile on her face, always ready to laugh. Audrey and my brother-in-law, Bob Maeser, were married fifty-one years. She met him when she was at LSU and the Army sent him there. Bob was rather serious, an engineering student who would later finish at Northwestern in Evanston, Illinois. A famous story in our family was how Bob told Audrey when they met, "I don't care much for dancing."

"I don't care for it so much myself," she said.

The very next day the campus newspaper ran a column of "Bests" in which Audrey Pfeffer was named best jitterbug dancer on campus. Oops. Bob enjoyed telling that story for a long time.

I once told someone that all three of us worked but Audrey didn't have a "real job." That isn't quite true. She may not have worked from nine to five, but she did publicity for the Baytown, Texas, library; gave many book reviews to various groups; wrote for the local paper; and was active in the Texas Press Women's Association. Aside from that, she and Bob were both involved in the Baytown Little Theatre, directing plays—Audrey even wrote some. They were also extremely active in the Episcopal church, and Audrey directed plays that she wrote based on Bible stories. Along the way, she became interested in quilting, joined a bee, and made many beautiful quilts.

As my sisters and I talked about all our activities, I said, "I guess we don't sit around, us Pfeffer girls."

Audrey said, laughingly, "I can just hear Mother now: 'Busy hands are happy hands.' "

Audrey had finished two panels of a quilt with a "four

seasons" theme—winter and spring. One panel, spring, now hangs above my bed.

We had moments of great sadness, although these three days could not have been more perfect. As is so often the pattern in our family, we didn't talk about the fact that this was probably our one last visit together.

Audrey was in obvious pain and discomfort and slept a lot, but she was with us every waking moment. In these moments, we three remembered all kinds of things—silly things and tender, endearing things. We talked about our children—now and when they were babies. Audrey was so proud of me and the work I was embarking on.

Even though she was so ill, friends stopped in every day to visit. And their Episcopal priest visited one day and said a prayer that was so touching it just about undid me.

As I write this, I miss her so much. I can still see her, just a shadow of her former self, but still concerned with everyone else's well-being and comfort. I can only hope that when my time comes, I can be as brave and gracious as she was.

As I write about my sisters, I realize what wonderful role models they were. I'm not sure I've always lived up to their high standards, but more and more I'm trying.

Audrey died on September 6, 1997, two weeks after I visited. When Helen called to tell me, I was watching the funeral of Princess Diana. Loss seemed to blanket the world.

I flew back to Baytown for Audrey's funeral. As her priest gave a eulogy in a church that was filled to overflowing, I thought of Audrey's interest in angels and how, in the last few years, she had talked about wanting to write a book about them. She didn't get around to doing that—but now she is one.

SITTING AT THE Ivy on my birthday, I silently recall how I returned from the funeral just in time to attend the Emmy Awards and watch Ellen (and the rest of the team) receive her Emmy for Best Writing for the coming out episode. From the lowest lows to the highest highs—a real roller-coaster ride for me. And there were in-betweens too, like the bittersweetness I felt attending the last days of filming on the set of *Ellen* two months before.

The show hadn't officially been canceled yet, but all signs were pointing to it. I remember thinking about it with concern one afternoon in a grocery store; when I got to the checkout stand, the cashier said, "I hope they don't cancel Ellen's show. She is the nearest thing to Lucille Ball that we have." Of course, I couldn't have agreed more. It seemed that in all the hoopla of controversy this was something a lot of network and studio executives were overlooking. It was gratifying, for that reason, when so many entertainment greats took part in the last episode, which was, as Ellen called it, a "mockumentary" of her career and the history of TV. Included in this star-studded cast were Glenn Close, Diahann Carroll, Bea Arthur, Cindy Crawford, Tim Conway, Jada Pinkett Smith, Helen Hunt, Christine Lahti, Richard Benjamin, Ted Danson, Mary Steenburgen, Julianna Margulies, Woody Harrelson, and Linda Ellerbee as the interviewer.

Because it was to be an hourlong format of vignettes, the show was rehearsed and shot on different days. I stopped by on a few occasions and could feel how stressful this time was for Ellen. Clearly, the very last day of shooting was emotionally draining.

Fittingly, perhaps, the last scene of the last day was with two cast regulars—Joely Fisher and Jeremy Piven. It was a send-up of Lucy and Ethel's famous wine-making scene. Clea Lewis and Dave Higgins had already shot their funny bits for the show. After the last take, El, in a costume as a pregnant peasant woman, spoke to the cast and crew. She began simply, thanking them for their wonderful work and support. Very soon, though, she was crying to break her heart—and so were most people on the set. She just went on through her tears—apologizing for the times she had rushed out on Friday nights without thanking the crew for all their good work, thanking them for continuing to work and being supportive of the show whether or not they agreed with her position, hoping that somehow, somewhere, they would all work together again. It was without doubt one of the most difficult things she has ever done, and my heart broke for her.

The producers had planned a lunch for everyone, but El thought she couldn't pull herself together enough to attend. I left the set with her to go up to her dressing room, leaving through the same door that for the last four seasons she had used to enter the set, bounding through it exuberantly before running out to greet the audience. This time, she was going through it the opposite way, exiting stage right. Her sadness in those moments and the ones that followed was more profound than I can say.

And yet, none of this could detract from all that had been

accomplished—the changes that opened doors for vast numbers of people, people who are struggling with issues brought out on the episodes and people whose minds are open and who aren't afraid to look at what our gay family members face every day of their lives.

In Howard Rosenberg's rave review in the *Los Angeles Times* of this last episode, he really hit the nail on the head by saying that Ellen's basic ordinariness is what threatened antigay bigots, who seem to feel that gays should be portrayed only in stereotypical extremes.

He's right; Ellen isn't threatening to anybody. Truly, she disarms bigoted opposition with her goodness and her honesty, being as likable and normal as anyone can be. And, as we saw on our trip to London in April, she is doing that not just in our country but all over the world.

This trip was another high—compliments of BBC's Channel 4. In conjunction with the coming out episode, which it was airing in England for the first time, Channel 4 had made a documentary about the filming of the historic show and had flown Ellen, Anne, and me to London to be part of three days of festivities. Brief though this was, it was a great introduction and whetted my appetite to return and stay longer.

We were treated royally, with me feeling very much like the Queen Mother as we attended official activities that included a press conference at the BBC, a dinner party overlooking the Thames, and a huge celebration that was televised for later viewing.

As a matter of fact, we were showered with attention and

love everywhere we went in London. We strolled around areas such as Soho and Covent Garden and the expensive stores in the high-end shopping districts—so the twins, as we call them, could indulge in one of their favorite pastimes. I was amazed at how many autographs they signed. They still managed to acquire lots of beautiful new clothes. Neither one even looked at a price tag. With my Depression-era background, I did, only to get dizzy. Ellen said, "Why bother looking at prices? You know you're spending a lot of money when they say, 'Would you like something to drink?' "

On our last day in London, I walked from our hotel all around Buckingham Palace, snapping pictures all the way. Then, with time running out, I went with our driver and Ali, one of our bodyguards, to Westminster Abbey. Much to my dismay, Ali and I approached the entrance as they were turning people away for the day. Ali, an imposing-looking ex-prizefighter, said he'd talk to them.

As I waited anxiously, I saw Ali talking quietly to an official who was dressed in a red robe. The man's face lit up, and he motioned for me to come through.

"Ali," I whispered as we walked in together, "what did you tell him?"

He smiled and answered, "That you've been trying to get here every day and that this is your last day here. . . . Oh, and that you're Ellen's mom."

What fun! I couldn't wait to get back and tell El that I got into Westminster Abbey because I'm her mom.

• • •

SO NOW IT'S my birthday and my three kids are celebrating with me at the Ivy, making me feel good about what my being their mom has done for them.

Speaking of which, Ellen says, it's a good thing I talked her into doing *Larry King Live!* when she was in New York to receive the prestigious Peabody Award. With the *Ellen* series finale airing in two nights, doing Larry's show made a lot of sense to me, but when I talked to El she was overwhelmed and was thinking about not doing it. As she said, it was a good thing that I had persuaded her to do it, because she was just great, answering questions and speaking honestly with her typical wit, intelligence, and congeniality. It was a positive, upbeat interview—just the right note for what she said would be the last one for a while.

"And what about your trip?" Vance asks me.

I'm glad he asked that. I had just come back from the last official spokesperson trip that I'll have time to tell about in this book. And how perfect—of all places, it was a trip to my hometown, New Orleans. Talk about coming full circle.

To make it even more perfect, Helen drove in from Pass Christian to share a week of it with me. This was the icing on the cake.

I invited her to stay with me after I arrived at the Claiborne Mansion and saw my elegant, expansive accommodations. The brochure says, "The opulent home overlooking Washington Square Park has been restored to its 1850s Greek revival style with spacious rooms, 14-foot ceilings, and exquisite finishing details." There were gorgeous chandeliers and fireplaces with marble mantels throughout, and my suite even had a baby grand piano. The courtyard was large and lush with huge oak trees; a pool, where Helen swam every morning; and a pool house with ceiling fans and tables and chairs for lounging. I was truly living in "opulent decadence," and I like it there! This was certainly coming home in style.

The week was a happy mix of exciting scheduled activities and lazy downtime for doing old familiar things such as riding the ferry across the Mississippi River to Algiers and back. One day there was time for a streetcar ride up oak-tree-lined St. Charles Avenue, one of my favorite drives. Passing stately homes now interspersed with townhouses and condos, I spotted all the familiar sights—Audubon Park, Tulane and Loyola universities. Our final destination was the Camellia Grill, a favorite of New Orleanians for many, many years. The waiters have a reputation for staying there forever. This was where El and I used to stop in often for a sliver of cheesecake so rich that a sliver was plenty. I looked for the waiter who would always greet her the same way, "Hi, star," to tell him how prophetic he had been, but he wasn't there.

My HRC and P-FLAG events were like family affairs. I had a bit of a surprise at the first event, which took place on Mother's Day. It was a P-FLAG gathering in City Park which I had assumed would be an informal event. Wrong. When I arrived, I saw before me a highly organized scene complete with a large roped-off area for a catered reception and, off to another side, several hundred chairs facing a stage.

This was actually the New Orleans P-FLAG chapter's annual champagne reception to award scholarships to deserving young gay men and women. And when I looked at a program, to my further surprise, I saw that I was listed as the keynote speaker.

Generally, at informal events, I need to say only a few words, and I'm comfortable with spontaneous remarks. For longer speeches, I keep my notes in front of me, so that I can glance at them and not have to rely on my memory. "Keynote speaker" definitely sounded like more than spontaneous remarks.

Nonetheless, when it was time for my keynote address, I just got up and talked to everyone, speaking from my heart and keying in on the thoughts I most wanted to share with them.

It must have been OK. In thanking me, several people made the comment, "I felt like you were talking just to me—like we were having a conversation."

I wanted to say: Well, as a matter of fact, we were! Instead, I just thanked them for the compliment.

One of the mothers who is also a member of HRC was bemoaning that my year as spokesperson was soon going to be over.

"Haven't you heard?" I said. "I've been asked to stay on."

"And?" She asked tentatively.

"And I said yes," I told her. "I'll keep talking as long as my message is needed."

This setting at City Park Carousel was quite familiar, with its beautiful old merry-go-round housed in its own building that had all open doors and windows. There's also a wading pool and swings, and giant live oaks draped with moss. Recalling the many happy hours I spent there when Vance and

Ellen were little made this a very nostalgic evening. And how appropriate that it was Mother's Day!

Though Helen has always been entirely supportive of Ellen, that has pretty much been the extent of her exposure to homosexuality. So this experience was really educational for her. Everybody loved Helen, and Helen loved everybody. At one of the events, there was a woman whom both Helen and I knew, though neither of us had any idea that she had a gay child. She told us that she hadn't attended P-FLAG events before but she and her husband had come because they heard I'd be there. They have six children, and one daughter is gay. The mother and father are most certainly supportive and accepting, and all the siblings are too—except one brother.

I later commented to Helen, "How strange. I wonder why one young man would be homophobic when the rest of the family isn't?" Helen found it sad as well.

At another event, we met a young woman from Pass Christian whose mother lives not far from Helen.

The young woman told us that her mother is not accepting of her being gay. Helen instantly asked, "Would you like me to call and invite her over and talk to her?"

I love it. Next year Ellen's aunt will be the HRC spokesperson!

One of the most memorable nights was dinner at Commander's Palace, truly one of the world's great restaurants. We were a group of seven, and three of us were proud, supportive mothers of gay daughters. And we had every right to be. Their two daughters are highly successful in the business world, and my two are highly successful in the entertainment world. The dinner was sublime—the food and service were perfect. We ordered seven different desserts and shared. All the desserts were splendid but crème brulée and praline cream-cheese cheesecake topped my list. I knew there was a reason I had dieted for a few weeks before my trip to New Orleans.

Before leaving town, I visited Jackie in her French Quarter home. I had known her in grammar school, high school, and college. Her daughter, Jill, and Ellen were friends when they were in junior high. Jill also came over with her two little girls.

Jill told me a funny anecdote about when she and Ellen were in the eighth grade. "Ellen used to call me and ask me to bring her over two aspirin because her daddy wouldn't let you all have any in the house."

"What did she need aspirin for?" I asked Jill.

"Because she drank too much strawberry wine the night before," Jill said, laughing. More things mothers don't know!

Jackie told me, "I used to tell Jill to invite Ellen over to spend the night because Ellen was so funny."

Jill added, "And watching her on TV is like being with her back then—she's so natural and real. She hasn't changed at all."

WELL, ONE THING is certain: Ellen hasn't changed a bit when it comes to how loving and giving she is.

What a lucky mom I am! As I blow out the candle on

my Ivy birthday cake, looking at yet one more table laden with fabulous desserts, it's hard to know what else to wish for. But these three have more in store for me.

There is a beautiful pottery vase from Vance with a handmade card featuring his cartoonish male wishing me a happy birthday. Anne, a talented artist, has given me a painting of one of the fantastic, dreamy people that she draws. The dreamy figure in my painting just happens to have short gray hair and wears little round glasses. The painting is full of symbolism, and I love it.

And a gift from my best friend, best teacher and daughter, another Ellen DeGeneres poetic masterpiece entitled, "Sixty-Eight," portions of which follow:

Oh my Mama Oh my
What she's accomplished
What she's done with her life
To come so far
To do so much
To start so shy
And be so tough
A teacher a leader an activist . . .

Poised is how she always stays
She fights the fight day after day
She could stay home
But no—no way
She's our Joan of Arc
She's making her mark

On society—on the world
She's the greatest—She's my Mama
I'm so proud to be her girl.
Thanks for making me
Carrying me
Having me
Raising me
Loving me
Unconditionally.
Elle

Here I am on the happiest birthday of my life. My kids are with me, and our lives are rich and full. For a second, I think back to those two women on the beach in Pass Christian, that mother and that daughter, as though they were two people I once knew a long, long time ago. El and I have both shed our skins a few times.

I think of what we have been through as a family—everything, the good and the bad. From the toughest and most challenging days to these glorious times, I would change very little. After struggling and learning, we're all finding our place in life—purpose, wholeness, authenticity, fulfillment, love.

I couldn't be more grateful.

WELL, AS FOR what's next—as they say in show business, stay tuned!

Ellen and I have been through many chapters in our lives, many openings and closings. Without fail, the closing of a chapter has led to the opening of a bigger and better one. I'm grateful for our journey together so far, and I look forward to whatever lies ahead.

That great philosopher, Charles Schultz, has said, "Just remember, once you are over the hill you begin to pick up speed."

This is certainly true in my case. If sixty-five is considered over the hill, I am zipping along at quite a clip—on a faster track than ever—and loving every minute of it.

Not long ago, I was inspired by a short piece by Robert J. Hastings called "The Station." He uses a train as a metaphor for our journey through life. He says that like many passengers on trains, instead of enjoying the sights and the scenery along the way, we think only of getting to the station—the station being "when I get a promotion," "when I pay off the mortgage," "when I meet Prince Charming," and so on. Hastings speaks of the importance of realizing that there is no station, that "the true joy of life is the trip." What an important message.

I think this applies very well to my own message about love and acceptance. If we all focused on being grateful for every day and looking for the good in everything and everyone around us, much of our hate and bigotry and fear would fall away.

I don't mean to paint too rosy a picture. I understand that as long as there are human beings on this earth, there will be differences—as I said at the beginning of this book; however, there are some things that would make our differences so easy to live with.

In my fondest dreams:

People of different races treat each other with respect.
Members of different religions respect each other's differences and, since we're all God's children, treat each other with kindness and love.
All of us who read and study the Holy Bible understand that some people take every word of the Bible literally and some don't. We respect each other's interpretations and emphases.
Those with strong philosophical opinions live peaceably with opposing philosophies.
No one feels a need to proselytize.

And, last but certainly not least, in my fondest dreams:

Our gay family members will be embraced and celebrated by all their loved ones.
They will be appreciated and secure in the workplace.
They will not face physical or mental abuse; rather, they will be treated fairly and equally throughout our nation. This, of course, includes the right to marry.

So this is where I sign off for now. I hate writing this part. It means that this particular journey is over. For me, it's been enlightening and edifying. I've loved the whole process. I'll miss writing. I'll miss my sessions with Mim, who has been jogging my memory and keeping me organized and on track.

I hope you enjoyed coming on this journey with me. Thank you for making the trip. I hope you saw some sights that made you think or laugh or cry. I hope it has somehow enriched your life and your own journey.

Rather than say good-bye, I'd like to send you off with my own incurably optimistic version of Paul Monette's admonition:

Go with love, joy, peace, and happiness in your heart. Heal the world.

Resources

P-FLAG
1101 14th St. N.W., Suite 1030
Washington, DC, 20005
202-638-4200

Human Rights Campaign (HRC)
919 18th St. N.W., Suite 800
Washington, DC, 20006
202-628-4160

National Coming Out Project 1-800-866-6263
http://www.hrc.org

You can call the 800 number above to receive HRC's excellent booklet "Resource Guide to Coming Out." In it you will also find names and addresses of other support organizations, along with a list of resources that includes helpful books and other reading material.

Two I recommend are *Shared Heart: Portraits and Stories Celebrating Lesbian, Gay, and Bisexual Young People*, with photographs by Adam Mastoon (William Morrow, 1997) and *Straight Parents/Gay Children* by Robert A. Bernstein (Thunder's Mouth Press, Avalon Publishing Group, 1995).

Lagniappe—A Little Something Extra

MY "LAGNIAPPE" TO YOU, dear readers, is an invitation to send in your questions, comments, and letters for possible inclusion in a follow-up book. We still have a long way to go, and I hope I have "miles to go before I sleep." I would like to continue documenting our progress in this struggle for fairness and equal rights for our gay family members.

Finally, as I say at the end of my Human Rights Campaign speeches: I love you all. Celebrate yourselves. Feel good about yourselves.

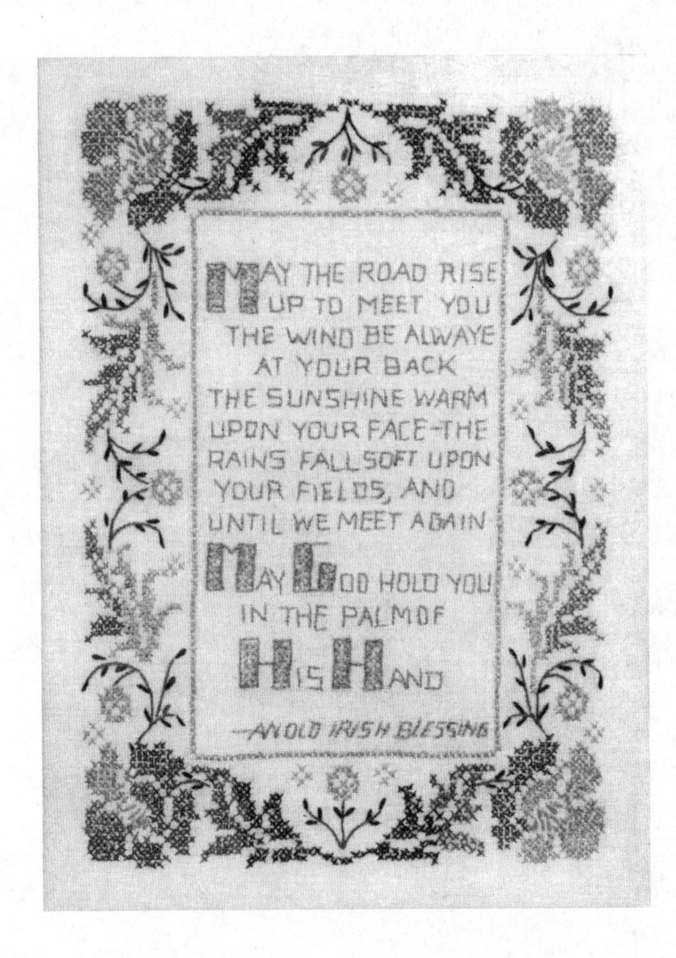

One of my mother's favorite sayings. Her handiwork is captured in this embroidered version, which hangs in my house.

Embroidery by Mil Pfeffer
Photography by Jan Sonnenmair